浙江省普通高校“十三五”新形态教材

国家级一流本科课程配套教材

经典英美文化
五维课堂

主编 骆蓉 文晓华

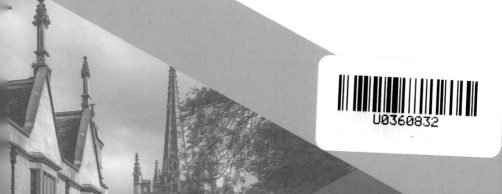

British and American Culture: A Multi-dimensional Class

清華大學出版社
北京

内 容 简 介

本教材共有 10 个章节，分别介绍了英语的历史与当代发展、英国国家概况、美国国家概况、英美历史与社会变迁、英美政治制度特征、英美教育体系与知名高校、英美传统与新媒体文化、英美美食风格与类别、英美艺术流派与特色、英美节日文化与对比等内容。每章包含 Text A、Text B、Text C 三篇课文，分为课前预习、课中阅读、课后思考三个教学环节。此外，学生可以在课后扫描二维码，获取 Text D 及音视频资源，促进对每个章节的全面理解。本教材另配有练习答案和 PPT 教学课件，可登录"清华社英语在线"（www.tsinghuaelt.com）进行下载。

本教材既适用于需要提高英语综合素养及跨文化交际能力的英语专业学生，又适用于已经具备了一定英语语言能力、希望开拓视野的非英语专业学生。

图书在版编目（CIP）数据

经典英美文化：五维课堂 / 骆蓉，文晓华主编 .—北京：清华大学出版社，2024.3

国家级一流本科课程配套教材

ISBN 978-7-302-62809-5

Ⅰ. ①经… Ⅱ. ①骆… ②文… Ⅲ. ①英语－阅读教学－高等学校－教材②文化－概况－英国③文化－概况－美国 Ⅳ. ① H319.4: G

中国国家版本馆 CIP 数据核字（2023）第 034672 号

责任编辑：倪雅莉
封面设计：李伯骥
责任校对：王荣静
责任印制：曹婉颖

出版发行：清华大学出版社

网　　址：https://www.tup.com.cn, https://www.wqxuetang.com
地　　址：北京清华大学学研大厦A 座　　**邮　　编：**100084
社 总 机：010-83470000　　**邮　　购：**010-62786544
投稿与读者服务：010-62776969, c-service@tup.tsinghua.edu.cn
质量反馈：010-62772015, zhiliang@tup.tsinghua.edu.cn

印 装 者：三河市龙大印装有限公司
经　　销：全国新华书店
开　　本：185mm×260mm　　**印　　张：**16.75　　**字　　数：**330千字
版　　次：2024年3月第1版　　**印　　次：**2024年3月第1次印刷
定　　价：68.00 元

产品编号：091969-01

前　言

PREFACE

新时代的中国作为全球第二大经济体，已经成为全球治理的参与者。我国高等教育迫切需要培养大批具有国际视野、通晓国际规则、能够参与国际事务和竞争的国际化人才。《大学英语教学指南》(2020) 和《英语专业教学指南》(2020) 均提出应提高学生的跨文化交际能力，培养学生成为合格的人才。作为跨文化交际类新形态教材，《经典英美文化：五维课堂》结合国家级精品在线课程“印象英美——穿越时空之旅”，采用混合教学理念，将线上资源与线下课堂有机衔接，旨在提供动态交互的立体课堂，让学习者既有身临其境的网络学习体验，也有真实碰撞的课堂交互氛围。

1. 适用对象

本教材立足时代需求，旨在培养具有国际意识的跨文化交际人才，适用于以下院校和学生：

· 有国际化、复合型外语人才培养要求的高层次院校；

· 在课程思政、大学英语教学改革中做出特色的普通院校；

· 需要提高英语综合素养及跨文化交际能力的英语专业学生；

· 已经具备了一定英语语言能力、希望开拓视野的非英语专业学生。

2. 教学目标

通过拓展大学生的英美社会文化知识、开拓国际视野，提高跨文化交际能力，有助于培养兼具语言素养和国际意识的人才。本教材具体目标为：

· 拓展国际视野：基于跨文化交流视角，了解英美国家社会概况及现实问题；

· 提升语言技能：通过学习全英文教材，掌握西方文化概念的地道英语表达；

· 提高交际能力：透过中西方文化差异，提升跨文化交流的包容性和沟通力；

· 讲述中外故事：结合当下中国国情，培养讲述中外故事的外语叙事能力。

3. 编写理念与特色

1）重视跨文化思辨能力培养与提高

本教材介绍了英美国家的语言概况、人文地理、政治经济、教育媒体、风俗礼仪等文化知识，提高学生对西方文化的赏鉴能力和跨文化交际能力，培养文化包容性；引导学生进行跨文化对比思辨，客观看待中西方文化差异，积极借鉴英美社会发展中的成功经验，同时，对西方社会的问题和不足进行了理性的分析和批判。

2）突显立德树人的核心目标

与传统英美文化教材不同，本教材在介绍英美文化的同时，立足中国国情，将经典中国文化与西方文化展开对比赏析，培养学生的中西文化互鉴能力，尤其是批判思维能力和综合观察能力。本教材以立德树人为核心目标，以实现语言知识技能提升与思政育人的双重目标，引导学生站在全球化高度学习和鉴赏不同文化，在提高跨文化交际能力的同时，兼顾价值观的塑造。

3）打造新形态教材和混合教学模式

本教材采用新形态教材理念编写，厘清线上和线下功能，明晰课前线上学习、线下课堂交互与课后发散思考的分阶段教学目标，设计大量服务翻转课堂的教学活动。学生通过扫描教材二维码，可进入教材“云空间”，观看视频、收听音频、阅读文档、在线做题，实现实体课堂与课下自学相互补充。

4. 教材章节与内容设计

1）教材章节

本教材总共 10 个单元，从多个方面详细介绍了英美社会与文化，各单元的内容如下：

	Contents
Chapter 1	English as a Lingua Franca
Chapter 2	The UK: A Country of Countries
Chapter 3	The US: A Country of Cultural Diversity

(cont.)

	Contents
Chapter 4	Great Events of the UK and the US: Legends in History
Chapter 5	Political Systems in the UK and the US
Chapter 6	An Overview of Education in the UK and the US
Chapter 7	Public Media in the UK and the US
Chapter 8	A Culinary Adventure of the UK and the US
Chapter 9	Arts in the UK and the US
Chapter 10	Festivals and Holidays in the UK and the US

2) 内容设计

本教材每个单元包含 Text A、 Text B、 Text C 三篇课文，分为课前预习（Pre-class Preparation）、课中阅读（In-class Reading）、课后思考（Post-class Thinking）三个教学环节。此外，学生可以在课后扫描二维码，获取 Text D 及其他补充资源，促进对每个章节的全面理解。

· **课前预习环节**

课前预习环节是每篇课文教学的开端，该环节设计了两个预习活动：观看慕课和预习思考题。通过预习慕课视频，学生可先行了解本篇课文的知识点，为接下来开展的混合式学习提供了知识储备。课前思考题方便学生对课文的核心问题展开预测。

· **课中阅读环节**

课中阅读环节提供了与慕课内容主题一致的课文，佐之以文化词汇和文化点注释，方便学生深入掌握学习要点。为服务混合式教学实践，教材设计了丰富的课堂练习与教学活动，用于检测学生对慕课视频的掌握和理解。课堂活动包括讨论、辩论、角色扮演、迷你剧表演等形式，体现了以学生为中心的教学理念，教师可采用合作式教学、基于任务式教学方式展开教学。本教材专设了“中西文化对比与反思”板块，引导学生在学习英美文化的同时，积极思考相应的中国文化现象，进行中西文化对比赏鉴，提升跨文化思辨能力。

· **课后思考环节**

为提升课程的高阶性和挑战度，本教材在课文内容教学之后设计了课后思考环节。课后思考环节的思路来自课本、高于课本，要求学生在学习慕课与课文基础上进行深入思考。练习类型包括填补思维导图、进行基于课本内容的反思性写作、撰写社会调查报告等。通过课后思考环节中的语言产出类活动，学生可以加强对英美文化知识的深度掌握与灵活应用。

鉴于编者水平有限，编写时间仓促，书中如有纰漏，恳请读者批评指正。

编者

2023 年 1 月

CONTENTS

Chapter 1
English as a Lingua Franca

Among more than 5,000 languages used in the world, English has become a real global lingua franca. It is the native language of many countries, including the United Kingdom, the United States, Canada, Australia, New Zealand and a number of Caribbean nations. When combining the number of both native speakers and language learners, English is the most commonly used language in the world and is widely used in international cultural, political and economic affairs. This chapter will introduce the evolvement of English from a local language used in medieval England to a global lingua franca.

Text A English as a Lingua Franca

Pre-class Preparation

MOOC Watching

Watch the MOOC video "English as a Lingua Franca" to prepare for Text A.

Pre-reading Questions

1. What is a lingua franca? Which language has served as a regional lingua franca and which language has served as a global lingua franca?
2. Which countries speak English as a first language and which countries speak it as a lingua franca?

In-class Reading

English as a Lingua Franca

1 A **lingua franca** is a common language used to make communication possible between people who do not share a native language. **English as a lingua franca (ELF)** refers to the use of English as a global means of communication between people of different languages. By the middle of the 19th century, the British Empire had spread English through the colonies of "the empire on which the sun never sets". The rise of the United States in the 20th century, along with worldwide broadcasting in English by BBC and other broadcasters, significantly **accelerated** the spread of the language

accelerate
v. 使增速；加快，增加

across the world. Since the foundation of the United Nations at the end of World War II, English has become the main worldwide language in diplomacy and international relations. It is one of the six **official languages** of the United Nations. Many international organizations, including the European Union[1], European Free Trade Association[2], Asia-Pacific Economic Cooperation (APEC)[3] and the International Olympic Committee[4], set English as a major or sole working language. Now English is the world's most widely used language in mass media, book publishing, scientific research, international trade, and international **telecommunications**.

telecommunication *n.* 电信，远程通信

2 English is spoken as a majority language in the United States, the United Kingdom, Canada, Australia, New Zealand and Ireland. And it is used as either the official language or one of the official languages in more than 60 **sovereign** states. In the 21st century, English is more widely spoken and written than any other language. **Potential** ELF users include both those who speak English as an additional language and those who speak English as their main language. If you are speaking English with someone who speaks English as a second language, whether or not English is your main language, you are both using ELF. Now, Modern English family includes a large number of **varieties** spoken in diverse countries. This includes American English, Australian English, British English, Canadian English, Caribbean English, Nigerian English, New Zealand English, Philippine English, Singaporean English and South African English. This wide spread of English use has made English communication acceptable in most international contexts.

sovereign *adj.* 有主权的，至高无上的 *n.* 君主

potential *adj.* 潜在的，可能的

3 British linguist Jennifer Jenkins points out that ELF is not a new phenomenon. What makes ELF a **novel** phenomenon is the extent to which it is used in spoken, written and **computer-mediated communication**. A typical ELF conversation might involve an Italian and a Korean professor chatting at an international academic conference held in Berlin, a Spanish tourist asking a local for the way in Japan, or an Arabian negotiating with a

novel *adj.* 革新的

Chinese salesperson in New York. In a general sense, ELF communication concentrates on function rather than form. That means communicative **efficiency** (i.e. getting the message across) is more important than correctness. Although English is not the official language for many countries, it serves as a bridge between people from different cultural backgrounds. Therefore, Modern English is regarded as the first global lingua franca or the first world language.

efficiency
n. 效率，功效

Cultural Terms

1. lingua franca 通用语（指不同母语国家可以相互交流的共同语言）
2. English as a lingua franca (ELF) 英语作为国际通用语（指不同母语使用者将英语作为全球性交流媒介）
3. official language 官方语言（经国家、政府或其他权威机构认定具备法定地位的语言文字）
4. variety 英语的变体（指英语在不同国家、地区使用的不同形式）
5. computer-mediated communication 计算机为中介的沟通（也称网络沟通）

Cultural Notes

1. the European Union

   欧洲联盟，简称“欧盟”，是欧洲多国建立的政治经济联盟，创立于 1993 年。它目前有 27 个成员国，为世界第三大经济实体，其中 19 个国家接受欧元作为流通货币。

2. European Free Trade Association

   欧洲自由贸易联盟，是欧洲促进贸易的政府间组织，成立于 1960 年，目前成员国有冰岛、挪威、瑞士、列支敦士登四国。

3. Asia-Pacific Economic Cooperation (APEC)

   亚太经济合作组织，是亚太地区促进经济合作与贸易投资的论坛，成立于 1989 年，现有 21 个成员经济体。

4. International Olympic Committee

   国际奥林匹克委员会，是一个非政府、非营利国际体育组织，负责组织举办夏季奥林匹克运动会、冬季奥林匹克运动会、残疾人奥林匹克运动会和青年奥林匹克运动会，其总部位于瑞士洛桑。

Exercise

True or False

Directions: *Determine whether the following statements are true (T) or false (F).*

1. "English as a lingua franca" refers to the use of English as a global means of communication between people of different languages.
2. The rise of the British Empire in the 20th century significantly accelerated the spread of the language across the world.
3. In the 21st century, English is the second most widely spoken language in the world only after Mandarin Chinese.
4. In a general sense, ELF communication focuses more on function than form.
5. Although English is not the official language in China, it serves as a bridge for Chinese people to know about the world.

Critical Thinking

Directions: *Talk about the following topic with your group members. Then choose one speaker to express his or her opinion on behalf of the whole group.*

Nowadays, China is developing at a fast speed and has attracted more and more attention from the whole world. Do you think Mandarin Chinese will replace English as the first language or global lingua franca in the future? Share your reasons and evidence with your partners.

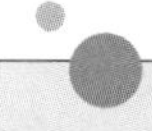

Post-class Thinking

Blank Filling

Directions: *Scan the QR code to fill in the blanks of the mind map of Text A and you will have a better understanding of the structure of the text.*

Text B A Brief History of the English Language

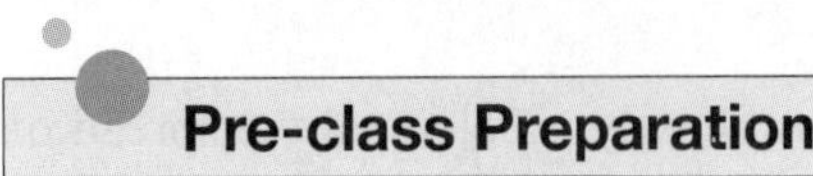

Pre-class Preparation

MOOC Watching

Watch the MOOC videos “The Origin and Development of the English Language” and “Modern English: A Voyage to Be a Global Language” to prepare for Text B.

MOOC video “The Origin and Development of the English Language”

MOOC video “Modern English: A Voyage to Be a Global Language”

Pre-reading Questions

1. Do you know any differences between English in the past and at the present?
2. How many stages are there in the development of the English language?

In-class Reading

A Brief History of the English Language

1 How did English become a global language? Who created the English language and who brought it to the other parts of the world? A brief history of the English language will provide answers to the above questions. The following parts will introduce the origin of the English language and four

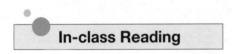

important periods in its development.

2 English is a West Germanic **Anglo-Frisian language** belonging to the **Indo-European language** family. English is classified as a **Germanic language** because it shares common features with other Germanic languages such as Dutch, German, and Swedish. Meanwhile, English shares other features with Frisian, so it is also classified as an Anglo-Frisian language. English was brought to Britain by Germanic people from what is now called northwest Germany and the Netherlands. It uses a vocabulary unlike other European languages of the same era. A large portion of the modern English vocabulary comes from **Anglo-Norman languages**.

3 The history of English is complex and **dynamic**. Generally speaking, there are four periods in the development of the English language: Old English, Middle English, Early Modern English, and Late Modern English.

dynamic
adj. 动态的

★ Old English (550–1066 AD)

4 The history of English started with the arrival of three Germanic **tribes** who invaded Britain in the 5th century. They are Angles, Saxons and Jutes who crossed the North Sea from today's Denmark and northern Germany. Later, they mixed their Germanic dialects to form a language called **Englisc**, from which Old English was derived. Before the arrival of the Germanic tribes, the Celts had been living in Britain for thousands of years. They were then either killed or chased to other areas and their **Celtic languages** had a slight influence on today's English. The Romans had brought Latin to Britain, which was a part of the Roman Empire for four hundred years (55 BC–410 AD). By the 7th century, the Germanic language of the Anglo-Saxons became **dominant** in Britain, replacing Latin and the Celtic languages which were used during Roman Britain.

tribe
n. 部落，部族

dominant
adj. 占优势的

5 In 597, the arrival of **St. Augustine** introduced **Christianity** into England. This brought more Latin words into English. Words concerning churches and ceremonies such as "church", "**bishop**", "monk" and

Christianity
n. 基督教

bishop
n. （基督教）主教

baptism
n. 洗礼
script
n. 书写字母
alphabetic
adj. 字母的

"**baptism**" came indirectly from Greek through Latin. It is from Latin that English took its **script** and **alphabetic** system. Old English was written down using the Latin alphabet. In the middle of the 9th century, Scandinavian words entered the English language with the invasion by Norwegian and Danish **Vikings**. Their northern Germanic words and speech had a fundamental influence on English. Many English words used today come from these ancient Vikings. Words like "sky", "egg", "window", "husband", "lift" and "take" are from the old languages of these northern countries.

6 In Modern English, about 25,000 words are from Old English. Many of today's words are from Old English—nouns like "friend", "son", "daughter", "home" and "ground", prepositions like "in", "on", "by" and "from", and verbs like "come", "go", "love" and "sing". However, Old English does not sound like Modern English at all and words have complex endings and vowel change, which differs greatly from the language we use today. Therefore, Old English is almost **unintelligible** to English speakers in the 21st century.

unintelligible
adj. 令人费解的

★ Middle English (1066–1500 AD)

7 From the 8th to the 12th century, Old English gradually transformed into Middle English. In 1066, William the Conqueror, the Duke of **Normandy**, invaded and conquered England. The French king brought French to England. Old French then took over as the language of Royal court, administration and culture. Latin remained a primary language used mostly for written language, especially that of the church. English, however, was reduced to the language of the lower class and was considered a vulgar tongue.

8 Standing side by side with the other two languages, English has survived and **assimilated** many words from French. After England and France split in the 14th century, English became dominant in England again

assimilate
v. 吸收，同化

and was developed into Middle English. Middle English form showed many signs of French influence, both in vocabulary and spelling. About ten thousand French words poured into English and covered every realm of culture and society. The words with French roots in English vocabulary are words of power and legislation, such as "castle", "crown", "army", "duke", "governor", "romance" and "parliament". In order to **reconcile** Old Norse and Old English, Middle English greatly simplified the inflectional system. Middle English literature is represented by Geoffrey Chaucer's *The Canterbury Tales*[1], and Malory's *Le Morte d'Arthur*[2]. Middle English continued to be spoken until 1500 when Modern English was gradually shaped.

reconcile
v. 使和谐一致，调和

★ **Early Modern English (1500–1700 AD)**

9 Early Modern English was characterised by the Great Vowel Shift[3] (1350–1700), inflectional simplification, and linguistic **standardisation**. The Great Vowel Shift affected the pronunciation of long vowels of Middle English and explained why English vowel letters have very different pronunciations from the same letters in other languages. Vowel sounds were made further to the front of the mouth and the letter "e" became silent at the end of words.

standardisation
n. 标准化

10 In 1476, William Caxton brought the printing press to England. Printing brought standardisation to English spelling. Grammar became fixed and the dialect of London became standard. Between the end of the 16th century and the early 17th century, the rise of Renaissance[4] in England greatly boosted the development of Early Modern English. The revival of classical literature brought many Latin and Greek words into the language. English grew, flowered and exploded with new words. Literature began to flourish in this period. It was during this period that William Shakespeare[5] (1564–1616), one of the greatest writers in English, produced most of his works. His works contributed to the standardisation of the English language.

★ **Late Modern English (1700–Present)**

11 From around 1700, the Late Modern English period started. In the 19th century, Britain became "the empire on which the sun never sets" and English was spread through its colonies and geographical dominance. The rise of the British Empire not only introduced English to the world, but also assimilated new words from all major languages in the world. Moreover, the Industrial Revolution brought forth many new inventions, which made it necessary to create more new words and English greatly facilitated international trade and business. Commerce, science and technology, diplomacy, and formal education all contributed to English becoming the first global language.

12 After World War II, the growing economic and cultural influence of the United States and its status as a superpower, enabled the English language to spread across the world much faster. Thousands and thousands of new words from other languages poured into the English language to express new ideas, inventions and scientific achievements. *The Oxford English Dictionary* lists more than 250,000 distinct words, not including many technical, scientific, and slang terms. As Modern English developed, standard usage of English was put forward and spread through public education and publications. In 1755, Samuel Johnson published his *A Dictionary of the English Language*[6] , which introduced standard spellings of words and usage norms. In 1828, Noah Webster published *An American Dictionary of the English Language*[7], trying to establish an American English norm which was independent of the British standard.

T Cultural Terms

1. Anglo-Frisian language 盎格鲁弗里希语（属于西日耳曼语，古英语、低地苏格兰语、古弗里希语都属于这一分支。）
2. Indo-European language 印欧语系（世界上分布最广泛的语系，欧洲、南亚、美洲和大洋洲的大部分国家都采用印欧语言作为母语或官方语言。印欧语系包括 400 多种语言和方言，使用人数超过 32 亿。）

3. Germanic language 日耳曼语言（印欧语系下的一个语言分支，全球有 5 亿多人以日耳曼语为母语，分布在欧洲、北美洲和大洋洲南部。全球使用最广泛的日耳曼语为英语。）
4. Anglo-Norman language 盎格鲁诺曼语（法国诺曼族人征服英格兰之后，在英格兰等不列颠群岛地区使用的古诺曼语，是一门混杂语言。）
5. Englisc 古英语（来自盎格鲁人的英语的最早记录方式，也是“English”一词的由来。）
6. Celtic language 凯尔特语言（属于印欧语系下的分支，古代英国的爱尔兰、苏格兰、威尔士等地多使用凯尔特语。）
7. St. Augustine 圣奥古斯丁（公元 6 世纪晚期，他受罗马教皇格里高利一世的派遣去英国传教，后成为坎特伯雷首位大主教。）
8. Viking 北欧维京人（别称北欧海盗，是由商人、探险家、海盗组成的松散族群，从公元 8 世纪到 11 世纪一直侵扰欧洲沿海和不列颠岛屿，足迹遍布从欧洲大陆至北极的广阔疆域，欧洲这个时期被称为“维京时期”。）
9. Normandy 诺曼底（法国西北部沿海地区的一个区，历史上曾是法国的一个公国。）

Cultural Notes

1. *The Canterbury Tales*

《坎特伯雷故事集》，是一部诗体短篇小说，作者为英国诗人乔叟。书中呈现了 29 位朝圣者前往坎特伯雷路途中各自讲述的故事。主要包括爱情和骑士探险传奇、宗教和道德故事、滑稽故事、动物寓言等 24 个故事，大多数用双韵诗体写成。

2. *Le Morte d'Arthur*

《亚瑟之死》，是至今以英语写作的亚瑟王传奇中最著名的作品，作者是托马斯·马洛。书中汇集了一些英文及法文版本亚瑟王骑士文学的作品，包含了马洛的部分原创故事以及一些以马洛的观点重新诠释的旧故事。

3. Great Vowel Shift

元音大迁移，是英语发展史上的一次主要的语音转变，开始于 14 世纪，大体完成于 15 世纪中期。元音发音的较大改变奠定了现代英语的发音基础。元音发音的转变主要体现在英语长元音的变化上。最先开始对这一现象进行研究的是丹麦语言学家奥托·叶斯柏森，“元音大迁移”的说法就是由他提出的。

4. Renaissance

文艺复兴，一场发生在14世纪至17世纪欧洲的文化复兴运动，起源于意大利中部的佛罗伦萨、威尼斯等城市，即意大利文艺复兴，后扩展至欧洲各国。其词源为意大利语"Rinascimento"。

5. William Shakespeare

威廉·莎士比亚，是英国文学史上最杰出的戏剧家，也是西方文学史上最杰出的作家之一。他流传下来的作品包括38部戏剧、154首十四行诗、两首长叙事诗和其他诗歌。

（扫描二维码，观看慕课片段"Shakespeare: The Greatest Writer in the English Language"）

6. *A Dictionary of the English Language*

《英语大词典》，由英国文学家塞缪尔·约翰逊编纂的英文词典，于1755年4月15日出版。它是英语历史上最具影响力的词典之一，是英语发展史上的一个里程碑。

7. *An American Dictionary of the English Language*

《美国英语词典》，由被誉为"美国学术和教育之父"的诺亚·韦伯斯特编纂。在美国，韦伯斯特的名字等同于"词典"，而他首版于1828年的现代《韦氏词典》尤为著名。现在韦伯斯特词典多指美国梅里厄姆-韦伯斯特公司编写的词典。

Exercises

I. Matching

Directions: *For each period in the history of the English language, find out the corresponding historical events that played an indispensable role in the development of the language.*

1. Old English ________________	**A.** Great Vowel Shift **B.** The rise of the British Empire **C.** Norman Conquest in 1066
2. Middle English ________________	**D.** The arrival of Angles, Saxons and Jutes **E.** Renaissance **F.** The creation of *The Canterbury Tales*

(cont.)

3. Early Modern English ____________	**G.** Industrial Revolution **H.** The status of the United States as a superpower after World War II **I.** The introduction of Christianity to England in 597 **J.** The introduction of the printing press to Britain
4. Late Modern English ____________	

II. Etymology Exploration

Directions: *Look into a dictionary to find the origin of the following English words. Which languages are they derived from and have they changed their meanings?*

pajamas: ______________________________

litchi: ______________________________

yoghurt: ______________________________

mutton: ______________________________

shampoo: ______________________________

abandon: ______________________________

ketchup: ______________________________

church: ______________________________

Critical Thinking

Directions: *Tell a story about the English language from the first person perspective. You can share stories with your partners and you can also co-work in telling one story.*

You can start your story with the following sentences.

Hi! I am English, the most widely used language in the world nowadays. I come from...

Post-class Thinking

Extensive Reading

Directions: *Read and listen to the prologue of* The Canterbury Tales *and* Shall I Compare Thee to a Summer's Day. *How do you feel about these two famous poems and can you sense the features of English in the authors' periods?*

The prologue of *The Canterbury Tales*

Shall I Compare Thee to a Summer's Day

Text C British English and American English

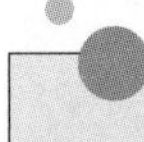

Pre-class Preparation

MOOC Watching

Watch the MOOC video "British English and American English" to prepare for Text C.

Pre-reading Questions

1. What are the differences between British English and American English?
2. When and where do you use different varieties of English?

British English and American English

1 In the global spread of English, a large number of dialects, **pidgins** and **creoles** have evolved all over the world. Among all these English varieties, British English and American English are two typical standards of English dialects. There is an old saying that America and Britain are "two nations divided by a common language". The last two centuries have witnessed how these two **Englishes** have grown together, sometimes in harmony, sometimes in competition.

★ British English

2 British English is an English dialect spoken and written in the UK and throughout the British Isles. British English represents the **uniformity** in written English within the UK. However, the forms of spoken English vary considerably in most other areas of the world where English is spoken, so there is no uniform concept of British spoken English. Due to historical reasons, English spoken in London and the East Midlands became standard English within the court, and ultimately became the basis for generally accepted use in the law, government, literature and education in Britain. That explains why **Received Pronunciation**, or RP has traditionally stood out to be regarded as the standard accent of British English. Now the term "British English" refers to the various varieties of English spoken in member states of **the Commonwealth of Nations**.

uniformity
n. 一致，统一

★ American English

3 From around 1600, the English colonization of North America resulted in the creation of a new variety of English—American English. Coupled

with the influence of the languages of native Americans, German, Irish, and Spanish that came with the new waves of immigrants, American English has formed its own characteristics. **General American (GA)**, which is spread over most of the United States, is more typically the model for the United States. In 1828, the publication of *An American Dictionary of the English Language* written by Noah Webster, the first American dictionary, showed that the United States now speaks a different dialect from Britain. In the 20th century, the growing economic and cultural influence of the United States and its status as a superpower following World War II have **consolidated** the position and influence of American English.

consolidate *v.* 巩固

4 A large number of native American words have entered the English language. There are place names such as "Mississippi", "Roanoke", and "Iowa", and Indian-sounding names like "Idaho", which had no native American roots. But many other words like "raccoon", "tomato", "canoe", "barbecue", "**savanna**", and "**hickory**" have native American roots. Spanish also has an influence on American English. "Mustang", "canyon", "ranch", "stampede", and "vigilante" are all examples of Spanish words that made their way into English through the settlement of the American West. A less number of words have entered American English from French and West African languages.

savanna *n.* 热带草原

hickory *n.* 山核桃树

★ **Differences between British English and American English**

5 Now both British English and American English are used today in international communication. Although spoken American English and British English are generally mutually intelligible, there are enough differences to cause misunderstandings or embarrassment. In the 21st century, **approximately** two thirds of the world's native speakers of English live in the United States. Today, American English is more influential due to the dominance of mass media, television, trade, science and technology of the United States. British people and American people can always understand each other—but there are a few notable differences between

approximately *adv.* 大约

British English and American English. Their major differences lie in pronunciation, vocabulary, spelling and grammar.

1) Pronunciation

6 The best known British pronunciation is Received Pronunciation (RP). RP is spoken by the British upper class and is also called the Queen's English. It is the pronunciation style broadcast in BBC or taught in textbooks published by Oxford and Longman. American pronunciation usually refers to General American (GA) pronunciation. Most parts of the United States speak GA except the south of America. GA is the pronunciation style broadcast in VOA and described in Webster dictionary.

7 One **noticeable** pronunciation difference between British English and American English is the pronunciation of the letter "r". GA is **rhotic** which means /r/ sound needs to be pronounced, while RP is non-rhotic, which means the letter "r" is always silent. Compare words "car", "art", and "farm". Second, /t/ sound is often pronounced as /d/ sound in American English. Then for many long vowels in British English, American English tends to simplify them or change them into different vowels. These differences can be found in Table 1-1.

noticeable
adj. 显而易见的
rhotic
adj. 发 /r/ 音的（辅音前的 /r/ 全部读出）

Table 1-1 Differences between British English pronunciation and American English pronunciation

Words	British English pronunciation	American English pronunciation
bath	/bɑ:θ/	/bæθ/
job	/ dʒɒb/	/dʒɑ:b/
vase	/vɑ:z/	/veɪs/
tomato	/tə'mɑ:təʊ/	/tə'meɪtoʊ/

2) Vocabulary

8 The most noticeable difference between American and British English is vocabulary. There are hundreds of everyday words that are different. Their differences in vocabulary can be found in every aspect of our daily life,

such as food, clothing, places, transportation, time, buildings, etc. There are British words which many Americans will not understand and vice versa. There are also words which exist in both British English and American English but have very different meanings. Some of the differences between British English vocabulary and American English vocabulary are listed in the following categories of expressions.

Table 1-2 Differences between British English vocabulary and American English vocabulary

British English vocabulary	American English vocabulary
crisps	chips
chips	French fries
fizzy drink	soda
jam	jelly
biscuit	cookie
jumper	sweater
trousers	pants
pants	underwear
trainers	sneakers
flat	apartment
phone box	phone booth
ground floor	first floor
chemist’s	drugstore/pharmacy
queue	line
motorway	highway
pavement	sidewalk
lorry	truck
lift	elevator
underground	subway

3) Spelling

9 The differences between British English spelling and American English spelling lie in the different standards they adopt. Current British English spellings follow Samuel Johnson's dictionary of 1755, while most characteristic American English spellings were influenced by Noah Webster's dictionary of 1828. Generally speaking, both British English and American English spellings are acceptable but it is important to be consistent, which means that we'd better not mix their spellings in one single piece of writing. They have many long-existing and systematic spelling differences, some of which can be found in the following examples.

Table 1–3 Differences between British spelling and American spelling

British English spelling	American English spelling
colour	color
organise	organize
centre	center
defence	defense
neighbour	neighbor
recognise	recognize
fibre	fiber
offence	offense

4) Grammar

10 British people and American people have no problem understanding each other. However, there are some interesting variations existing in their grammar. British English and American English tend to use different past participle of the same verb, for example, British English uses "proved" instead of "proven". In American English, both forms are acceptable. In British English, perfect tense is often used when American English would prefer to use the past tense. For example, British people would be more

likely to say “I have been to that place once”, whereas American people would prefer to say “I went to that place once”.

11 In British English, “have got” is often used for the possessive sense of “have” and “have got to” is informally used for “have to”. This is much less common in American English. For example, British English has expressions like “I’ve got two sisters” and American English just uses “I have two sisters”. And British people would say “I’ve got to go now” when American people say “I have to go now”.

T Cultural Terms

1. pidgin 皮钦语（又称混杂语言，两个或两个以上的群体没有共同语言，为了彼此沟通而发展出的语言。皮钦语的地位通常低于官方语言或通用语言。）
2. creole 克里奥尔语（当皮钦语进一步发展，成为母语，出现完整语法，则形成稳定版本的混杂语——克里奥尔语。）
3. Englishes 各种英语形式（指不同国家或其他环境下使用的不同英语形式，如英式英语、美式英语、澳大利亚英语、新加坡英语、中国英语等。）
4. Received Pronunciation (RP) 也被称为女王 / 国王的英语（Queen’s/King’s English）、牛津英语（Oxford English）或 BBC 英语（在 20 世纪前期一度被认为是更权威、更有影响力的发音，如今英国社会认为 RP 并不优于其他英国地方发音。）
5. the Commonwealth of Nations 英联邦（指 50 多个英国的旧殖民地和自治领组成的国际互助组织，并不是一个统一的联邦，英国君主为公共元首。）
6. General American (GA) 通用美式英语（美式英语的标准化口音，被认为代表了最纯正的美式英语。）

* Exercises

I. True or False

Directions: *Determine whether the following statements are true (T) or false (F).*

1. RP, or Received Pronunciation, used to represent the standard accent of British English.
2. American English was thought to be a classless sort of English.
3. *An American Dictionary of the English Language* edited by Noah Webster was the first

American dictionary.

4. In American English, double letters were reduced to single ones, like the "l" in "traveller" and "g" in "waggon".
5. A person in New York will use the word "lift" instead of "elevator".

II. Blank Filling

***Directions:** Fill in the blanks with the appropriate British or American expressions for each picture.*

	British English expression: ____________ American English expression: ____________
	British English expression: ____________ American English expression: ____________
	British English expression: ____________ American English expression: ____________
	British English expression: ____________ American English expression: ____________
	British English expression: ____________ American English expression: ____________

Critical Thinking

***Directions:** Have an in-class debate based on the following topic. Choose one position and come up with views and evidence to support this position.*

The number of English speakers continues to increase and many people think that English provides them with opportunities for better education and employment. However, other people argue that the wide spread of English has quickened the assimilation of English vocabulary into other languages, which has led to language discrimination and even language death in countries where minority languages might be forgotten due to the increased use of English. Which of the opinions do you support, convenient intercultural communication or language diversity?

Position A: We should promote the global spread of English regardless of its possible threat to other languages.

Position B: We should protect language diversity in every country and prevent the global spread of English.

The debate process should go as follows:

- The two sides make opening statements;
- Side A presents its arguments;
- Side B rebuts Side A's arguments and presents its arguments;
- Side A rebuts Side B's arguments;
- The two sides make closing statements.

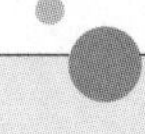

Post-class Thinking

Discussion

Directions: *Watch the 1964 film* My Fair Lady *starring Audrey Hepburn and discuss the following questions.*

1. What did Eliza's pronunciation sound like at the very beginning of the film?
2. How did Professor Higgens train Eliza into an elegant lady who could speak standard Received Pronunciation? What methods did he use in training Eliza and were they effective?

Supplementary Resources

1. Extensive Reading

Read Text D "New Englishes" and watch the MOOC video "New English Varieties". Then discuss the following questions with your partner.

1) How many new Englishes are there in Modern English family?

2) What do you think of Chinese English?

Text D "New Englishes"

MOOC video "New English Varieties"

2. Documentaries

1) Documentary: *The Adventure of English* （《英语历险记》）

The Adventure of English is a British television series (ITV) on the history of the English language, which ran in November 2003. The series is cast as an adventure story, covering the history of the language from its modest beginnings around 500 AD as a minor Germanic dialect to its rise as a global language.

2) Documentary: *Shakespeare Uncovered* （《揭秘莎士比亚》）

Shakespeare Uncovered combines history, biography, iconic performances and new analyses to tell the stories behind Shakespeare's greatest plays. It provides a crash course in Shakespeare's best-known plays, presented in hour-long documentary form and guided by film and theater stars like Morgan Freeman, Kim Cattrall, Ethan Hawke, and Helen Hunt.

3. Books

Bolton, K. 2004. World Englishes. In A. Davies & C. Elder (Eds.), *The Handbook of Applied Linguistics*. New Jersey: Blackwell, 367–396.

Drout, M. 2006. *A History of the English Language*.

Freeborn, D. 2009. *From Old English to Standard English.* 上海 : 上海外语教育出版社 .

Jenkis, J. 2007. *English as a Lingua Franca: Attitude and Identity*. Oxford: Oxford University Press.

Kachru, B. B. 1992. World Englishes: Approaches, issues and resources. *Language Teaching*, *25*: 1–14.

Seidlhofer, B. 2011. *Understanding English as a Lingua Franca*. Oxford: Oxford University Press.

李赋宁 . 1991. 英语史 . 北京：商务印书馆 .

Chapter 2
The UK: A Country of Countries

The UK is the first industrialized country in the world and one of the four largest national economies of Europe. It is one of the five permanent members of the UN Security Council and has established the global time standard of Greenwich Mean Time. The UK used to be the most powerful country in the world and still has great international influence today. In this chapter, we'll introduce the four components of the UK and the geographical features as well as the history of the country.

Text A A Brief Introduction to the UK

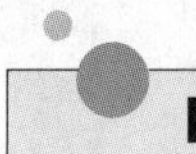

Pre-class Preparation

MOOC Watching

Watch the MOOC video "Splendid Landscape in Britain" to prepare for Text A.

Pre-reading Questions

1. When you think of the UK, what will jump into your mind first? Buckingham Palace, William Shakespeare, fish and chips, or the British Museum? Talk with your partners about your impressions of the country.
2. Who are the British people and who are the ancestors of people from England, Scotland, Wales and Northern Ireland?

In-class Reading

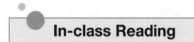

A Brief Introduction to the UK

1 When people refer to **Britain**, they often think of different names—**England**, **Great Britain**, the United Kingdom, and **the British Isles**. Are these terms the same or different?

2 The official name of Britain is "**The United Kingdom of Great Britain and Northern Ireland**", commonly known as the United Kingdom, or the UK for short. It is a sovereign country in northwestern Europe, off the north-western coast of the European mainland. The United Kingdom comprises

the island of Great Britain, the northeastern part of the island of Ireland, and many smaller islands within the British Isles.

3 The United Kingdom of Great Britain and Ireland was established in 1801. In 1921, British rule in most part of Ireland came to an end and only Northern Ireland remained in the United Kingdom. That is why the name of the country was changed to "The United Kingdom of Great Britain and Northern Ireland" in 1927. The UK is known as the home of both modern parliamentary democracy[1] and the Industrial Revolution[2]. Its capital is London, which is among the world's leading commercial, financial, and cultural centres. Other major cities include Birmingham, Liverpool, and Manchester in England, Edinburgh and Glasgow in **Scotland**, Cardiff and Swansea in **Wales**, and Belfast and Londonderry in **Northern Ireland**.

★ **The United Kingdom in the international arena**

4 The United Kingdom is one of the four largest national economies of Europe. It is one of the five **permanent** members of **the UN Security Council** and the first member of the Commonwealth of Nations, **the Council of Europe**, **the G20**, and **the World Trade Organization (WTO)**. The United Kingdom was the world's first **industrialized** country and the world's foremost power during the 19th and early 20th centuries. Today, the United Kingdom still has considerable economic, cultural, scientific, technological, and political influence internationally.

permanent *adj.* 永久的

industrialized *adj.* 工业化的

5 The United Kingdom became a member of the European Union in 1973. Many British people, however, were reluctant EU members, believing in the words of British wartime Prime Minister Winston Churchill, who **sonorously** remarked, "We are with Europe, but not of it. We are linked, but not comprised. We are interested and associated, but not absorbed." On January 31, 2020, after much negotiation, the **withdrawal** agreement on "Brexit[3]" (British Exit from the EU) was **ratified** by both the EU and the UK. Thus, the United Kingdom became the first country to withdraw

sonorously *adv.* 响亮地

withdrawal *n.* 撤回

ratify *v.* 批准

formally from the EU.

★ **Countries within a country: The United Kingdom**

6 The United Kingdom consists of four constituent countries: England, Scotland, Wales, and Northern Ireland. The UK Prime Minister's website has used the phrase "countries within a country" to describe the United Kingdom. Although the United Kingdom is a **unitary sovereign country**, Scotland, Wales and Northern Ireland have gained a degree of autonomy and have their own legal systems. The three countries also have separate national governing bodies for sports and compete separately in many international sporting competitions, including the Commonwealth Games and **the FIFA World Cup**. However, since the first Olympic Games, the UK has chosen to be represented by one team. It is normally called "Team GB", meaning "Team Great Britain and Northern Ireland".

unitary
adj. 统一的

7 Many people get confused about the difference between "England", "Great Britain" and "British Isles". England is the largest country of Great Britain and the UK. It is sometimes, wrongly, used in reference to the whole United Kingdom, or the entire island of Great Britain. This is not only incorrect but can cause offence to people from other parts of the UK. Great Britain is not a country but a **landmass**. It is known as "Great" because it is the largest island in the British Isles, and houses the countries of England, Scotland and Wales within its shores. It is sometimes used as a loose **synonym** for the United Kingdom as a whole. The British Isles refer to a group of islands off the north-western coast of continental Europe, consisting of the islands of Great Britain, Ireland, the Isle of Man, the Hebrides and over 6,000 smaller islands. It is a geographical name instead of a political term.

landmass
n. 大片陆地

synonym
n. 同义词

8 The Union Flag of the United Kingdom, popularly known as the Union Jack, symbolises the union of the countries of the UK. It is made up of the individual flags of three countries in the Kingdom and represents the political

union of three kingdoms—England, Scotland and Northern Ireland.

★ **Who are the British people?**

9 People from the UK are called British although they have different nationalities. The adjective "British" is commonly used to represent things relating to the United Kingdom and is used in law to refer to the United Kingdom citizenship. People of countries within the United Kingdom use different terms to describe their national identity and may identify themselves as being British, English, Scottish, Welsh, or Northern Irish. The official **designation** for a citizen of the United Kingdom is "British citizen".

designation *n.* 名称，称呼

10 The United Kingdom has made significant contributions to the world economy, famous for the **innovations** of technology brought by the Industrial Revolution starting from the 18th century. Since World War II, however, the United Kingdom's global influence has gradually declined. Now most of its **prominent** exports have become cultural, including literature, theatre, film, and popular music. Up until now, Britain's greatest export has been the English language, which is currently spoken in every corner of the world as one of the leading international media of cultural and economic exchange.

innovation *n.* 创新

prominent *adj.* 主要的

T Cultural Terms

1. Britain 不列颠（英国的简称）
2. England 英格兰（英国最大的组成国，位于大不列颠岛的南部）
3. Great Britain 大不列颠（指包含英格兰、苏格兰和威尔士的大不列颠岛）
4. the British Isles 英吉利群岛（指包含大不列颠岛、爱尔兰岛和周围岛屿的总称）
5. The United Kingdom of Great Britain and Northern Ireland 大不列颠及北爱尔兰联合王国（英国的全称）
6. Scotland 苏格兰（英国组成国之一，位于大不列颠岛的北部）
7. Wales 威尔士（英国组成国之一，位于大不列颠岛的西南部）
8. Northern Ireland 北爱尔兰（英国组成国之一，位于爱尔兰岛的北部）

9. the UN Security Council 联合国安全理事会（联合国六大主要机构之一）

10. the Council of Europe 欧洲委员会（欧洲政府间国家组织）

11. the G20 二十国集团（在 1999 年成立的七国集团基础上发展而来的二十国首脑会议）

12. the World Trade Organization (WTO) 世界贸易组织

13. sovereign country 主权国家

14. the FIFA World Cup 国际足联世界杯（足球界最高荣誉的国际赛事）

Cultural Notes

1. parliamentary democracy

议会民主制， 也称为议会制或内阁制，是一种政治制度，特点是“议会至上”。政府首脑（总理或首相）的权力来自议会，一是通过议会改选后的多数议席支持，二是政府首脑赢得议会的信任投票。在这样的政体下，国家元首需获得议会支持才能工作，一般认为英国是全世界最早实行议会民主制的国家。

2. the Industrial Revolution

工业革命，又称产业革命，准确地说是第一次工业革命，指发生在 18 世纪 60 年代发源于英国的机器代替人力的生产与科技革命。在这段时间里，人类生产与制造方式逐渐转为机械化，机器逐渐取代人力和畜力，大规模的工厂生产逐渐取代手工生产，引发了现代的科技革命。

3. Brexit（British Exit）

脱欧，指英国脱离欧盟，使英国不再受欧盟法律、欧洲单一市场及若干自由贸易协定的约束，并可取回对移民政策的控制权。英国于 2020 年 1 月 31 日晚上 11 点正式退出欧盟，随后进入脱欧过渡期，至 2020 年 12 月 31 日结束。

Exercises

I. Multiple Choice

Directions: *Below each statement there are four choices. Decide which of the following choices is the most appropriate answer.*

1. ________ is the official name of Britain.

A. The United Kingdom　　B. England

C. British Isles　　D. Great Britain

2. The full name of Britain is "The United Kingdom of ________ Britain and ________".

A. / ; Northern Ireland B. Great; Northern Ireland

C. /; Ireland D. Great; Ireland

3. There are ________ parts in Great Britain and ________ parts in Britain.

A. three; four B. three; three C. four; three D. four; four

4. The British Isles include two large islands: ________ and Ireland island.

A. Britain B. the UK C. Great Britain D. England

5. Britain withdrew from the EU in January of ________.

A. 2018 B. 2019 C. 2020 D. 2021

II. Matching

Directions: *Match the countries with their corresponding national flags.*

________ 1. England

________ 2. Wales

________ 3. Scotland

________ 4. (Old) Ireland

________ 5. the United Kingdom

________ 6. the Republic of Ireland

A  B  C

D  E  F

III. Oral Report

Directions: *Report to the whole class the relationship between Britain, England, Scotland, Wales, Northern Ireland, Great Britain and the British Isles. You can refer*

to the following picture.

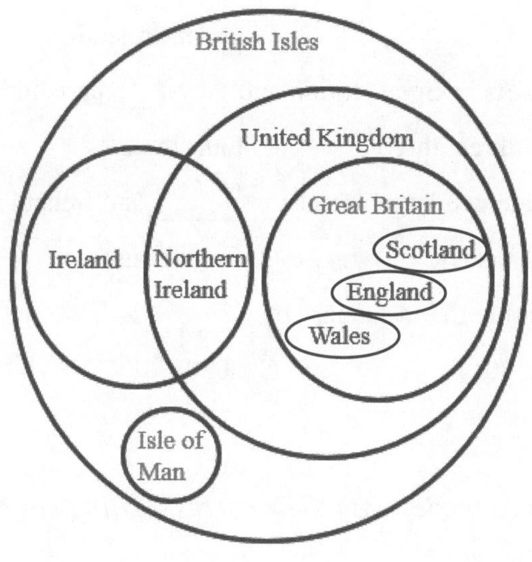

____

____

____

____

____

____

____

Post-class Thinking

Blank Filling

Directions: *Scan the QR code to fill in the blanks of the mind map of Text A and you will have a better understanding of the structure of the text.*

Text B England and Its Cultural Heritages

Pre-class Preparation

MOOC Watching

Watch the MOOC video "England: Jewel of Britain" to prepare for Text B.

Pre-reading Questions

1. Speaking of England, do you know any historical or cultural heritages there? Describe your impressions of any national cultural symbols of England.
2. How many cities in England do you know about? Do you agree with Samuel Johnson's comment "If one man is tired of London, he is tired of life"? Why or why not? Think about this question again when you finish reading Text B.

In-class Reading

England and Its Cultural Heritages

★ Land and climate in England

1 The name "England" originated from the old English name "Englaland", meaning "the land of the Angles", who came from continental Germany and invaded Britain in the late 5th century with the Saxons and Jutes. The term has been used in another sense meaning "the land inhabited by the English people". England used to be an ancient kingdom that existed from the 10th century to 1707. Now England is a constituent country within the United Kingdom.

2 England covers the central and southern two thirds of Great Britain and includes over 100 small islands. The country is bordered by two other countries of the UK: to the north by Scotland and to the west by Wales. Geographically England is close to **continental Europe** and is separated from France by **the English Channel**.

terrain
n. 地形

rolling
adj. 起伏的

3 Most of England's landscape consists of low hills and plains, with upland and mountainous **terrain** in the north and west of the country. Green lowlands and **rolling** hills are in the central and southern regions of the country. **The Pennines**, known as the "backbone of England", are the oldest mountain range in the country. **The Severn** is the longest river flowing through England (354 km). However, **the Thames** is the longest river entirely in England, which is 346 km in length. There are many lakes in England and the largest is Windermere within the area of **the Lake District**. The Lake District is a popular holiday destination and famous for its associations with **William Wordsworth** and other Lake Poets.

temperate
adj. 温和的

4 In England, the climate is **temperate maritime** and is greatly influenced by the ocean. In general, summers are warm and winters are cool. The summers in England are cooler than those on the European continent, but the winters are milder. Spring in England is very cool and summer is always the best season in England. July is the best month in a year and the west wind from the Atlantic is the warmest. That is why William Shakespeare wrote *Shall I Compare Thee to a Summer's Day* and **Percy Shelley** created the famous *Ode to the West Wind*.

★ People in England and British gentleman culture

descendant
n. 后代

5 Today's British people are a mixture of different ethnic groups. In a narrow sense, "English people" refer to the **descendants** of the English-speaking Anglo-Saxons who conquered the native Celts in England in the 5th century. English people attach great importance to keeping traditional British social system and customs. The monarchy and **the Upper House**

have been **retained** in the political system. In daily life, many house owners still keep fireplaces in their houses which are of little use today. British gentleman culture is another good example to represent typical British norms and customs.

retain
v. 保持

6 In novels, cartoons and movies, we often find images of typical English gentlemen with a **fedora** hat and a small **moustache**. Their polite and courteous manners, as well as their great respect for ladies have left a deep impression on people around the world. The term "gentleman" first appeared in Chaucer's *Canterbury Tales*. From the 15th century to the 17th century, men from upper-class families are called "gentlemen". In the Victorian Age, the term was preferred to express manners of people rather than their social class. *The Oxford English Dictionary* describes a gentleman as "a man in whom gentle birth is accompanied by appropriate qualities and behavior; hence, in general, a man of **chivalrous** instincts and fine feelings". Today, the word is widely used to indicate politeness in social communications.

fedora
n. 男士软呢帽
moustache
n. 小胡子

chivalrous
adj. 侠义的

★ Important cities in the UK

7 For centuries, England has been a center of government, as well as the scene of countless important historic events. There are numerous cultural heritages in Britain and many of them are located in England, such as **Stonehenge, Durham Castle and Cathedral**, and Maritime Greenwich. England is also home to a great number of cities that have held an important position in Britain and even Europe.

8 "When a man is tired of London, he is tired of life; for there is in London all that life can afford." Samuel Johnson highly praised London in a discussion with his friend in 1777. The whole world gradually got to know the charm of London in the following 200 years. London is the capital of both England and the UK. Standing on the River Thames, London has been a major transport **hub** for two millennia. Its history goes back to the time of

hub
n. 中心

metropolitan *adj.* 大都市的

the Romans and it became the largest **metropolitan** city during the Victorian Era. It has been rebuilt after many fires and has recovered from the disaster of World War II.

9 Now, London is one of the world's most important global cities. It is a leading center of commerce, education, entertainment, fashion, finance, media, tourism and transportation. In 2012, London became the first city to host three modern Summer Olympic Games. London is home to highly ranked education institutions such as University College London, Imperial College London, and the London School of Economics. London is home to numerous museums, galleries, libraries and other cultural institutions. **The British Museum** has a permanent collection of over 7 million objects. It is one of the largest and most comprehensive museums in the world, illustrating and documenting the story of human culture from its beginning to the present.

forefront *n.* 前沿

10 London is a city steeped in history and yet always at the **forefront** of fashion. The city includes a long list of world-renowned places as Westminster Abbey, **Buckingham Palace** and the Tower of London. Take a stroll in **Trafalgar Square**, go shopping on Oxford Street and don't miss a ride on the **London Eye**, which is a giant Ferris Wheel commanding stunning views of the city. For museum fans, the British Museum and the Science Museum are amongst the best anywhere. **The National Gallery** and **the Tate Gallery** have collections of some of the world's greatest art works. Theatre lovers will enjoy **phenomenal** plays and shows in **London's West End**. Other landmarks include **Piccadilly Circus, St. Paul's Cathedral, Tower Bridge**, and **the Shard**.

phenomenal *adj.* 非凡的

11 There are four World Heritage Sites[1] in London: the Tower of London[2]; Kew Gardens[3]; the Palace of Westminster[4] and Westminster Abbey, including St. Margaret's Church and Greenwich Maritime[5] where Royal Observatory Greenwich is located. Table 2–1 lists some of the most famous scenic spots in London.

Table 2–1 The most famous scenic spots in London

Scenic spots	Photos	Descriptions
The Tower of London		The Tower of London is a historic castle on the north bank of the River Thames in central London. Its official title is "Her Majesty's Royal Palace and Fortress of the Tower of London". The Tower of London has played a prominent role in English history. It has served as an armoury, a treasury, a public record office, and the home of the Crown Jewels of England. It has been used as a prison of political figures since the late 15th century, such as Elizabeth I before she became queen.
Kew Gardens		Kew Gardens, which was founded in 1840, is a botanic garden in southwest London. It houses the largest and most diverse botanical and mycological collections in the world. It is one of London's top tourist attractions and is a World Heritage Site. You can discover the world of science behind its botanical collections containing 50,000 living plants.
The Palace of Westminster		The Palace of Westminster, informally known as the Houses of Parliament, serves as the meeting place for the two Houses of the Parliament of the United Kingdom. The name of the palace derives from Westminster Abbey and now refers to a building complex on the north bank of the River Thames. The Palace of Westminster has become a metonym for the UK Parliament and the British government. The Elizabeth Tower, which is referred to by the name of its main bell, Big Ben, has become an iconic landmark of London and even the UK.

(cont.)

Scenic spots	Photos	Descriptions
Westminster Abbey		Westminster Abbey is a large, mainly Gothic abbey church in London. The abbey is formally titled the Collegiate Church of St. Peter at Westminster. It is one of the United Kingdom's most notable religious buildings as well as the traditional place of coronation. The Abbey is the burial site of more than 3,300 persons, usually of prominence in British history: at least 16 monarchs, 8 prime ministers, poets laureate, actors, scientists and military leaders.
Maritime Greenwich		Maritime Greenwich, a World Heritage Site in London, is described by the UNESCO as having "outstanding universal value" and reckoned to be the "finest and most dramatically sited architectural and landscape ensemble in the British Isles". It can be divided into the groups of buildings along the riverfront, Greenwich Park and the Georgian and Victorian town centre.
Buckingham Palace		Buckingham Palace is the official London residence and administrative headquarters of the monarch of Britain. Originally known as Buckingham House, the building was a large townhouse built for the Duke of Buckingham in 1703 and was later enlarged to be the residence of Queen Victoria in 1837. Now it has been a focal point for the British people at times of national rejoicing and mourning. The State Rooms contain some of the best pieces of the Royal Collection and stunning French furniture. Guests can visit some of the apartments inside the Palace.

(cont.)

Scenic spots	Photos	Descriptions
St. Paul's Cathedral		St. Paul's Cathedral, dating back to the late 17th century, was designed in the English Baroque style. It is now an Anglican cathedral in London. Its dedication to Paul the Apostle dates back to the original church on this site, founded in 604 AD. The cathedral is the second biggest cathedral in Britain and the fifth biggest cathedral in the world. Its dome, framed by the spires of Wren's City churches, has dominated the skyline for over 300 years.

12 Besides London, there are many places in England of historical importance and cultural significance. In Oxford, you'll find the oldest university in Britain—Oxford University. Go to Cambridge and stand by the bridge where Xu Zhimo wrote his famous poem "Saying Goodbye to Cambridge". Birmingham is the second largest city, urban area and metropolitan area in England and the United Kingdom. Manchester is the first industrialized city in the world and was known as the world's centre of textile manufacturing during the Industrial Revolution. Football fans might be crazy about the Manchester United Football Team. Named after ancient Roman baths, Bath has been a **wellbeing** destination and famous for its natural **thermal** hot springs. Bristol, Liverpool, New Castle and York are all great places of historical interests.

wellbeing
n. 安康，幸福
thermal
adj. 热的

13 From the middle ages to the present time, people in England have created brilliant cultural heritages. As the largest country in the UK, England has a deep cultural and economic impact on the whole world. The English language, the Anglican Church, the English law and the British parliamentary system have been widely adopted all over the world. That is why many people believe that the national symbols of England can represent British culture to a certain extent.

T Cultural Terms

1. continental Europe 欧洲大陆（欧洲主体大陆，不包括岛屿）
2. the English Channel 英吉利海峡（分隔英国与欧洲大陆的法国，并连接大西洋与北海的海峡）
3. the Pennines 奔宁山脉（英国英格兰北部的主要山脉和分水岭，被称为“英国的脊梁”）
4. the Severn 塞文河（英国境内最长的河流）
5. the Thames 泰晤士河（英国的母亲河，完全在英格兰境内的最长河流）
6. the Lake District 湖区（英格兰西北部的乡村地区，以湖泊和群山著称，著名旅游景区。）
7. William Wordsworth 威廉·华兹华斯（英国浪漫主义诗人，与雪莱、拜伦齐名，湖畔诗人的代表，与塞缪尔·泰勒·柯勒律治合著《抒情歌谣集》。）
8. temperate maritime 温带海洋性气候
9. Percy Shelley 珀西·雪莱 （英国浪漫主义诗人、作家）
10. the Upper House 英国上议院（也被称为贵族院，是英国议会两院之一）
11. Stonehenge 巨石阵（位于伦敦西南 100 多千米，欧洲著名的史前时代文化神庙遗址，1986 年巨石阵、埃克伯里及相关遗址被列入世界文化遗产。）
12. Durham Castle and Cathedral 达勒姆城堡和大教堂（1986 年被列入世界文化遗产）
13. Buckingham Palace 白金汉宫（英国君主在伦敦的居住地和办事处，皇家庆典的主要举办场地）
14. Trafalgar Square 特拉法尔加广场（伦敦著名广场，坐落在伦敦市中心）
15. the London Eye 伦敦眼（坐落在伦敦泰晤士河畔，世界上首座观景摩天轮）
16. the British Museum 大英博物馆（又名不列颠博物馆，位于伦敦牛津街附近的罗素广场，世界四大博物馆之一）
17. the National Gallery 英国国家美术馆（又译为国家艺廊，主要收藏绘画作品）
18. the Tate Gallery 泰特美术馆（因丰富的艺术藏品和建筑特色而闻名）
19. London’s West End 伦敦西区（与纽约百老汇齐名的世界两大戏剧中心之一，是表演艺术的国际舞台，也是英国戏剧界的代名词）
20. Piccadilly Circus 皮卡迪利广场（位于伦敦市中心的著名商业街区）
21. St. Paul’s Cathedral 圣保罗大教堂（著名的巴洛克风格的教堂，世界第五大教堂，英国第二大教堂）
22. Tower Bridge 伦敦塔桥（一座上开悬索桥，位于英国伦敦，横跨泰晤士河，因在伦敦塔附近而得名，是伦敦的象征。）

23. the Shard 碎片大厦（位于伦敦泰晤士河南岸，高达309.6米，目前是全欧洲第二高的大厦。）

Cultural Notes

1. World Heritage Sites

   世界遗产，由联合国教科文组织管理、世界遗产委员会决议通过的具有重要意义的地标或区域，包括自然遗产、文化遗产及兼具两者的复合遗产。被列入世界遗产的地点，必须对全世界人类都具有“突出的普世价值”。

2. the Tower of London

   伦敦塔，伦敦标志性的宫殿和要塞，曾是堡垒、军械库、国库和监狱，关押上层社会的囚犯，1988 年被列入世界文化遗产。

3. Kew Gardens

   英国皇家植物园林，坐落在伦敦三区的西南角，是世界上著名的植物园之一，2003 年被列入世界文化遗产。

4. the Palace of Westminster

   威斯敏斯特宫，也是英国的议会大厦，与威斯敏斯特教堂和圣玛格丽特教堂一起于 1987 年被列入世界文化遗产。

5. Greenwich Maritime

   格林威治海岸地区，以格林威治公园为主体，包括旧皇家天文台、航海博物馆、格林威治码头在内的整片区域，于 1997 年被列入世界文化遗产。

Exercises

I. Multiple Choice

Directions: *Below each statement there are four choices. Decide which of the following choices is the most appropriate answer.*

1. The longest river in Britain is ____________.

   A. River Severn B. River Thames C. River Mississippi D. River Shannon

2. Britain enjoys a ____________ climate.

   A. hot maritime B. temperate maritime C. warm continental D. cold continental

3. “If winter comes, can spring be far behind?” comes from *Ode to the* ____________ *Wind*

by Shelley.

A. East B. South C. West D. North

4. The Acts of Union in 1707 made the kingdoms of England and __________ united to form Great Britain.

A. Wales B. Scotland C. Wales D. Northern Ireland

II. True or False

Directions: *Determine whether the following statements are true (T) or false (F).*

1. July is normally the best month in a year and the west wind from the Atlantic is the warmest.
2. Jane Austen wrote *Pride and Prejudice*, *Sense and Sensibility* and other four novels.
3. "Ladies and gentlemen" only refer to those cultured and refined men and women.

Group Games

I. A DIY Trip in London

Directions: *You are supposed to stay in London for a week. How will you plan your trip using the London Pass? Search for the best price of the London Pass on the Internet. You will be given 300 pounds to buy tickets for all your destinations, including tourist attractions, subway tickets and three meals (not including accommodation). Each group needs to make a travel plan making good use of the London Pass. The group which proposes the best and most sensible travel plan covering the most tourist destinations using the least money will win.*

II. Role Play

Directions: *Two students form a group. One plays role A and the other plays role B. Start your discussion based on the following information.*

Role A: You are a tour guide in Britain. You are going to arrange a 6-day tour for a group of travelers from China. They hope they can have a wonderful trip in Britain and want to enjoy natural sceneries, historical buildings as well as British food. Make a travel plan for them including tourist destinations, hotels and restaurants.

Role B: You are the head of a group of travelers from China. Your group wants to tour around Britain for 6 days. You have a lot of questions to ask before starting your trip. Take a note of your group members' questions and talk with your tour guide to make sure everything will be fine for your trip.

Critical Thinking

Directions: *Discuss with your partners the following questions.*

Similar to gentlemen culture in the West, *Junzi* in Chinese traditional culture refers to respectable people with humane conduct and high moral standards. Look for 3–5 proverbs about *Junzi* in Chinese classical works and discuss with your partners the following questions:

1. What is your understanding of *Junzi* in the past and at the present?

2. What qualities should we college students possess to become a *Junzi* in modern China?

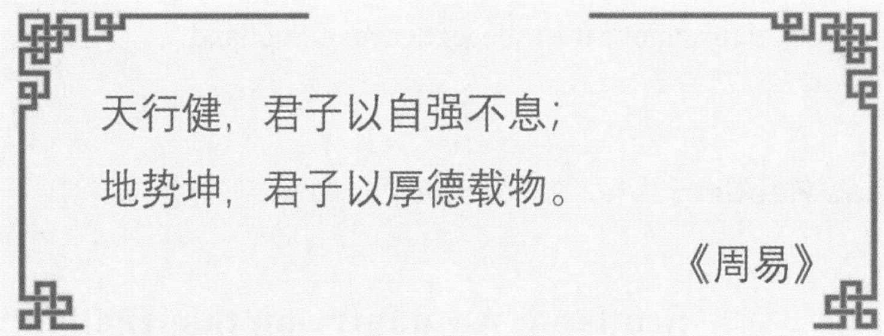
天行健，君子以自强不息；
地势坤，君子以厚德载物。
《周易》

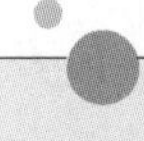

Post-class Thinking

Blank Filling

Directions: *Scan the QR code to fill in the blanks of the mind map of Text B and you will have a better understanding of the structure of the text.*

Text C Scotland: A Country on the Highlands

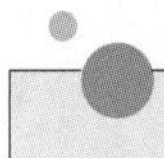

Pre-class Preparation

MOOC Watching

Watch the MOOC video "The Song of Freedom—Scotland" to prepare for Text C.

Pre-reading Questions

1. Do you know any legends or stories related to Scotland? Share your personal knowledge of Scotland with your partner.
2. Have you watched the British movie *The Brave Heart*? Why did people like William Wallace fight so hard to achieve the independence of Scotland?

In-class Reading

Scotland: A Country on the Highlands

★ Land and people in Scotland

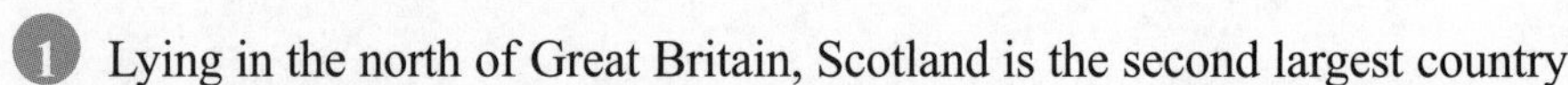

1 Lying in the north of Great Britain, Scotland is the second largest country

of the United Kingdom. In the 17th century, Scottish poet Robert Burns[1] wrote such a poem to show his deep **affection** to Scotland, his motherland.

affection
n. 感情；喜爱

My heart's in the highlands, my heart is not here;
My heart's in the highlands, chasing the deer;
Chasing the wild deer, and following the roe,
My heart's in the highlands, wherever I go.

2 The name "Scotland" derives from the Latin word "Scoti", meaning "land of the Scots", a Celtic people from Ireland who settled on the west coast of Great Britain in the 5th century BC. Scotland occupies one third of the island of Great Britain. The country borders England to the southeast and is surrounded by the Atlantic Ocean with the North Sea to the northeast and the Irish Sea to the west. It also has more than 790 islands. The Highlands are a wild, mountainous and rocky plateau and occupy the northern half of Scotland. **Ben Nevis**, the highest point in the UK, is located here. There is **Loch Ness**, where people claimed to have seen a monster in the lake, which still remains a mystery today. The Central Lowlands of Scotland average about 152 meters and contain Scotland's largest lake, **Loch Lamond**. The Southern Uplands feature the Scottish **moor** lands with their many rivers and **dells**. The capital of Scotland is **Edinburgh**. **Glasgow** is the largest city in terms of population.

moor
n. 沼泽
dell
n. 小溪谷

3 The population of Scotland accounts for about 8% of the population of the UK. Most of its population, including its capital Edinburgh, is concentrated in the **Scottish Central Lowlands**, the plain between the **Scottish Northern Highlands** and the **Scottish Southern Uplands**. Most of Scottish people are descendants of **the Celts,** and **Scottish Gaelic** has been a main language in the country since the 5th century. Although different languages are used in today's Scotland, Scottish Gaelic has held an indispensable position in people's life along the history of Scotland.

Scottish Northern Highlands

★ **The pursuit of independence**

4 On September 18, 2014, a **referendum** on Scottish independence was held in Scotland. Voters needed to vote "Yes" or "No" to decide whether Scotland should be an independent country. 55% of Scottish people voted against it and Scotland remained a part of Britain. This was not the first time for the Scottish to pursue freedom from the United Kingdom. For centuries, Scotland has been a land invaded again and again. The recorded history of Scotland begins with the arrival of **the Roman Empire** in the 1st century. It is generally believed that in the 9th century, the Kingdom of Scotland was united under the descendants of King Kenneth, the first king of a united Scotland. In 1296, Edward I of England invaded Scotland and took the Stone of Scone, which is also called the Stone of Destiny, away from Scotland and hid it in the Westminster Abbey in London. During the war time between England and Scotland in the 13th century, there arose a national hero in Scotland, whose name was William Wallace[2], who led the Scots in the First War of Scottish Indcpcndcncc against King Edward I of England.

5 After fighting a series of wars during the 14th century, James VI of Scotland became James I of England in 1603. In 1707, the Acts of Union[3] merged the Kingdom of Scotland and the Kingdom of England into a new state, the Kingdom of Great Britain. Scotland has remained a separate legal system from those of England and Wales and Northern Ireland, and

Scotland constitutes a distinct **jurisdiction** in public and private law. The distinctive feature of education, religion and legal systems has formed a unique Scottish culture and national identity.

jurisdiction
n. 司法权

6 Since the 1920s, the Labor Party of Scotland has been committed to home rule for Scotland. The Scottish National Party grew and gained a national prominence in the 1970s. A referendum on **devolution** in 1979 was unsuccessful as it did not achieve the necessary support of 40% of the electorate. In 1999, the newly elected Prime Minister of Britain, Tony Blair, who was brought up in Scotland, helped to push the independence of Scotland in a peaceful way. He opened a way for constitutional change and the new Scottish Parliament was established and first elected on May 6, 1999. In that year, the Scottish National Party became the official **opposition** in Scottish Parliament. This party is devoted to the independence of Scotland from the United Kingdom and had promised a referendum on the destiny of Scotland in 2014. The results showed that more than half of Scottish people voted to remain in the territory of the United Kingdom for the time being.

devolution
n. 权力下放

opposition
n. 反对派

★ Scotland in the world

7 **Kilt**, tartan and **bagpipe** are all characteristics of Scotland. A kilt is a type of knee-length short dress with pleats at the back, originating in the traditional dress of Gaelic men and boys in the Scottish Highlands. The kilt is most worn as an item of male clothing on formal occasions and has not been adapted to be used by both men and women all over the world on all occasions. Tartan is particularly associated with Scotland and Scottish kilts almost always have tartan patterns. Since 1782, tartan has been adopted as symbolic national dress of Scotland. The bagpipe is the national instrument of Scotland and the Scottish Great Highland bagpipes are the best known examples around the world. The name "bagpipe" has almost become synonymous with its best-known form, Great Highland Bagpipe.

kilt
n. 苏格兰短褶裙

bagpipe
n. 风笛

Great Highland Bagpipe

8 During the Scottish Enlightenment and the Industrial Revolution, Scotland became one of the commercial, intellectual and industrial powerhouses of Europe. Many great inventors and scientists came from Scotland. **James Watt** improved the steam engine. **Alexander Bell** invented telephone and **John Baird** invented TV. **Adam Smith** laid a foundation for modern economy. The great milestone in medicine—**penicillin** was discovered by a Scottish scientist **Alexander Fleming**. Scotland was home to the sports of golf and **curling**. And the curling team of Scotland ranked in the top three in the world.

penicillin
n. 盘尼西林（青霉素）
curling
n. 冰壶

9 Glasgow is the largest and the most populous city in Scotland. At the **onset** of the Industrial Revolution, Glasgow was once the "Second City of the British Empire" for much of the Victorian Era and the Edwardian Era. Edinburgh is the capital and the second largest city. It was the hub of the Scottish Enlightenment of the 18th century, which transformed Scotland into a commercial, intellectual, and industrial country. If you pay a visit to Scotland, **the Castle of Edinburgh** is a must for you. Built on a dead volcano, this big castle can be seen from all places in the city.

onset
n. 开始

T Cultural Terms

1. Ben Nevis 本尼维斯山（位于苏格兰高地区域内）
2. Loch Ness 尼斯湖（位于苏格兰高原北部峡谷中，相传湖中有神秘水怪）
3. Loch Lamond 罗蒙湖（苏格兰第二长湖，也是最深的湖）

4. Edinburgh 爱丁堡（苏格兰首府）
5. Glasgow 格拉斯哥（苏格兰第一大城市）
6. Scottish Central Lowlands 苏格兰中部低地
7. Scottish Northern Highlands 苏格兰北部高地
8. Scottish Southern Uplands 苏格兰南部高地
9. the Celts 凯尔特人（欧洲主要民族之一，公元前 5 世纪进入不列颠岛）
10. Scottish Gaelic 苏格兰盖尔语（也被称为高地盖尔语，曾是苏格兰代表性的语言）
11. referendum 全民公投（由全体国民集体投票，一般为重大事件举行）
12. the Roman Empire 罗马帝国（曾是横跨欧、亚、非三大洲的大帝国）
13. James Watt 詹姆斯·瓦特（苏格兰著名的发明家和机械工程师，曾改良了蒸汽机）
14. Alexander Bell 亚历山大·格拉汉姆·贝尔（苏格兰企业家，获得了世界上第一台可用的电话机的专利权，创建了贝尔电话公司）
15. John Baird 约翰·贝尔德（苏格兰发明家，发明了世界上第一套电视系统）
16. Adam Smith 亚当·斯密（苏格兰哲学家和经济学家，所著的《国富论》成为第一本试图阐述欧洲产业和商业发展历史的著作）
17. Alexander Fleming 亚历山大·弗莱明爵士（苏格兰生物学家、药学家、植物学家，1923 年发现溶菌酶，1928 年发现青霉素）
18. the Castle of Edinburgh 爱丁堡城堡（苏格兰和爱丁堡的重要象征，坐落在爱丁堡市内的城堡岩顶上）

Cultural Notes

1. Robert Burns

罗伯特·彭斯，著名苏格兰诗人，从小熟悉苏格兰民谣和古老传说。他搜集整理苏格兰民歌，并用苏格兰语写作。他的诗歌通俗流畅，便于吟唱，在民间广为流传，被认为是苏格兰的民族诗人。

2. William Wallace

威廉·华莱士，苏格兰独立战争的重要领袖。他本是苏格兰的骑士、贵族、爱国人士，自 1296 年带领苏格兰人民开始了反对英格兰的斗争，后于 1305 年被英军杀害。

3. the Acts of Union

《1707 联合法令》，于 1707 年生效，苏格兰国会和英格兰国会合并，将苏格兰和英格兰合并为一个国家。历史学家 Simon Schama 指出，这最初带有敌意的合并意外形成了一个欧洲大帝国。

 Group Games

Role Play

Directions: *Two students form a group. One plays role A and the other plays role B. Start your discussion based on the following information.*

Role A: You are Scotland. You have been pursuing independence from Britain for hundreds of years. State the primary reasons to support your political opinion and try to justify your national independent movement.

Role B: You are England. You don't want Scotland to be an independent country. Explain your considerations from social, political, economic and cultural perspectives.

Post-class Thinking

Extensive Reading

Directions: *Scan the QR code to read and listen to the poem "My Heart's in the Highlands" by Robert Burns.*

Supplementary Resources

1. Extensive Reading

Scan the QR codes to read Text D "Wales and Northern Ireland". Then watch the MOOC video "Celts' Heritages—Wales and Northern Ireland". Think of the following questions:

1) Where is Wales? Do you know any famous people or cultural symbols from Wales?

2) What is the difference between Northern Ireland and the Republic of Ireland? How do they relate to each other in the past and at the present?

Text D "Wales and Northern Ireland"

MOOC video "Celts' Heritages—Wales and Northern Ireland"

2. Documentaries

1) Documentary: *Britain from Above* (《俯瞰英国》)

Britain from Above is a British television miniseries which films the skies over Britain to research aspects of past and present British life and their interconnections that make Britain what it is today. BBC described the series as "an epic journey revealing the secrets, patterns and hidden rhythms of our lives from a striking new perspective".

2) Documentary: *Michael Wood's Story of England* (《英格兰的故事》)

Michael Wood's Story of England is a BBC documentary series written and presented by Michael Wood. It tells English history from the Roman Era to modern times and focuses on tracing history through ordinary people in an ordinary English town, in which current residents of Kibworth tell what they know of their ancestors.

3) Documentary: *A History of Scotland* (《苏格兰史话》)

A History of Scotland is a documentary charting the birth and growth of the Scottish nation. Ten episodes bring a fresh perspective to tell Scotland's past and reveals how in the second half of the 18th century Scotland was transformed from a poor northern country into one of the richest nations on Earth.

4) Documentary: *Lolo's Jewels of Wales* (《威尔士的瑰宝》)

Lolo's Jewels of Wales is a BBC documentary series in which Lolo William introduces his favorite Welsh landscapes and wild life. It also focuses on mineral resources in Wales and tells how they are exploited.

3. Books

Marr, A. 2010. *The Making of Modern Britain: From Queen Victoria to V.E. Day*. St. Charles: Pan Books.

McDowall, D. 1989. *An Illustrated History of Britain*. Harlow: Longman.

Morgan, K. O. 2001. *The Oxford History of Britain* (3rd ed.). Oxford: Oxford Paperbacks.

戴维 · 雷诺兹 . 2021. 英国故事：从 11 世纪到脱欧动荡，千年历史的四重变奏 . 北京：中信出版社 .

桂涛 . 2019. 英国：优雅衰落 . 北京：生活 · 读书 · 新知三联书店 .

Chapter 3
The US: A Country of Cultural Diversity

The US is a highly developed capitalist country and has become the world's largest national economy after the Cold War. The White House, Silicon Valley, Wall Street, Hollywood, and Broadway all enjoy a worldwide reputation. The history of the US is short but unique; the culture of the US is not profound but has an everlasting influence. This chapter will introduce the geographical features, landscapes and landmarks, representative cities as well as the international influence of the US.

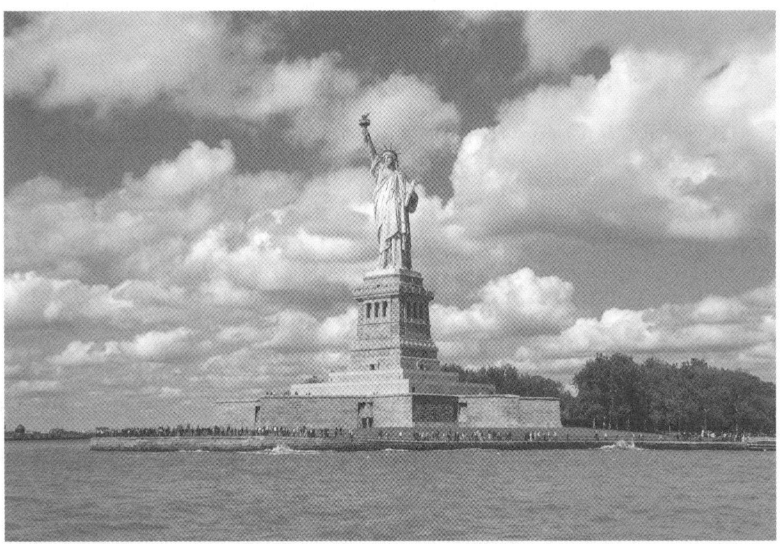

Text A　A Brief Introduction to the US

Pre-class Preparation

MOOC Watching

Watch the MOOC video "A Panoramic View of America" to prepare for Text A.

Pre-reading Question

What is your first impression of the US? New York City, the Statue of Liberty, Uncle Sam, KFC or Hollywood movies? Share with your partner what impresses you the most about the US.

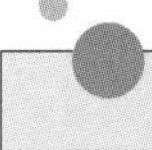

In-class Reading

A Brief Introduction to the US

primarily *adv.* 主要地

reservation *n.* 保护区

1 The United States of America, commonly known as the United States (US or USA), or simply America[1], is a country **primarily** located in North America. The United States is the second largest country in North America after Canada. It consists of 50 states, a **federal district**, five major **self-governing territories**, 326 Indian **reservations**, and some minor possessions. Besides the 48 **contiguous states** that occupy the middle part of North America, the United States includes the state of Alaska, at the northwestern extreme of North America, and the island state of Hawaii, in the mid-Pacific Ocean. The contiguous states border Canada to the north,

the Atlantic Ocean to the east, the Gulf of Mexico and Mexico to the south, and the Pacific Ocean to the west. With a population of more than 300 million people, the United States is the third most populous country in the world. Its national capital is Washington, DC, and the most populous city is New York City.

2 Because of its vast territory and wide **swath** of latitude, the United States has some of the world's most varied **topography** and diverse landscapes. The country houses a larger collection of distinct landscapes than most of other countries on the planet. Its physical environment ranges from **the Arctic** to the **subtropical**, from the moist rain forest to the arid desert, from the rugged mountain peak to the flat **prairie**. Although the total population of the United States is large by world standards, its overall population density is relatively low. The country embraces some of the world's largest urban concentrations as well as some of the most extensive areas that are almost devoid of **habitation**.

swath
n. 一片，一列
topography
n. 地形
subtropical
adj. 亚热带的
prairie
n. 大草原
habitation
n. 居住，住所

3 The United States is well known for its highly diverse population. Unlike a country such as China that mainly consists of **indigenous** peoples, the United States has a diversity of inhabitants that have come from an immense and sustained global immigration. The past decades have witnessed the rapid increase of racial and ethnic diversity in American population. Probably no other country has a wider range of racial, ethnic, and cultural types than the United States. In addition to the presence of surviving native Americans[2] (including **American Indians**, **the Aleuts** and **the Eskimos**) and the descendants of Africans taken as enslaved persons to the New World, the American national character has been enriched and constantly redefined by the tens of millions of immigrants. They have come to the United States hoping for better social, political, and economic opportunities than what they have in their motherlands. The American population is a unique **mosaic** of cultures. Based on the data from the US Census Bureau[3], almost 40%

indigenous
adj. 本地的
mosaic
n. 马赛克，也指不同要素的组合

of American people identified as racial or ethnic minorities in 2020. The Latino population is now the largest minority group, comprising of 18% of the total population. White people consist of 60% of the population, black people make a 12% and Asians make a 5.6% of the population. The first Chinese immigrants came to the United States in the mid-19th century as sailors, labors and merchants. In 1869, the first **transcontinental** railroad was completed with significant Chinese immigrant labor.

transcontinental *adj.* 跨州的

4 The United States is relatively young compared with other countries in the world, being less than 250 years old. The country achieved its current size only in the mid-20th century. It was the first of the European colonies to separate successfully from its motherland. In one and a half century after it was founded, the country was mainly preoccupied with territorial expansion and economic growth which ultimately led to Civil War and a healing period that is still not complete.

5 In the 20th century, the United States emerged as a world power, and since World War II it has been one of the **preeminent** powers. It is a founding member of the United Nations, **World Bank**, **International Monetary Fund**, **Organization of American States**, **NATO**, and other international organizations. The United States is a highly developed country and is the world's greatest economic power, measured in terms of **gross domestic product (GDP)**. The United States is the world's largest importer and the second largest exporter of goods. Although its population is only 4.2% of the world total, it holds 29.4% of the total wealth in the world. Making up more than a third of global military spending, the United States is the foremost military power in the world and is a leading political, cultural, and scientific force internationally.

preeminent *adj.* 卓越的

6 As a melting pot with immigrants from all over the world, the United States is known for its diverse cultures and ethnicities. This is a country

recognized as the world's **foremost** economic and military power, a prominent political and cultural force, and a leader in scientific research and technological innovations. Despite the country's proud boast of high ratings for human rights record, the United States has received some criticism in regard to inequality related to race, wealth and income, tens of thousands of deaths caused by gun violence, infamous political corruption, high **incarceration** rates, and lack of universal health care, among other issues.

foremost
adj. 首要的

incarceration
n. 监禁

Cultural Terms

1. federal district 联邦特区（美国联邦政府所在地）
2. self-governing territory 自治领地
3. contiguous state 临近州（指在美国地理上相邻的州）
4. the Arctic 北极，北极区域
5. American Indian 美洲印第安人（在前哥伦布时期就已经生活在北美洲、中美洲和南美洲的民族及其后代）
6. the Aleut 阿留申人（主要分布在美国阿拉斯加、阿留申群岛、加拿大魁北克一带，人口稀少）
7. the Eskimo 爱斯基摩人（居住在北美洲最北部的因纽特人和尤皮克人的总称，与阿留申人有亲缘关系）
8. World Bank 世界银行（为发展中国家提供贷款的联合国金融系统，国际金融机构）
9. International Monetary Fund 国际货币基金组织（与世界银行同为世界两大金融机构，致力于促进全球货币合作，确保金融稳定，促进国际贸易）
10. Organization of American States 美洲国家组织（一个以美洲国家为成员的国际组织，总部位于美国华盛顿特区，成员为美洲的 35 个独立主权国家）
11. NATO 北大西洋公约组织（简称北约，“二战”后，美国为了维护其在欧洲的主导地位，联合西欧一些国家成立该组织，其总部位于比利时布鲁塞尔）
12. gross domestic product (GDP) 国内生产总值（一定时期内一个区域的经济活动中所生产全部最终成果的市场价值，是国民经济核算的核心指标）

Cultural Notes

1. America/Americans

虽然“America”和“Americans” 经常用于表达“美国”和“美国人”，但是也可以分别指代“美洲”和“美洲人”。

2. native American

美国原住民，在美国 500 多个原住民部落中，有一半是印第安人的部落。因此，美国原住民主要指美国印第安人及阿拉斯加原住民。不过，如今美国原住民也包括夏威夷原住民及其他太平洋领地的原住民。

3. the US Census Bureau

美国普查局，是美国商务部经济和统计管理局下属的一个机关。美国宪法明文规定，美国普查局必须至少每十年进行一次人口普查，美国众议院的各州席次分配由此普查结果决定。除此之外，它还提供美国国家、人民和经济普查的统计数据。

Exercises

I. Multiple Choice

Directions: *Below each statement there are four choices. Decide which of the following choices is the most appropriate answer.*

1. The United States is made up of ________ contiguous states and ________ separate states.

   A. 50; 2　　B. 49; 2　　C. 48; 2　　D. 50; 0

2. The United States is the ________ largest country in North America and the ________ most populous country in the world.

   A. first; second　　B. second; third　　C. first; third　　D. second; second

3. Which of the following landscapes cannot be found within the territory of the United States?

   A. The Arctic.　　B. Flat prairie.　　C. The Antarctic.　　D. Rain forest.

4. Now surviving native Americans include the following except ________.

   A. American Indians　　B. the Aleuts

   C. the Maoris　　D. the Inuit

5. The United States became a preeminent superpower since ________.

   A. the Industrial Revolution B. World War I

   C. World War II D. the beginning of the 21st century

II. Chart Drawing

Directions: *Look for the population of the United States (2020) on the Internet. Draw a pie chart of the population composition and describe its population distribution.*

Your pie chart:

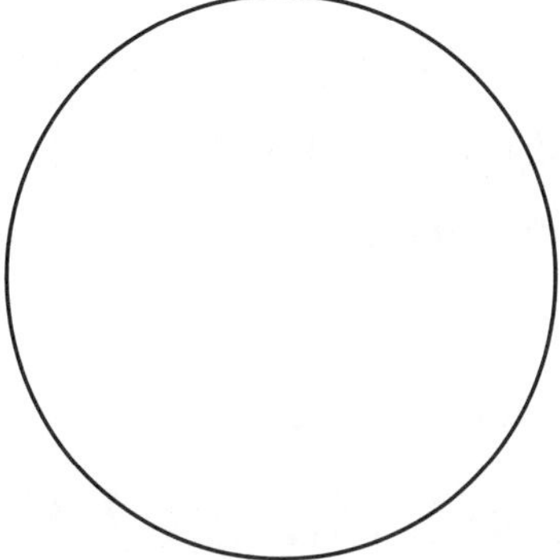

Your description: ____

____

____

____

____

Critical Thinking

Directions: *Talk about the following topic with your group members. Then one speaker will express his or her opinion on behalf of the whole group.*

The United States shares many commonalities with China since they both have a vast territory and a wide stretch of latitude. Based on your personal knowledge of China's geographical features, how do the two countries differ in terms of topography and landscapes?

Post-class Thinking

Blank Filling

Directions: *Scan the QR code to fill in the blanks of the mind map of Text A and you will have a better understanding of the structure of the text.*

Text B Landmarks in the US

Pre-class Preparation

MOOC Watching

Watch the MOOC video "United States Landmarks: Iconic Encapsulation" to prepare for Text B.

Pre-reading Questions

1. Can you list some representative landmarks in the US? How do these landmarks relate to the landscapes and history of the country?
2. How do landmarks in the US differ from landmarks in China in terms of history, geographical features and national spirit?

Landmarks in the US

1 From **natural wonders** thousands of years old to **legendary** monuments built within the last century, the US has countless landmarks for both native and international people to explore. Among thousands of landmarks across this vast country, there are tens of most internationally renowned historical and **natural landmarks**.

legendary
adj. 传奇的

★ **Historical landmarks**

2 **Historical landmarks** in the US **commemorate** the country's founding and record the ups and downs of the country in the past three hundred years. The Statue of Liberty, Independence Hall in Philadelphia, Washington Monument and Mount Rushmore take you right back to the time of the Founding Fathers of the United States.

commemorate
v. 纪念

1) Independence Hall

3 **Independence Hall** is in the center of **Independence National Historical Park** in Philadelphia, Pennsylvania. Here, you can explore the birth of the United States, where the founding fathers signed both **the Declaration of Independence** and **the US Constitution**. Known as the birthplace of America, the building was formerly known as the Pennsylvania State House. Today it is a UNESCO World Heritage Site. In other words, it is not easy to find another building that is loaded with such historical significance. Situated in the heart of Philadelphia, the red brick building stood as a symbol for freedom in the 13 colonies and is now one of America's most famous landmarks. When you enter its doors, you step back into history—**George Washington** and **Thomas Jefferson** used to debate

and write the most critical documents in American history.

2) Mount Rushmore

4 **Mount Rushmore National Memorial** is a sculpture carved into the granite face of Mount Rushmore in Black Hills, South Dakota. As tall as 60 feet (about 20 meters), Mount Rushmore pays patriotic tribute to four of the most famous presidents in American history—George Washington, Thomas Jefferson, **Abraham Lincoln**, and **Theodore Roosevelt**. The four presidents are chosen to represent nation's birth, growth, development and preservation respectively. Majestic figures of the presidents are surrounded by the beauty of the Black Hills of South Dakota. Mount Rushmore attracts more than two million visitors annually.

Mount Rushmore

3) The Statue of Liberty

5 Proudly standing 151 feet high, Lady Liberty remains the most recognizable symbol of American freedom—and unsurprisingly one of the best US landmarks to visit. **The Statue of Liberty** is a **colossal neoclassical** sculpture on Liberty Island in New York Harbor within New York City in the United States. This copper statue is a gift from the people of France to the people of the United States. The statue is a figure of **Libertas**, a robed Roman liberty goddess. She holds a torch above her head with her right hand and in her left hand carries a **tabula ansata** inscribed JULY IV MDCXXVI (July 4, 1776 in Roman numerals), the date of the US Declaration of Independence. After its dedication in 1886, the statue has

colossal *adj.* 巨大的
neoclassical *adj.* 新古典主义的

become an **icon** of freedom of the United States and is seen as a symbol of welcome to immigrants arriving by sea.

icon
n. 象征

The Statue of Liberty

4) The Lincoln Memorial

6 **The Lincoln Memorial** is a US national memorial built to honor the 16th president of the United States, Abraham Lincoln. It is on the western end of the National Mall in Washington, DC, across from the **Washington Monument**, and is in the form of a neoclassical temple. Considered as "the savior of the Union" by American people, Abraham Lincoln is known for his inspiring words of his Gettysburg Address[1] and as the signer of the Emancipation Proclamation[2]. Two years after Lincoln's **assassination**, Congress approved an association to build the Lincoln Memorial. The Memorial has become a symbolically sacred **venue** especially for the Civil Rights Movement[3]. The March on Washington[4] in 1963 brought 250,000 people to the National Mall and is famous for **Martin Luther King Jr.**'s "I Have a Dream" speech.

assassination
n. 暗杀

venue
n. 聚会地点

The Lincoln Memorial

5) The White House

7 **The White House** is the official residence and workplace of the president of the United States. The term "White House" is often used to represent the American president and their **advisers**. It is located at 1600 Pennsylvania Avenue NW in Washington, DC, and has been the residence of every US president since John Adams in 1800. The modern-day White House complex includes the Executive Residence, West Wing, East Wing, the Eisenhower Executive Office Building (the former State Department, which now houses offices for the president's staff and the vice president) and Blair House, a guest residence. In 2007, the White House was ranked second on the American Institute of Architects list of "America's Favorite Architecture".

adviser
n. 顾问

★ Natural landmarks

8 Within the 50 states of the country, there are incredible natural landmarks like **skyscraping** mountain ranges, rolling grasslands, tropical rain forests, desert plateaus and active volcanic zones. The following are some of the most famous natural landmarks in the United States.

skyscraping
adj. 高耸的

1) Yellowstone National Park

9 Yellowstone is the first national park in the US and also becomes the first national park in the world in 1872. It is located in the western United States, largely in the northwest corner of Wyoming and extending into Montana and Idaho. Many tribes and bands used the park as their home, hunting grounds, and transportation routes prior to and after European American arrival. The park is known for its wildlife and its many **geothermal** features, especially **Old Faithful Geyser**. Hundreds of species of mammals, birds, fish, reptiles, and **amphibians** have been documented, including several that are either endangered or threatened. The vast forests and grasslands also include some plants of unique species.

geothermal
adj. 地热的
amphibian
n. 两栖动物

2) Grand Canyon

10 The **Grand Canyon** is recognised as one of the seven natural wonders

in the world. Located in Arizona, **Grand Canyon National Park** is home to much of the immense Grand Canyon. Grand Canyon is unmatched in the incomparable **vistas** it offers visitors from the rim. It is known for its visually overwhelming size and its intricate and colorful landscape. Layered bands of colorful rock reveal millions of years of **geologic** history. For thousands of years, the area has been continuously inhabited by native Americans, who built settlements within the canyon and its many caves. **The Pueblo people** considered the Grand Canyon a holy site, and made **pilgrimages** to it. President Theodore Roosevelt was a major proponent of preservation of the Grand Canyon area and visited it on numerous occasions to hunt and enjoy the scenery.

vista
n. 远景

geologic
adj. 地质的

pilgrimage
n. 朝圣之行

Grand Canyon

3) Niagara Falls

11 **Niagara Falls** are a group of three waterfalls at the southern end of Niagara Gorge, spanning the border between the province of Ontario in Canada and the state of New York in the United States. The largest of the three is Horseshoe Falls, also known as Canadian Falls, which span the international border of the two countries. The smaller American Falls and Bridal Veil Falls lie within the United States. Located on the Niagara River, Niagara Falls have the highest flow rate of any waterfall in North America that has a **vertical** drop of more than 160 feet (50 meters). Niagara Falls are well known for their **pristine** beauty and as a valuable source of **hydroelectric** power.

vertical
adj. 垂直的

pristine
adj. 原始的，未开发的

hydroelectric
adj. 水力发电的

★ Other famous landmarks

⑫ Besides historical and natural landmarks, there are a large number of well-known landmarks across the vast territory of the United States. These include unique man-made architectures and buildings, as well as some magnificent **mega projects** accomplished by American people in the past hundreds of years.

1) Golden Gate Bridge

suspension *n.* 悬索桥，吊桥

⑬ The **Golden Gate Bridge** is a **suspension** bridge spanning the Golden Gate, the one-mile-wide (1.6 kilometers) strait connecting San Francisco Bay and the Pacific Ocean. Spanning 4,200 feet, this famous suspension bridge connects San Francisco and Marin County. The bridge is one of the most internationally recognized symbols of San Francisco and California. At the time of its opening in 1937, it was both the longest and the tallest suspension bridge in the world. It has been declared one of the Wonders of the Modern World[5] by the American Society of Civil Engineers. Now, it is the most famous and most photographed bridge in the United States.

Golden Gate Bridge

2) Empire State Building

skyline *n.* 地平线

sensational *adj.* 激动人心的

⑭ The **Empire State Building** is a 102-storey **Art Deco** skyscraper in Midtown Manhattan in New York City, the United States. It has been an iconic symbol of New York City's **skyline** since 1931. Standing 1,200 feet high, the Empire State Building allows travelers to take in **sensational** views of Manhattan from its observation areas on the 86th and 102nd floors. The Empire

State Building stood as the world's tallest building until the construction of the World Trade Center in 1970 and it was again the city's tallest skyscraper in 2012 after September 11 attacks. As of 2020, the building is the 7th tallest building in New York City, the 49th tallest in the world.

Empire State Building

3) Hoover Dam

15 **Hoover Dam** is a **concrete arch-gravity dam** standing on the border between the US states of Nevada and Arizona. It was constructed between 1931 and 1936 during the Great Depression. When Hoover Dam was finished in 1936, it was the world's largest hydroelectric power station. It was also the world's largest concrete structure at that time. Originally known as Boulder Dam from 1933, it was officially renamed Hoover Dam for President Herbert Hoover by a joint resolution of Congress in 1947. The purpose of a dam is to contain the flow of water, and now the dam's **generators** provide power for public and private utilities in Nevada, Arizona, and California. Hoover Dam is a major tourist attraction and nearly a million people visit the dam each year.

generator *n.* 发电机

4) Hollywood Sign

16 There is no landmark in Los Angeles more iconic than **Hollywood Sign**. Situated on Mount Lee in the Hollywood Hills area, Hollywood Sign is a cultural landmark overlooking Hollywood, Los Angeles. The sign was

upscale *adj.* 高档的

evocative *adj.* 唤起的

originally created in 1923 as an advertisement for the **upscale** Hollywood land housing development. But it quickly becomes an icon and has been imitated all over the world. After removing last four letters in 1949, the signs required constant repairs until it was completely rebuilt in 1978. For many American people, Hollywood Sign is more than just nine white letters spelling out a city's name; it's one of the world's most **evocative** symbols — a universal metaphor for ambition, success, and glamor.

Hollywood Sign

Cultural Terms

1. natural wonder 自然奇观
2. natural landmark 自然地标
3. historical landmark 历史性地标
4. Independence Hall 美国独立纪念馆（位于美国宾夕法尼亚州费城的一栋乔治风格的红砖建筑物）
5. Independence National Historical Park 国家独立历史公园（位于美国费城的一座国家历史公园，被称为“美国最有历史意义的一平方公里”）
6. the Declaration of Independence 《美国独立宣言》（北美 13 个英属殖民地宣布从大不列颠王国独立，也是美国最重要的立国文书之一）
7. the US Constitution 美国宪法（美国的根本大法，奠定了美国政治制度的法律基础）
8. George Washington 乔治·华盛顿（1775—1783 年美国独立战争时期的殖民地军总司令，于 1789 年当选为美国第一任总统）
9. Thomas Jefferson 托马斯·杰斐逊（美利坚合众国第 3 任总统，同时也是《美国独立宣言》主要起草人及美国开国元勋中最具影响力者之一）

10. Mount Rushmore National Memorial 拉什莫尔山国家纪念公园（常称美国总统公园、美国总统山、总统雕像山，是坐落于美国南达科他州基斯通附近的美国总统纪念设施）
11. Abraham Lincoln 亚伯拉罕·林肯（第 16 任美国总统，1861 年 3 月就任， 1865 年 4 月遇刺身亡。林肯领导美国南北战争，维护了联邦的完整并废除了奴隶制，推动经济的现代化）
12. Theodore Roosevelt 西奥多·罗斯福（第 26 任美国总统，曾任美国海军部副部长，参与美西战争，1900 年当选副总统）
13. the Statue of Liberty 自由女神像（位于美国纽约港自由岛的巨型古典主义塑像）
14. Libertas 罗马自由女神
15. tabula ansata 独立公约
16. the Lincoln Memorial 林肯纪念堂（为纪念美国总统亚伯拉罕·林肯而设立的纪念堂，位于华盛顿特区国家广场西）
17. Washington Monument 华盛顿纪念碑（美国首都华盛顿哥伦比亚特区的地标，为纪念美国总统乔治·华盛顿而建造）
18. Martin Luther King Jr. 小马丁·路德·金（美国牧师、社会运动者、人权主义者和非裔美国人民权运动领袖，也是 1964 年诺贝尔和平奖得主）
19. the White House 白宫（美国总统官邸与主要办公的地方，位于美国华盛顿哥伦比亚特区西北区，宾夕法尼亚大道 1600 号）
20. Yellowstone National Park 黄石国家公园（美国第一个国家公园，主要位于怀俄明州，部分位于蒙大拿州和爱达荷州）
21. Old Faithful Geyser 老忠实间歇泉（位于美国黄石国家公园的间歇泉，是黄石国家公园第一个被命名的间歇泉）
22. Grand Canyon 大峡谷（位于美国亚利桑那州西北部，是科罗拉多河经过数百万年的冲蚀形成的，色彩斑斓，峭壁险峻，1979 年大峡谷被列入世界遗产）
23. Grand Canyon National Park 大峡谷国家公园（美国西南部的国家公园，1979 年被列为世界自然遗产，以科罗拉多大峡谷景观闻名于世）
24. the Pueblo people 普罗布洛人（居住在美国西南部的美洲原住民普韦布洛社群）
25. Niagara Falls 尼亚加拉瀑布（位于加拿大安大略省和美国纽约州的交界处）
26. mega projects 超级工程（大规模的投资建设项目）
27. Golden Gate Bridge 金门大桥（美国旧金山的地标。它跨越连接旧金山湾和太平洋的

金门海峡，南端连接旧金山的北端，北端接通加州的马林县）

28. Empire State Building 帝国大厦（位于美国纽约州纽约市曼哈顿第五大道的一栋著名摩天大楼）
29. Hoover Dam 胡佛水坝（坐落于科罗拉多河黑峡谷河段之上的混凝土重力式拱坝，为美国最大的水坝，被誉为“沙漠之钻”）
30. concrete arch-gravity dam 混凝土拱形大坝
31. Hollywood Sign 好莱坞标志（位于美国加利福尼亚州洛杉矶，是当地地标，也是美国的重要文化象征）

Cultural Notes

1. Gettysburg Address

《葛底斯堡演说》，第 16 任美国总统亚伯拉罕·林肯最著名的演说，也是美国历史上为人引用最多的政治性演说。1863 年 11 月 19 日，也就是美国内战中葛底斯堡战役结束的四个半月后，林肯在宾夕法尼亚州葛底斯堡国家公墓揭幕式上发表此次演说，哀悼在长达五个半月的葛底斯堡战役中阵亡的将士。

2. the Emancipation Proclamation

《解放奴隶宣言》，美国总统亚伯拉罕·林肯于 1863 年 1 月 1 日发布的宣言，主张所有黑人奴隶应享有自由，然而，未脱离联邦的边境州及联邦掌控下的各州依然可以使用奴隶。此宣言为最终废除全美奴隶制度奠定了基础。

3. the Civil Rights Movement

非裔美国人民权运动，美国民权运动的一部分，是非裔美国人为争取与白人同等的地位而发起的群众性斗争运动，代表人物是马丁·路德·金。这项民权运动乃是经由非暴力的抗议行动争取非裔美国人民权的群众斗争。除了黑人外，它还得到了不少白人的支持。

4. the March on Washington

“向华盛顿的伟大进军”，美国历史上最大的一场人权政治集会，发生于 1963 年 8 月 28 日。集会的目的在于争取非裔美国人的民权和经济权利，马丁·路德·金在林肯纪念堂前发表了旨在推动族际和谐的著名演讲——《我有一个梦想》。

5. the Wonders of the Modern World

七大世界近现代工程奇迹，是指美国土木工程师协会于 1994 年评选出的 20 世纪最伟大的七大工程建筑，包括美国帝国大厦、金门大桥、巴拿马运河、荷兰三角洲工程、巴西伊泰普大厦、加拿大国家电视台和英法海底隧道。

Exercises

I. Matching

Directions: *Match the following landmarks in the United States with their corresponding descriptions.*

1. Hollywood Sign	________
2. Independence Hall	________
3. Golden Gate Bridge	________
4. Grand Canyon	________
5. the White House	________
6. the Lincoln Memorial	________

A. the place where the founding fathers signed both the Declaration of Independence and the US Constitution

B. a sacred venue especially for the Civil Rights Movement and the location where Martin Luther King Jr. delivered the speech "I Have a Dream"

C. the official residence and workplace of the president of the United States

D. located in Arizona, known as one of the seven natural wonders in the world

E. one of the seven Wonders of the Modern World of the 20th century

F. an iconic and cultural landmark of Los Angeles representing ambition, success and glamour

II. True or False

Directions: *Determine whether the following statements are true (T) or false (F).*

1. Yellowstone is the first national park in the US and is also widely known to be the first national park in the world.
2. The faces of George Washington, Thomas Jefferson, Abraham Lincoln, and Franklin Roosevelt are carved into Mount Rushmore.
3. Look at the Statue of Liberty and you will find Lady Liberty holds a torch with her left

hand which represents freedom.

4. The 105-storey Empire State Building has been an iconic symbol of New York since 1931.
5. Independence Hall, Grand Canyon, Yellowstone National Park and Golden Gate Bridge are all included in the World Heritage Site list.

Post-class Thinking

I. Extensive Reading

Directions: *Scan the QR code to read the transcription of the Stone Engraving of the Parchment Declaration of Independence.*

II. Extensive Writing

Directions: *Write an essay based on the following questions.*

There are many historical and natural landmarks in different countries. Can you compare some similar landmarks in China, the UK and the US? What are their differences in history, geographical features and popularity, such as Buckingham Palace v.s. the Forbidden City; Mississippi River v.s. Yangtze River; London Tower Bridge v.s. Golden Gate Bridge; Route 66 v.s. the Silk Road?

____

____

____

____

____

____

____

____

____

Text C Mirrors of a Country: Cities in the US

Pre-class Preparation

MOOC Watching

Watch the MOOC video "Snapshot of American Cities: The Past and Present" to prepare for Text C.

Pre-reading Questions

1. How many American cities can you list? Introduce one or two of them in your own words, including its location, famous landmarks or people, and history.
2. Compare a city in the US with one in China. How are they similar to or different from each other?

In-class Reading

Mirrors of a Country: Cities in the US

1 A country is always known to the outside world by its famous cities. Cities serve as a mirror reflecting the origin, development and transformation of the country in the past hundreds or even thousands of years. Some cities lay the foundation of the country and others record the change of the nation in detailed ways shown in the ups and downs of the cities' history. The following six cities put together a **holistic** picture of the United States, providing the **fragments** of its development from different perspectives.

holistic
adj. 整体的
fragment
n. 碎片

★ Washington, DC

2 Washington, DC, formally the District of Columbia, is the capital city of the United States. It is located on the Potomac River bordering Maryland and Virginia. As the seat of the US federal government and several international organizations, the city is an important world political capital. Washington, DC was named after George Washington, the first president of the United States and a founding father, and the federal district is named after Columbia, a female personification of the nation. The name "Columbia" derived from explorer Christopher Columbus, who discovered the "new world" in 1492 and introduced America to the Western Europe for the first time.

3 In 1791, the city of Washington was founded to serve as the national capital. In 1801, the land which was formerly part of Maryland and Virginia became recognized as the federal district. The US Constitution provided a federal district under the exclusive **jurisdiction** of **US Congress**. Therefore, Washington, DC is not a part of any US state.

jurisdiction
n. 司法权

4 The three branches of the US federal government are centered in the District: Congress (legislative), the president (executive), and the Supreme Court (judicial). Washington is home to many national monuments and museums, primarily situated on or around **the National Mall**. The city hosts 177 foreign embassies as well as the headquarters of many international organizations, trade unions, non-profits, **lobbying groups**, and professional associations, including the World Bank Group, the International Monetary Fund, the Organization of American States, **the National Geographic Society**, **the Human Rights Campaign**, **the International Finance Corporation**, and **the American Red Cross**.

5 Visitors can find a big number of historical sites in Washington, DC, which records and shapes the history of the country vividly. The National Mall is a large, open park in downtown Washington between the Lincoln Memorial and **the United States Capitol**. The Washington Monument

and **the Jefferson Pier** are near the center of the mall, south of the White House. Also on the mall are the National World War II Memorial at the east end of **the Lincoln Memorial Reflecting Pool, the Korean War Veterans Memorial,** and **the Vietnam Veterans Memorial**.

★ **New York City**

6 New York City, simply called New York, is the largest city in the United States. With an estimated population of more than 8 million in 2019, New York City is the most densely populated major city in the United States. Located at the southern tip of the State of New York, the city is the center of the New York **metropolitan** area, the largest metropolitan area in the world. The Big Apple has been a nickname for the city since the colonists arrived in 1624.

metropolitan
adj. 大都市的

7 Situated on one of the world's largest natural harbors, New York City is composed of five **boroughs**—Brooklyn, Queens, Manhattan, the Bronx, and Staten Island. The city and its metropolitan area constitute the **premier** gateway for legal immigration to the United States. Now New York is home to more than 3.2 million residents born outside the United States. As many as 800 languages are spoken in New York, making it the most linguistically diverse city in the world.

borough
n. 区
premier
adj. 首要的

8 The origin of New York City can be traced back to a trading post on Lower Manhattan founded by colonists from **the Dutch Republic** in 1624. The post was named New Amsterdam in 1626. The city and its surroundings came under British control in 1664 and were renamed the Province of New York after King Charles II of England granted the lands to his brother, the Duke of York. New York City was the capital of the United States from 1785 until 1790, and has been the largest US city since 1790. In the 21st century, it is one of the world's most populous **megacities** and is a symbol of freedom and cultural diversity. This global power city has exerted a significant influence on the world's commerce, finance, media,

megacity
n. 超级城市

art, fashion, education, technology and entertainment.

9 Many districts and landmarks in New York City are internationally well known, such as **Manhattan, Wall Street** and **the Broadway Theater District**. Manhattan is the smallest of the five boroughs of New York City and is the urban core of the New York metropolitan area. Manhattan serves as the city's economic and administrative center, cultural identifier, and historical birthplace. Famous for Wall Street in the Financial District of Lower Manhattan, New York City has been called the world's leading financial center and is home to the world's two largest stock exchanges by total market **capitalization**, **the New York Stock Exchange** and **NASDAQ**. Broadway Theatre District, together with London's West End, represents the highest commercial level of live theater in the English-speaking world. The city has over 120 colleges and universities, including Columbia University, New York University, Rockefeller University, and the City University of New York system, which is the largest urban public university system in the United States.

capitalization
n. 资本化

★ **Boston**

10 Boston is the capital and the largest city of the state of Massachusetts and is located on the banks of Massachusetts Bay. Like New York, it features fine natural ports as one of the oldest cities in the United States. Boston was founded in 1630 by Puritan settlers from England. During the American Revolution, the city was known for historical events, such as the Boston Massacre and the Boston Tea Party upon American independence from Great Britain. The city continued to be an important port and manufacturing hub, as well as a centre for high-quality education in the United States.

11 After World War II, Boston changed from "mill-based" to "mind-based" industries, with major corporations dominating electronics, telecommunications, and digital research. Later, Boston firms took the lead

in software design, computer architecture, data processing, and biomedical technologies. Today, Boston is a thriving center of scientific research. The colleges and universities in Boston area make it a world leader in higher education, including law, medicine, engineering and business, and the city is considered to be a global pioneer in innovation and **entrepreneurship**, with nearly 5,000 **startups**. Boston's economic power lies in its finance, business services, biotechnology, information technology, and government activities. Households in the city claim the highest average rate of **philanthropy** in the United States. Businesses and institutions rank among the top in the country for environmental sustainability and investment.

entrepreneurship *n.* 企业家精神
startup *n.* 创业
philanthropy *n.* 慈善

★ Philadelphia

12 Philadelphia, simply known as Philly to the American people, is the largest city in the State of Pennsylvania and the sixth most populous city in the United States. It is one of the oldest **municipalities** in the United States founded in 1682. Philadelphia is considered to be the birthplace of the United States. During the American Revolution, Philadelphia played an indispensable role as the meeting place for the Founding Fathers of the United States, who signed the Declaration of Independence in 1776 at the Second Continental Congress, and the Constitution at the Philadelphia Convention of 1787.

municipality *n.* 自治市

13 Philadelphia remained the nation's largest city until being **overtaken** by New York City in 1790. The city used to be one of the nation's capitals during the revolution, serving as temporary US capital while Washington, DC was under construction.

overtake *v.* 赶上

14 In the 19th and 20th centuries, Philadelphia became a major industrial center and a railroad hub. Today's Philadelphia is the center of economic activity in Pennsylvania and is home to five ***Fortune* 1000 Companies**. The Philadelphia area has a big number of universities and colleges, making it a top study destination, as the city has evolved into an educational and economic

hub. The city became a member of the Organization of World Heritage Cities in 2015, as the first World Heritage City in the United States.

★ Los Angeles

15 Los Angeles, officially the City of Los Angeles and often abbreviated as LA, is the largest city in California. With an estimated population of nearly four million people, it is the second most populous city in the United States (after New York City) and the third most populous city in North America (after Mexico City and New York City). Los Angeles is known for its Mediterranean climate, ethnic diversity, Hollywood entertainment industry, and its **sprawling metropolis**.

sprawl
v. 蔓延
metropolis
n. 大都会

16 The city was founded on September 4, 1781 and became a part of Mexico in 1821 following the Mexican War of Independence. In 1848, at the end of the Mexican-American War, Los Angeles and the rest of California were purchased and thus became part of the United States. Los Angeles was established as a municipality on April 4, 1850, five months before California achieved **statehood**. The discovery of oil in the 1890s brought rapid growth to the city. Los Angeles has a diverse economy and hosts businesses in a broad range of professional and cultural fields. Today the Los Angeles metropolitan area is the third-largest area by GDP in the world, after the Tokyo and New York City metropolitan areas. Los Angeles hosted the 1932 and 1984 Summer Olympics and will host the 2028 Summer Olympics.

statehood
n. 州的地位

★ Chicago

17 Chicago, officially the City of Chicago, is the most populous city in the US State of Illinois, and the third most populous city in the United States. Chicago is the principal city of the Chicago metropolitan area and constitutes the third most populous urban area in the United States after New York City and Los Angeles. Located on the shores of **freshwater Lake Michigan**, Chicago was incorporated as a city in 1837 near a **portage**

freshwater
adj. 淡水的
portage
n. 运送

between the Great Lakes and the Mississippi River **watershed** and grew rapidly in the mid-19th century.

watershed
n. 流域

18 Today Chicago has become an international hub for finance, commerce, industry, education, technology, transportation and telecommunication. The city is home to several *Fortune* 500 Companies, including **Allstate**, **Boeing**, **Caterpillar**, **McDonald's**, **Sears**, **United Airlines Holdings**, **US Foods**, and **Walgreens**. Landmarks in the city include Millennium Park, Navy Pier, the Magnificent Mile, the Art Institute of Chicago, Museum Campus, the Willis (Sears) Tower, Grant Park, the Museum of Science and Industry, and Lincoln Park Zoo. Among all the colleges and universities in Chicago area, the University of Chicago, Northwestern University, and the University of Illinois at Chicago are classified as "highest research" doctoral universities.

T Cultural Terms

1. US Congress 美国国会
2. the National Mall 国家广场（在华盛顿特区的中心区）
3. lobbying group 游说集团（为了实现某种政治经济利益而游说的组织）
4. the National Geographic Society 美国国家地理学会（一个非营利性的教育科学组织）
5. the Human Rights Campaign 人权运动
6. the International Finance Corporation 国际金融公司
7. the American Red Cross 美国红十字会
8. the United States Capitol 美国国会山（美国立法机构所在地）
9. the Jefferson Pier 杰弗逊码头石（标志美国第二本初子午线）
10. the Lincoln Memorial Reflecting Pool 林肯纪念堂倒影池(位于林肯纪念堂前方的长方形水池)
11. the Korean War Veterans Memorial 韩战老兵纪念碑（位于华盛顿特区）
12. the Vietnam Veterans Memorial 越战退伍军人纪念碑（位于华盛顿特区）
13. the Dutch Republic 荷兰共和国（1581—1795 年在现今的荷兰和比利时北部存在的一个国家）
14. Manhattan 曼哈顿（纽约市五个区中最小且人口最稠密的一个区）
15. Wall Street 华尔街（位于纽约曼哈顿的一条街道，汇集了美国及世界顶尖的金融机构）

16. the Broadway Theater District 百老汇剧院区（美国戏剧和音乐的发源地，音乐剧的代名词）
17. the New York Stock Exchange 纽约证券交易所
18. NASDAQ 纳斯达克证券交易所
19. *Fortune* 1000 Companies 《财富》美国 1000 强（美国营业额最多的 1000 家公司）
20. Lake Michigan 密歇根湖（五大湖区中唯一完全属于美国的湖）
21. Allstate 好事达（保险公司）
22. Boeing 波音（航空公司）
23. Caterpillar 卡特彼勒（重型工业制造公司）
24. McDonald's 麦当劳 （快餐连锁公司）
25. Sears 西尔斯（百货公司）
26. United Airlines Holdings 联合航空控股公司
27. US Foods 美国食品控股公司
28. Walgreens 沃尔格林（连锁药局）

Exercise

Matching

Directions: *For each city in the left column, identify the corresponding descriptions and important events in the right column.*

1. New York ________________	**A.** It is the second most populous city in the United States. **B.** It is the most densely populated major city in the United States.
2. Philadelphia ________________	**C.** It is home to Harvard University. **D.** It will host the 2028 Summer Olympics.
3. Boston ________________	**E.** It is home to the world's leading financial center Wall Street. **F.** It is considered to be the birthplace of the United States.
4. Los Angeles ________________	**G.** It is the most populous city in the US State of Illinois. **H.** It served as temporary US capital from 1790 to 1800 while Washington, DC was under construction.
5. Chicago ________________	**I.** It is the largest city of the State of Massachusetts. **J.** It is home to Northwestern University.

Critical Thinking

Directions: *Some Chinese provinces and American states (cities) are similar in their geographic environment, economic power and international popularity. Try to compare the following pairs of cities and province/state in the two countries and find out their similarities and differences.*

1) Beijing / Washington, DC

____

2) Shanghai / New York

____

3) Shenzhen / Los Angeles

____

4) Hainan / Florida

____

Post-class Thinking

Comparison and Analysis

Directions: *American Census Bureau reports that from 2010 to 2020, populations in cities in the southern and western regions of the United States experienced rapid growth. The south leads the way with 10 of the top 15 fastest-growing large US cities, with a population of 50,000 or more. Among the 15 most populous US cities or towns in 2020, nine are located in the south, four in the west, and one each in the northeast and the midwest. In China, there is a similar population flow in recent decade and more people are migrating to cities in the south of China. What are the social, economic and political reasons behind the population flow in the two countries?*

Supplementary Resources

1. Extensive Reading

Scan the QR codes to read Text D "The Road in American Culture" and watch the MOOC video "Culture of Road: A Nation on Wheels". Then discuss the following questions with your partner.

1) Why do roads play such an important role in America's transportation and even national culture?

2) Do you know anything about the Silk Road in China? How did it foster the cultural communication between China and other countries?

Text D "The Road in American Culture"

MOOC video "Culture of Road: A Nation on Wheels"

2. Documentaries and Videos

1) Documentary: *America: The Story of Us*（《美国，我们的故事》）

Produced by Nutopia, *America: The Story of Us* portrays more than 400 years of American history focusing on how American creation of new technologies has had effects on the nation and the world. It spans time from the successful English settlement of Jamestown beginning in 1607, through to the present day. The series recreates many historical events by using actors dressed in the style of the period and computer-generated special effects.

2) Documentary: *Aerial America*（《俯瞰美国》）

Aerial America is a television series and each episode is an aerial video tour of a US state or destination in the United States. The narrative show consists entirely of aerial scenes, which features flyovers of historical landmarks, natural areas such as national parks, and well-known buildings and homes in urban areas. The series has aired an episode for each state that has showcased popular destinations such as Hollywood and small towns in the US.

3) Documentary: *Aerial Cities*（《航拍美国：城市 24 小时》）

The document *Aerial Cities* films America's most prominent cities, all captured from breathtaking heights. From the creators of *Aerial America*, this adventure takes you on epic, sky-high journeys over Las Vegas, Chicago, Seattle, Miami, San Francisco, and Los Angeles, and celebrates the nation's most treasured and bustling metropolises and the people who keep them running.

4) Song: *Get Your Kicks on Route 66*（《驰骋在 66 号公路上》）

Get Your Kicks on Route 66 is a popular rhythm and blues song, composed in 1946 by American songwriter Bobby Troup. The lyrics follow the path of US Route 66 (US 66), which traversed the western two-thirds of the US from Chicago, Illinois, to Los Angeles, California. The song became a standard, with several renditions appearing on the record charts.

As the song by Bobby Troup goes:

If you ever plan to motor west
Travel my way, the highway that's the best
Get your kicks on Route 66!

3. Books

Jane, J. 1992. *The Death and Life of Great American Cities*. Visalia: Vintage.

Raitz, K.B. 1996. *The National Road*. Baltimore: The Johns Hopkins University Press.

约翰 · 斯坦贝克 . 2018. 愤怒的葡萄 . 胡仲持译 . 上海：上海译文出版社 .

Chapter 4
Great Events of the UK and the US: Legends in History

As the first country to establish constitutional monarchy and the first to complete the Industrial Revolution, the UK occupied nearly one quarter of the world in its heyday. The US began to expand its territory after winning its independence from the UK and grew into a super power parallel to the UK, even exceeding it in some fields. This chapter will mainly introduce great historical events related to British feudalism, British Empire, American beginnings, American independence and expansion of the US.

Text A Ups and Downs of British History Before 1689

Pre-class Preparation

MOOC Watching

Watch the MOOC video "Ups and Downs of British History Before 1689" to prepare for Text A.

Pre-reading Questions

1. What dynasties do you know about in British history?
2. Can you name some of the British kings or queens and tell about their stories?

In-class Reading

Ups and Downs of British History Before 1689

1 Britain is a northwest European country with a long history, dating back to the Celtic culture about 2,000 years ago. Long before the Celts arrived, some other peoples had inhabited there, who left monumental architectures. For instance, Stonehenge, the most famous prehistoric monument in Britain, remains a mystery as for how and why it was built.

★ **From Roman invasion to Norman Conquest**

2 There occurred four invasions to Britain in history, beginning from the Roman invasion in 43 AD. The famous wall, named **the Hadrian's Wall**, was built by the Romans in 122 AD. The Anglo-Saxons came from northern Europe to invade and colonize England in the 5th and 6th centuries. They introduced

new farming methods and founded **self-sufficient** villages, which constructed the basis of English society. In the 8th century, the Vikings came to Britain and conquered the islands around Scotland and part of Ireland, but they were defeated by **King Alfred** when they attempted to conquer England.

self-sufficient *adj.* 自给自足的

3 Norman Conquest of 1066 is the last invasion in record, led by **Duke William**, who killed King Harold at the Battle of Hastings[1] and became **William the Conqueror**. The year of 1066 is thus viewed as the most important landmark and even the real start of British history. Along with William the Conqueror, a new kind of feudal system was introduced into Britain: The land in England was owned by William and given to the Norman soldiers who had helped him conquer the country; in return, the soldiers swore their loyalty to the king. In 1086, King William ordered his officials to compile ***the Domesday Book,*** a detailed record of the people and their possessions across his land.

★ From Magna Carta to the feudal war

4 Faced with the possible threat of the civil war, King John had to accept the charter of liberties in 1215, known as Magna Carta[2] or the Great Charter. The charter placed England's **sovereigns** within a rule of law to avoid abuses of power and guaranteed the liberties of the **elite** classes. But the majority of common people were still at the bottom of the social ladder, lacking a voice in government.

sovereign *n.* 君主
elite *adj.* 精英的；上层的

King John Signing the Magna Carta (from *The Guardian*)

5 In the middle of the 14th century, due to the labor shortage resulted from

the Black Death[3], as well as the increasing importance of trade and towns, the traditional ties established within the feudal structure were therefore weakened. Finally, the constant feudal conflict between Lancastrians and Yorkists led to the Wars of the Roses[4]. Three decades later, the war ended in 1485, when Henry Tudor (Lancastrian) defeated Richard III (Yorkist) and rose to the **throne** to be King Henry VII, hence the beginning of the Tudor Dynasty (1485–1603).

throne
n. 王位；王权

★ Tudor monarchy

6 Henry VIII (1509–1547) is well-known for the Reformation[5] he launched. During the Reformation, the king replaced the pope as the head of the church in England, causing a bitter divide between Catholics and Protestants. The church was briefly reunited with Rome during the reign of Mary I (1553–1558) but separated once again under Elizabeth I. Although a talented leader, he was not interested in government stuff, so it's natural for the Tudor Dynasty to adopt a new government structure, appointing **professionals** to run the government instead. In this way, the existing feudal **aristocracy** seemed no longer so much in need. Later on, monarchs had to ask the House of Commons for agreement to issue their policies, because the House was mainly made up of the newly powerful merchants and landowners.

professional
n. 专门人员
aristocracy
n. 贵族

7 During the reign of Queen Elizabeth I, the English navy succeeded in defeating **the Spanish Armada** in 1588, which not only enabled England to dominate the sea, but also guaranteed England's foreign trade with the other countries.

★ The decline of feudalism

8 From the 16th through the 19th century, the Enclosure Movement[6] swept across Britain. Under England's former feudal system, most of the rural area was set aside for common people to live on. But when more and more lands were enclosed with fences for the **exclusive** use of the

exclusive
adj. 专用的

wealthy landowners, the lower classes became landless and had to move to cities for jobs. They formed the cheap labor force for the growing Industrial Revolution. Thus, the Enclosure Movement was an important step for England to develop capitalism.

9 The link between religion and politics became intense while Parliament established its **supremacy** over the monarchy in the 17th century. The Stuart monarchs could not raise any money until they got the agreement of the Commons first. Not satisfied with the way the king governed, a group of **Catholics** planned secretly to blow up the Parliament as well as the king, hence the Gunpowder Plot[7] in 1605. But their plot failed in the end, i.e., a victory of **Protestant** parliament over Catholic leadership.

supremacy
n. 最高权威

Catholic
n. 天主教信徒

10 When *the Authorized Version of the Bible*[8] was published, conflicts got tense with the Puritans[9], which finally caused the civil war to break out. The war ended with Charles I's execution in 1649, and the **parliamentary** forces won the complete victory. **Oliver Cromwell**, the Puritan leader of the army, led Britain into a republic.

parliamentary
adj. 议会的

11 But not long later, the monarchy was restored in 1660 when King Charles II was brought to the throne. Along with the Glorious Revolution breaking out in 1688, England formally established the constitutional monarchy, restricted by laws, such as **the Bill of Rights 1689**.

T Cultural Terms

1. the Hadrian's Wall 哈德良城墙
2. King Alfred 阿尔弗雷德大帝（849—899，是盎格鲁－撒克逊英格兰时期国王，他率众抗击北欧海盗维京人的侵略，被尊称为"英国国父"）
3. Duke William 威廉公爵
4. William the Conqueror 征服者威廉
5. the Domesday Book（1086 年威廉一世颁布的）土地调查清册
6. the Spanish Armada 西班牙无敌舰队

7. Protestant 新教教徒（16 世纪脱离罗马天主教）

8. Oliver Cromwell 奥利弗·克伦威尔（英国革命家、军事家、政治家和宗教领袖）

9. the Bill of Rights 1689 英国 1689 年《权利法案》（确立了议会主权，限制王权）

Cultural Notes

1. the Battle of Hastings

黑斯廷斯战役，1066 年英格兰国王哈罗德的军队与诺曼底威廉公爵的军队在黑斯廷斯地区交战。同年 10 月 14 日，战役以公爵战胜英王告终，公爵遂被称作“征服者威廉”。此次战役被视为欧洲中世纪盛期开始的标志。

2. Magna Carta

《大宪章》，英国封建时期的重要宪法性文件之一。1215 年 6 月 15 日，金雀花王朝约翰王（1199—1216 年在位）在大封建领主、教士、骑士和市民的联合压力下被迫签署该文件。主要内容是保障封建贵族和教会的特权及骑士、市民的某些利益，限制王权。

3. the Black Death

黑死病，一般指鼠疫。鼠疫在世界历史上曾有多次大流行，文中指 1347—1353 年席卷整个欧洲的“黑死病”，夺走了 2 500 万欧洲人的性命，占当时欧洲总人口的 1/3。

4. the Wars of the Roses

玫瑰战争，又称蔷薇战争（1455—1485），是英国兰开斯特和约克两大家族之间为争夺英格兰王位而发生的断断续续的内战。“玫瑰战争”因两个家族所选的家徽而得名，兰开斯特选用红蔷薇，约克选用白蔷薇。不过当时并未使用该名称，而是在 16 世纪莎士比亚历史剧《亨利六世》中以两朵玫瑰被拔作为战争开始的标志后，该名称才成为普遍用语。

5. the Reformation

英国宗教改革，也称作 the Protestant Reformation。随着人文主义和宗教改革思想的传播，英国社会各阶层的反罗马教会情绪日益高涨。在此背景下，英王亨利八世发起宗教改革运动，破除教皇对英国的控制，重新确立教会与国家的关系，英国民众的民族意识被大力激发起来。

6. the Enclosure Movement

圈地运动，最早出现在 12 世纪，在 14、15 世纪农奴制解体过程中，英国新兴的资产阶级和新贵族通过暴力把农民从土地上赶走，强占农民土地及公有地，并把强占的土地圈占起来，变成私有的大牧场、大农场。

7. the Gunpowder Plot

火药阴谋案，发生于 1605 年，天主教徒密谋炸毁英国国会大厦，并杀害正在其中进行国会开幕典礼的英国国王詹姆斯一世，但阴谋败露而未成功。现今每年 11 月 5 日的盖伊·福克斯之夜（或篝火节之夜，Guy Fawkes Night）正是为纪念这个历史事件而设定的英国传统节日。

8. *the Authorized Version of the Bible*

《钦定版圣经》，于 1611 年出版，是由英王詹姆斯一世下令翻译的版本，或称英王钦定版、詹姆斯王译本或英王詹姆斯王译本等。

9. the Puritans

清教徒是指要求清除英国国教中天主教残余的改革派，也是最为虔敬、生活最为圣洁的新教徒。《圣经》被认为是唯一的最高权威，任何教会或个人都不能成为传统权威的解释者和维护者。他们认为通过阅读《圣经》，每个个体都可以与上帝直接对话，主张简单、实在、上帝面前人人平等的信徒生活。

Exercise

Blank Filling

Directions: *Complete the following blanks based on Text A.*

1. In British history, Britain went through four invasions: ________, ________, ________, and ________.
2. Duke William defeated the English army at ________.
3. The Wars of the Roses was fought between ________ and ________ from ________ to 1485.
4. During Queen Elizabeth I's reign, the English navy defeated ________ and dominated the ________.
5. The Gunpowder Plot in 1605 failed in the end, which symbolized a victory of ________ parliament over ________ leadership.

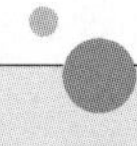

Post-class Thinking

Blank Filling

Directions: *Scan the QR code to fill in the blanks of the mind map of Text A and you will have a better understanding of how feudalism in England developed through the time.*

Text B The Rise and Fall of the British Empire

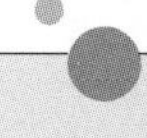

Pre-class Preparation

MOOC Watching

Watch the MOOC video "The Rise and Fall of the British Empire" to prepare for Text B.

Pre-reading Questions

1. Which countries and areas did Britain colonize from the early 17th century to the end of the 20th century?
2. Why was Britain ever called "an empire on which the sun never sets"?

The Rise and Fall of the British Empire

1 The British Empire, **spanning** from the early 17th century to the end of the 20th century, was a worldwide colonial system under the control of Great Britain. It may be dated back to the year of 1601, shortly after the formation of the East India Company chartered by Queen Elizabeth I in 1600. First for wealth, the Company later shifted its interest and focus on British **imperialism** in India.

span
v. 跨越；持续

imperialism
n. 帝国主义

★ Early exploration

2 During the 15th and 16th centuries, known as "Age of Discovery" or "Age of Exploration", the leading European nations, particularly Portugal and Spain, launched voyages abroad hoping to find wealth and undiscovered lands. Starting in about 1420, the Portuguese zipped along the African coast and came back with **spices**, gold, slaves and other goods from Asia and Africa to Europe. Eager to share the riches of the "Far East[1]", Spain also turned its attention to exploration and conquest in other areas of the world. In 1492, the Spanish monarch sponsored Christopher Columbus's voyage by sailing west across the Atlantic. However, the "assumed" Indies he landed on were later proved to be a new continent.

spice
n. （调味）香料

3 England also joined the exploration actively and had exerted great efforts in exploring the unknown overseas area ever since the end of the 15th century. In 1497, King Henry VII sent John Cabot[2] on an **expedition** to discover a route to Asia via the Atlantic. In 1502, Henry VII **commissioned** another voyage to North America. In 1552, English naval officer arrived in **Guinea**. In 1554, Sir Hugh Willoughby[3] searched for a northeast route to the Far East. In 1588, the English navy defeated the Spanish Armada.

expedition
n. 远征

commission
v. 正式委托

All these efforts paved the way for England's future connection with and colonization of the other lands.

John Cabot Landing on the East Coast of North America

★ **The founding of settlements**

4 In 1607, New England, **Virginia**, and **Maryland**, beyond which some other British settlements were also set up in **Bermuda**, Honduras, Antigua, Barbados, and **Nova Scotia**. More land on North America was **ceded** to Britain along with the Treaty of Paris in 1763, including Florida, and the areas of Lower Canada (land up to the Mississippi).

cede
v. 割让

5 In 1769, English Captain James Cook made his way to New Zealand and claimed New South Wales, the east coast of Australia for the British Crown the next year. Cook's detailed accounts of New Zealand attracted much European interest as well as attention. With an aim to alleviate overcrowding in British prisons, in 1788, the British ships first carried 1,500 **convicted** criminals from England to Botany Bay, Australia, making Australia its **penal colony**.

convicted
adj. 定罪的

6 On the African Continent, the first permanent British settlement was made in the Gambia River in 1661. **Senegal** was ceded to Britain in 1763 based on the terms of the Treaty of Paris. **Sierra Leone** became a British possession in 1787 although slave trading had begun earlier there. Besides, the Cape of Good Hope (now in South Africa) was brought under Britain's control in 1806.

7 In the former two centuries of the Empire beginning from 1607, the

British government exerted control over its colonies primarily in trade and shipping. Normally the colonies provided raw materials for England and in return, they were expected to serve as markets for British manufactured goods. Not until 1776 when the American colonies declared to be independent was a free-trade movement underway.

8 The Treaty of Amiens[4] in 1802 added Trinidad and Ceylon (now Sri Lanka) officially to Britain, and the Treaty of Paris in 1814 ceded Tobago, Mauritius, **Saint Lucia**, and Malta from France to Britain. In addition, the Empire extended its power over **Malacca** in 1795, and Singapore in 1819.

★ Summit of the British Empire

9 The British Empire ascended to its summit in the 19th century. After New Zealand was officially colonized in 1840, systematic colonization around the Pacific Ocean followed rapidly, extending to Fiji, Tonga, Papua, and other **adjacent** islands. British influence was soon further expanded in the Far East, **Myanmar**, Somalia, southern Arabia, **the Persian Gulf**, **Cyprus**, **Brunei** and **Sarawak**.

adjacent
adj. 邻近的

10 However, the control over Africa is viewed as the greatest 19th-century British extension, including Egypt, Sudan, Nigeria, Ghana and Gambia, followed by Kenya, Uganda, Zimbabwe, Zambia, and Malawi. Thus, British territories stretched from South Africa northward to Egypt, i.e., extending "from the Cape to Cairo". By the end of the 19th century, the British Empire covered nearly one-quarter of the world's landmass and more than one-quarter of its total population.

★ Collapse of the British Empire

11 Entering the 20th century, Britain was no longer the world's richest country. In 1839 Canada first put forward the proposal of self-government and later won a "responsible self-government" or "**dominion**". The newly-proposed system spread rapidly in Britain's other colonies, so that more and more dominions had replaced the previous colonies by 1907. When World

dominion
n. 英联邦自治领

War I ended in 1918, the dominions represented themselves to sign the peace treaties. By 1919, the British Empire was already becoming less of an empire and more of a **confederation**, which was often referred to as the British Commonwealth[5].

confederation
n. 联盟

12 The Statute of Westminster[6] in 1931 recognized the dominions as independent countries "within the British Empire, equal in status" to the United Kingdom. In the 25 years following World War II, the British Empire gradually collapsed, no longer a superpower in the world. India declared independence from Britain in 1947. British troops were withdrawn from Palestine in 1948. Sudan gained independence in 1956, closely followed by Ghana the next year. British colonies in Africa declared independence one after another before 1966 except Namibia in 1990. Numerous other countries across the globe also followed suit.

13 By then, **virtually** nothing remained of the empire. The former British colonies mostly joined the British Commonwealth for both practical cooperation and mutual development with the United Kingdom.

virtually
adv. 几乎

T Cultural Terms

1. Guinea 几内亚（位于西非西岸）
2. Virginia 弗吉尼亚（位于美国东部大西洋沿岸）
3. Maryland 马里兰州（位于美国东海岸）
4. Bermuda 百慕大群岛（北大西洋西部群岛）
5. Nova Scotia 新斯科舍（加拿大省名）
6. penal colony 罪犯流放地
7. Senegal 塞内加尔（位于非洲西部凸出部位的最西端）
8. Sierra Leone 塞拉利昂（位于西非大西洋岸）
9. Saint Lucia 圣卢西亚岛（位于东加勒比海）
10. Malacca 马六甲海峡（连接印度洋和太平洋的水道）
11. Myanmar 缅甸（东南亚国家，东北与中国接壤，首都为内比都）
12. the Persian Gulf 波斯湾（阿拉伯海西北伸入亚洲大陆的一个海湾）

13. Cyprus 塞浦路斯（地中海东北部的一个岛国）
14. Brunei 文莱（东南亚国家）
15. Sarawak 砂拉越州，简称砂州（马来西亚最大的州）

Cultural Notes

1. the Far East

远东，西方国家开始向东方扩张时对亚洲最东部地区的通称，即以欧洲为中心，把东南欧、非洲东北称为“近东”，把西亚附近称为“中东”，把更远的东方称为“远东”。“远东”一般包括今天的东亚（包括俄罗斯的东部）、东南亚和南亚，即阿富汗、哈萨克以东、澳洲以北、太平洋以西、北冰洋以南的地区。

2. John Cabot

约翰·卡伯特，意大利航海家。1497 年，他为英王亨利七世航行到达今天的加拿大，却以为是亚洲东海岸，次年他又到达了如今的美国东海岸。英王根据他的报告，将他所发现的北美大陆宣称属英国所有，为日后英国的殖民扩张奠定所谓“合法”的基础。

3. Sir Hugh Willoughby

休·威洛比爵士（1495—1554），英国探险家、航海家，为寻找东北航道而进行北极地区的探险航行，在探险途中不幸献身。

4. the Treaty of Amiens

《亚眠条约》。1802 年，法国及其盟国西班牙、荷兰同英国在法国北部的亚眠签订的条约，它标志着第二次反法联盟的最后破产。可是《亚眠条约》在订立以后，并未得到双方全面的遵守。

5. the British Commonwealth

英联邦，相当于大英帝国延续的一个国际组织，成员国大多为前英国殖民地或保护国。各国志愿加入，谋求在贸易、金融、国防、教育、技术、医药等各个方面的友好协作和共同进步，以发展经济为主要目的。

6. the Statute of Westminster

《威斯敏斯特法案》，于 1931 年通过，正式确立英国和各自治领的关系。法案规定英联邦是一个自由、平等国家的松散联合，肯定了各自治领的独立地位和与宗主国的平等立法权，成为现代英联邦的法律基础，被称为《英联邦的大宪章》。

Exercise

Matching

Directions: *Match the years in the left column with the countries or areas Britain colonized in the right column based on Text B.*

1. 1607 – ________	**A.** Ceylon
2. 1763 – ________	**B.** Singapore
3. 1770 – ________	**C.** the Cape of Good Hope
4. 1787 – ________	**D.** New Zealand
5. 1788 – ________	**E.** Mauritius
6. 1795 – ________	**F.** Jamestown
7. 1802 – ________	**G.** New South Wales
8. 1806 – ________	**H.** Florida
9. 1814 – ________	**I.** Malacca
10. 1819 – ________	**J.** Australia
11. 1840 – ________	**K.** Sierra Leone

Post-class Thinking

Comparison and Analysis

Directions: *During the 15th century, Western Europe, led by Portugal, Spain and England, launched voyages to explore the outer world. Looking back at China, Zheng He of the Ming Dynasty led seven expeditions (1405–1433), reaching Persia, Arabia and East Africa. Make a comparison between China and Western Europe around the 15th century, and further analyze why England continued to explore and expand its influence to the other countries but China stopped the exploration abroad after Zheng He's expeditions.*

Text C Four Colonial Patterns Founded in the New World

Pre-class Preparation

MOOC Watching

Watch the MOOC video "American Beginnings: Stories in the New World" to prepare for Text C.

Pre-reading Questions

1. Comparatively speaking, America has a much shorter history than Britain. How long is American history?
2. What important events have happened in American history?

In-class Reading

Four Colonial Patterns Founded in the New World

1 Long before **Christopher Columbus** set foot on the new land in 1492, all parts of America had been **inhabited** by various native tribes, now all grouped into the term "Indians". Their original arrival may probably be dated back to 20,000 to 35,000 years ago from Asia to North America by way of **the Bering Strait**. But their previous life underwent complete changes upon the arrival of Europeans. Among the Europeans were especially English explorers and settlers, who set up one after another colony in **the New World**.

inhabit
v. 居住在

2 In the 17th and 18th centuries, 13 English colonies came into being

along the eastern Atlantic coast of North America. The colonies were divided into New England, the Middle Colonies and the Southern Colonies based on the geographic location. At the beginning period of American history, four colonial patterns took shape step by step on the new land.

★ **Virginia settlement**

3 **Jamestown** Virginia, named after the then English King James I, was the first successful English colony established in 1607. Chartered by the king and financed by the London Virginia Company[1], the explorers first aimed to look for gold in the new continent. Their first years in America were extremely difficult, and soon they ran short of food. Many people died from disease and starvation or from wars with local Indians.

rigid
adj. 严格的

tobacco
n. 烟草

4 Faced with such severe crises, Captain John Smith[2] put forward a **rigid** discipline that everyone should work. Later, John Rolfe[3] succeeded in the experiment with **tobacco** planting and in return, tobacco cultivation brought them huge profits. With the quick spreading of tobacco plantation, the colony survived and flourished by selling tobacco to Europe.

★ **Puritan New England**

doctrine
n. 教义

persecute
v. （因种族、宗教或政治信仰）迫害

5 **New England** today refers to the six states lying in the northeast of the USA—Massachusetts, Connecticut, New Hampshire, Vermont, Maine and Rhode Island. After the Protestant Reformation started by Henry VIII, the Church of England[4] was set up in place of the Catholic Church. But Puritans held that the Church of England was too similar to Catholicism and wanted to "purify" the church. Furthermore, they believed that the Bible was the authority of their **doctrine**, and that every Puritan was able to have a direct individual contact with God by reading the Bible. Holding different religious beliefs from the Church of England, Puritans were cruelly **persecuted** in Britain and even thrown into prison or executed. As a result, some Puritans fled to other countries to seek religious freedom.

6 They took the ship Mayflower to North America in 1620, and an agreement called the Mayflower Compact[5] was drawn up and signed before landing. Abiding by the agreement, they built their own religious community and a civil government for their common interests. In 1630, a much larger Puritan colony was founded in the Boston area and more Puritans moved to nearby Connecticut by 1635. Today, Puritans are no longer in existence due to the frontier environment and the **mobility** of the population. However, Puritans as well as their beliefs have left a far-reaching influence on American society and culture, including such values as individualism, hard work, and respect of education.

mobility
n. 流动性

★ **Catholic Maryland**

7 George Calvert[6] (First Lord Baltimore), a member of the English Parliament, was at first interested in the colonization of the New World for commercial reasons. But later his attention was drawn to creating a refuge for English Catholics. Then he visited America twice and wanted to gain a settlement for his fellow Catholics. As a response to his **petition**, King Charles I agreed and granted him land—Maryland within the Southern Colonies.

petition
n. 请愿书

8 But unfortunately, Lord Baltimore suffered ill health and died before his wish got fulfilled. His son, Second Lord Baltimore, was **subsequently** granted the royal charter for Province of Maryland in 1632. Just as his father had hoped, thousands of British Catholics migrated to Maryland and the land eventually became a refuge for Catholic settlers. The charter didn't impose any guidelines on religion, which further encouraged more Catholics to come and settle down in Maryland.

subsequently
adv. 后来

★ **Quaker Pennsylvania**

9 The fourth colonial pattern is Pennsylvania founded by William Penn in 1681 with the grant by King Charles II of England. Pennsylvania was named after William's father, while "Sylvania", an Italian word, means "forest", hence, "Penn's Woods". The colony was set up in order to

help solve the problem of the growing Society of Friends[7] or "Quaker" movement in England.

10 Although the Quakers were Protestants, they held very different religious beliefs from the Catholics, Puritans and other Protestant **denominations** as well. They denied both the church and the Bible as the highest authority; instead, they believed that humans could communicate with God directly, i.e., needless to rely on the church or the priests as the **mediator**. In their eyes, everyone had an inner light of God, and they could worship God anywhere. Based on this, all were born equal, and all were brothers and sisters. Penn wrote his First Frame of Government while still in England, outlining the governmental structure for the colony and promising certain rights to its citizens. All those who came to settle in Pennsylvania would enjoy religious freedom, which attracted thousands of people with different religious backgrounds to the land. What's more, William Penn carried out the policy of separation of state and church in Pennsylvania, an American religious **convention** till today.

denomination *n.*（基督教）教派

mediator *n.* 调停者

convention *n.* 惯例

Cultural Terms

1. Christopher Columbus 克里斯托弗·哥伦布(意大利探险家、航海家,相信"大地球形说",认为从欧洲西航可达东方的印度和中国)
2. the Bering Strait 白令海峡（位于亚欧大陆最东点的俄罗斯杰日尼奥夫角和美洲大陆最西点的美国威尔士王子角之间)
3. the New World 美洲新大陆（相对欧洲旧大陆而言)
4. Jamestown 詹姆斯敦（1607 年英国在美洲建立的一个殖民地)
5. New England 新英格兰（包括马萨诸塞、康涅狄格、新罕布什尔、佛蒙特、缅因和罗得岛诸州的美国东北部地区)

Cultural Notes

1. the London Virginia Company

伦敦弗吉尼亚公司, 1606 年成立, 全称"伦敦城弗吉尼亚第一殖民地冒险家与殖民者公司"。

股东有商人、地主和冒险者，英国政府特许其在北美弗吉尼亚进行殖民地经营。1607 年建立居民点詹姆斯敦，后沿詹姆斯河任意占领土地，建立许多烟草种植园。

2. Captain John Smith

约翰·史密斯船长（1580—1631），早期英国殖民者、探险家，在弗吉尼亚建立了第一个永久英国殖民地——詹姆斯敦。1607 年，他们踏上了美洲土地，但一开始与当地原住民之间不断爆发冲突。后来，史密斯改变策略，机智地解决了问题，缓解了双方的矛盾，并与印第安人和睦相处。

3. John Rolfe

约翰·罗尔夫（1585—1622），北美早期的英国殖民者之一，首次培育出弗吉尼亚殖民地的出口作物——烟草，被誉为“绿色黄金”。烟草种植业使这块殖民地迅速成为繁荣的商业中心。

4. the Church of England

英格兰教会，经 16 世纪英国宗教改革，脱离罗马教廷及天主教会而建立的新教教会。英格兰教会是基督教的宗派及教会之一，也是英格兰的国家教会，信仰新教的安立甘宗。英国国王担任英格兰教会的最高领袖。

5. the Mayflower Compact

《五月花号公约》，1620 年 11 月签署。签署人立誓创立一个自治团体，而且将依法而治。这份公约是美国历史上第一份重要的政治文献，签订至今一直影响着美国。它是美国建国的奠基，也是现在美国信仰自由、法律制定等所遵奉的根本依据。

6. George Calvert

乔治·卡尔弗特，巴尔的摩男爵一世（1579—1663），英国政治家。他曾计划在北美洲建立马里兰殖民地，努力为虔诚的天主教徒寻找一个安身之处。

7. Society of Friends

公谊会，亦称贵格会，兴起于 17 世纪中期的英国及其美洲殖民地，创立者为乔治·福克斯。“贵格”为英语 Quaker 一词之音译，意为“颤抖者”，该教会没有成文的信经、教义，最初也没有专职牧师，无圣礼与节日，而是直接依靠圣灵的启示指导信徒的宗教活动与社会生活。1688 年英国光荣革命后，该会在英国开始取得合法地位。

Exercises

I. Blank Filling

Directions: *Complete the following blanks based on Text C.*

1. The first successful English colony was ________, named after the English King James I, established in ________.
2. New England today refers to the ________ states lying in the ________ of the US—____.
3. Puritans have left such cultural values as ________, hard work and respect of ________, which exert a great influence on Americans.
4. George Calvert was first interested in the ________ of the New World for ________ reasons, but later he decided to create a ________ in America for ________.
5. The Quakers denied the highest authority of ________ and ________ because they believed that humans could ________ with God ________.

II. Matching

Directions: *For each colonial pattern founded in the New World, find out the corresponding events or beliefs characteristic of each pattern.*

1. Virginia Settlement ________________	**A.** All were born equal, and all were brothers and sisters. **B.** For their common interests, Puritans built their own religious community and a civil government.
2. Puritan New England ________________	**C.** Everyone should work. **D.** All those who came to settle down could enjoy religious freedom. **E.** Jamestown, the first successful English colony, was established in 1607.
3. Catholic Maryland ________________	**F.** Thousands of British Catholics migrated to the land, which later became a refuge for Catholic settlers. **G.** Church of England, too similar to Catholicism, was not a pure church.
4. Quaker Pennsylvania ________________	**H.** William Penn carried out the policy of separation of state and church. **I.** Puritan beliefs and values have left a far-reaching influence on American society and culture. **J.** George Calvert aimed at creating a refuge for English Catholics.

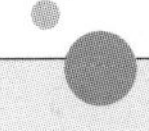

Post-class Thinking

Survey Report

Directions: *Based on Text C, discuss why the origins of America were mostly associated with religion, and make a brief report about American people's religion with the help of the following data you get by searching information online.*

Percentage of religious believers	
Top three religions	
The most religious state	
The least religious state	
Regular churchgoers (weekly, monthly, ...)	
The most religious race	
The least religious race	
Age groups of religious believers	

Blank Filling

Directions: *Scan the QR code to fill in the blanks of the mind map of Text C and you will have a better understanding of how the original colonial patterns were set up in North America.*

Supplementary Resources

1. Extensive Reading

Scan the QR codes to read Text D "Territorial Expansion of the US" and watch the MOOC video "Territorial Expansion of the US: From the Atlantic to the Pacific". Then discuss the following question with your partner: How did America expand its land from 13 to 50 states?

Text D "Territorial Expansion of the US"

MOOC video "Territorial Expansion of the US: From the Atlantic to the Pacific"

2. Documentaries

1) Documentary: *A History of Britain* （《英国史》）

This documentary was released by BBC in 2002, with 15 episodes: 1. Beginnings (3100 BC–1000 AD); 2. Conquest (1000–1087); 3. Dynasty (1087–1216); 4. Nations (1216–1348); 5. King Death (1348–1500); 6. Burning Convictions (1500–1558); 7. The Body of the Queen (1558–1603); 8. The British Wars (1603–1649); 9. Revolutions (1649–1689); 10. Britannia Incorporated (1690–1750); 11. The Wrong Empire (1750–1800); 12. Forces of Nature (1780–1832); 13. Victoria and Her Sisters (1830–1910); 14. The Empire of Good Intentions (1830–1925); 15. The Two Winstons (1910– present).

2) Documentary: *Britain's Bloody Crown: The Wars of the Roses* （《英国血腥王冠：玫瑰战争》）

This documentary is about the intermittent British civil war—the Wars of the Roses between 1455 and 1485 in British history, and the disputes between Lancastrian and Yorkist families for the throne of England.

3) Documentary: *America: The Story of Us* （《美国：我们的故事》）

This documentary tells about the history of the development of the United States, including 12 series: Rebels, Revolution, Westward Movement, Division, the Civil War, Hinterland, Cities, Prosperity, Depression, World War II, Superpower and Golden Age.

4) Documentary: *America: Imagine the World Without Her* （《假如美国不存在》）

It is an American political chronicle film directed by Dennis D'Souza, an Indian American director, and starring Barack Obama in 2014. From the founding of the United States to today's society, the documentary describes various political and social issues such as American elections, immigration, government, and medical bill. The opening scene reproduces the classic scenes of the American War of Independence, and then assumes where the United States will go if Washington dies in the war.

3. Books

Jones, D. 2015. *Magna Carta: The Birth of Liberty*. New York: Viking.

McCullough, D. 2005. *1776*. New York: Simon & Schuster.

O'Toole, F. 2019. *The Politics of Pain: Postwar England and the Rise of Nationalism*. New York: Liveright.

Taylor, A. 2002. *American Colonies: The Settling of North America, Vol. 1*. London: Penguin Books.

常俊跃，夏洋，赵永青 . 2016. 英国国情：英国历史文化 . 北京：北京大学出版社 .

Chapter 5
Political Systems in the UK and the US

The UK has adopted constitutional monarchy since 1689, which is considered a representative Western political system. Constitutional monarchy is characterized by a supreme power held by the parliament and a symbolic head of state. The US adopts a presidential democratic system. Its federal government is composed of three distinct branches: legislative branch, executive branch, and judicial branch, whose powers are vested in the Congress, the President, and the federal courts, respectively.

Text A The Political System in the UK

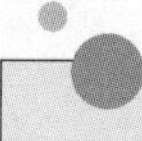

Pre-class Preparation

MOOC Watching

Watch the MOOC video "The Political System in the United Kingdom" to prepare for Text A.

Pre-reading Questions

1. What role does the monarch play in the political system of the UK?
2. Do you know any countries that adopt constitutional monarchy besides the UK?

In-class Reading

The Political System in the UK

unitary *adj.* 统一的

1 The UK is a **unitary** state governed within the framework of a parliamentary democracy[1] under a constitutional monarchy[2]. The monarch is the head of state, while the prime minister is the head of government.

devolve *v.* 权力下放
vest *v.* 授予，赋予

2 Executive power is exercised by the British government, on behalf of and by the consent of the monarch, and the **devolved** governments[3] of Scotland, Wales and Northern Ireland. Legislative power is **vested** in the two chambers of the UK Parliament, **the House of Commons** and **the House of Lords**, as well as the Scottish and Welsh Parliaments and the Northern Ireland Assembly. The judicial branch is independent of the executive branch and the legislative branch. The highest court is the Supreme Court of the United Kingdom.

★ **Constitutional monarchy**

3 Constitutional monarchy is a system of government in which a monarch shares power with a constitutionally organized government. The monarch may be the **de facto** head of state or a purely **ceremonial** leader. The constitution **allocates** the rest of the government's power to the legislature and judiciary.

de facto
adj. （拉丁语）实际上的
ceremonial
adj. 仪式性的
allocate
v. 分配

4 Britain became a constitutional monarchy under **the Whigs**. The monarch is the head of state but not the head of government. The British Parliament and the government—chiefly in the office of British Prime Minister—exercise their powers under **prerogative**: on behalf of the monarch and through powers still formally possessed by the monarch. Other constitutional monarchies in the world include Belgium, Cambodia, Jordan, the Netherlands, Norway, Spain, Sweden, and Thailand.

prerogative
n. 特权

5 In the Kingdom of England, the Glorious Revolution[3] of 1688 led to a constitutional monarchy restricted by laws such as the Bill of Rights 1689 and the Act of Settlement 1701, although limits on the power of the monarch were much older, such as Magna Carta in 1215. Constitutional monarchy has a far-reaching influence all over the world and initiates a new creative political system which strikes a balance between the sovereign and democratic government. Now there are several constitutional monarchies, which are known as Commonwealth realms. Unlike some of their continental European counterparts, the Monarch and his **Governors-General** in the Commonwealth realms hold significant reserved powers, which are to be **wielded** in times of extreme emergency or constitutional crises, usually to support parliamentary government. An instance of a Governor-General exercising such power occurred during the 1975 Australian constitutional crisis, when the Australian Prime Minister, Gough Whitlam, was **dismissed** by the Governor-General. Supporters of constitutional monarchy believe in the monarchy's value as a source of checks and balances against elected politicians who might seek excessive powers and ultimately as a safeguard against **dictatorship**.

wield
v. 行使（权力）
dismiss
v. 开除，解散
dictatorship
n. 专政，独裁

★ **The crown of the UK**

6 The British monarch, currently King Charles III, is the head of state of the United Kingdom. Nowadays, the king's role is mostly symbolic and ceremonial. Though the monarch takes little direct part in government, he has ultimate executive power over the government which covers a wide range of affairs, such as the issue and withdrawal of passports, the dismissal of the prime minister or even the declaration of war. No person may accept significant public office without swearing an oath of **allegiance** to the king. With few exceptions, the monarch is bound by constitutional convention to act on the advice of the government.

allegiance
n. 效忠

7 The monarchs in Britain used to have absolute power, but that was hundreds of years ago. 2015 was the 800th anniversary of the Magna Carta, or the Great Charter. The Magna Carta is regarded as the first statement of citizen rights in the world. The Bill of Rights 1689—which is still in effect—lays down limits on the powers of the crown and sets out the rights of Parliament and rules for freedom of speech in Parliament, the requirement for regular elections to Parliament, and the right to **petition** the monarch without fear of **retribution**.

petition
v. 请愿
retribution
n. 报应，惩罚

★ **The UK Parliament and the two-party system**

8 The UK Parliament possesses legislative supremacy and ultimate power over all other political bodies in the UK and the overseas territories. Parliament is **bicameral** but has three parts, consisting of the sovereign, the House of Lords, and the House of Commons (the primary chamber). The Commons is publicly elected. The party with the largest number of members in the Commons forms the government. **Members of the Commons** debate the big political issues of the day and proposals for new laws. The House of Lords is the second chamber of UK Parliament. It plays a crucial role in examining bills, questioning government action and investigating public policy. The two-party system acts as a check and balance for both Houses.

bicameral
adj. 两院制的

9 People vote in elections for Members of Parliament (MPs) to represent them. The party that gets the most seats in Parliament forms the government. The senior decision-making body of the government is **the Cabinet** chaired by the prime minister and its members include the Secretary of State and other senior ministers. **The Opposition Party** is usually the political party with the second-largest number of seats in the House of Commons. It aims to contribute to the creation of policy and legislation through constructive criticism and oppose government proposals they disagree with. Under the leadership of the Leader of the Opposition, **the Shadow Cabinet** forms an alternative cabinet to that of the government.

10 The British political system adopts a two-party system. Since the 1920s, the two dominant parties have been the Conservative Party and the Labor Party. Before the Labor Party rose in British politics, the Liberal Party was the other major political party, along with the Conservatives.

11 The Conservative Party is a centre-right political party in the UK. The party was founded in 1834 from **the Tory Party** whose supporters are primarily middle-class voters, especially in rural and suburban areas of England. Since the 1980s, the party has generally adopted liberal economic policies supporting free market economics with measures such as **privatisation** and **marketisation**. The famous leaders of the Conservative Party include Margaret Thatcher (1975–1990), John Major (1990–1997), David Cameron (2005–2016) and Theresa May (2016–2019). The Conservatives have adopted a clear pro-Brexit line under Boris Johnson, who led the UK to withdraw from the EU in January 2020.

privatisation
n. 私有化
marketisation
n. 市场化

12 The Labor Party is a centre-left political party in the UK. The party was founded in 1900, growing out of the trade union movement and socialist parties of the 19th century. It overtook the Liberal Party to become the main opposition to the Conservative Party in the early 1920s. Historically influenced by **Keynesian economics**, the party favoured government

intervention *n.* 干预

devolution *n.* 权力下放

intervention in the economy, and the redistribution of wealth. The party desired a **welfare state** and adopted free market policies since the late 1980s. In 1997, Tony Blair became the first leader of the Labor Party to win the general election. His political acts included the establishment of the national minimum wage, the **devolution** of power to Scotland, Wales and Northern Ireland and major changes to the regulation of the banking system. Gordon Brown is the most recent Labor Party leader and most recent Scottish politician to hold his office of prime minister.

13 Other big parties include **the Liberal Democrats**, **Scottish National Party**, **Plaid Cymru**, and **UK Independence Party**. Membership of political parties has been in decline in the UK since the 1950s.

T Cultural Terms

1. the House of Commons 下议院（英国议会的第一议院）
2. the House of Lords 上议院（英国议会的第二议院）
3. the Whigs 辉格党（产生于 17 世纪的英国政党，19 世纪演变为自由党）
4. Governors-General 总督（英国君主在英联邦各国的最高级代表）
5. Members of the Commons 众议院成员
6. the Cabinet 内阁（由首相和执政党高级官员组织的咨询机构）
7. the Opposition Party 反对党
8. the Shadow Cabinet 影子内阁（由反对党领袖领导的机构，攻击并制衡内阁的政治决议）
9. the Tory Party 托利党（产生于 17 世纪的英国政党，19 世纪演变为保守党）
10. Keynesian economics 凯恩斯经济学（建立在凯恩斯著作基础上的经济学理论，主张国家采用扩张性的经济政策，通过增加需求促进经济增长）
11. welfare state 福利国家（国家维护公民的社会经济利益）
12. the Liberal Democrats 自由民主党（由自由党和社会民主党合并而成）
13. Scottish National Party 苏格兰民族党（致力于苏格兰民族运动）
14. Plaid Cymru 威尔士党（信奉威尔士民族主义）
15. UK Independence Party 英国独立党（主张英国脱离欧盟）

Cultural Notes

1. parliamentary democracy

议会民主制，又称内阁制、议会民主制，是“议会至上”的政治制度。政府首脑（总理或首相）权力来自议会，议会是国家权力的中心，存在多个参与议会选举的政党。现代意义上的议会民主制可追溯到 18 世纪的英国，随着英国议会的逐渐民主化和议会权力的增大，议会开始控制英国政府，并最终能够决定君主必须任命谁来组建内阁。当今大多数西欧国家都采用议会民主制。

2. constitutional monarchy

君主立宪制，又称共和君主制或民主君主制，是区别于君主专制的一种君主制国家政体。君主立宪是在保留君主制的前提下，通过立宪赋予人民主权，限制君主权力，达成共和主义或民主主义理想。君主立宪制可分为二元制君主立宪制和议会制君主立宪制。英国实行的是议会制君主立宪制。

3. the Glorious Revolution

光荣革命，是英国于 1688—1689 年发生的一场政变，起因是英国国王与英国议会权力之争以及基督教新旧教（英国国教会及天主教会）之争。英国议会中辉格党以及部分支持新教（英国国教）的托利党人联合起义，将信奉天主教的国王詹姆斯二世驱逐，由詹姆斯之女玛丽二世与夫婿威廉三世共治英国。这场政变以不流血著称，被称为“光荣革命”。光荣革命诞生了《1689 年权利法案》，成为英国君主立宪制形成的重要基础。

Exercises

I. Blank Filling

Directions: *Fill in the following blanks according to Text A.*

1. The United Kingdom is a unitary state governed within the framework of a parliamentary democracy under a ________ monarchy.
2. In the Kingdom of England, the ________ Revolution of 1688 led to a constitutional monarchy which limited the power of the British monarch.
3. 2015 was the 800th anniversary of the ________, or the Great Charter.
4. Since the 1920s, the two dominant parties in the UK have been the ________ Party and the Labor Party.

5. The ________ Party aims to contribute to the creation of policy and legislation through constructive criticism and oppose government proposals they disagree with.

II. Matching

Directions: *Match the representatives of the Conservative Party and the Labor Party with their photos.*

1. Leaders of the Conservative Party: ________
2. Leaders of the Labor Party: ________

A. David Cameron　B. Margaret Thatcher　C. Boris Johnson

D. Tony Blair　E. Theresa May　F. Gordon Brown

Post-class Thinking

Blank Filling

Directions: *Scan the QR code to fill in the blanks of the mind map of Text A and you will have a better understanding of the structure of the text.*

Text B The Royal Family in the UK

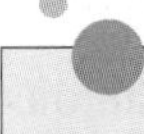

Pre-class Preparation

MOOC Watching

Watch the MOOC video "A Glimpse of the British Royal Family" to prepare for Text B.

Pre-reading Question

What are the duties and responsibilities that the British royal family members should fulfill in public?

In-class Reading

The Royal Family in the UK

1 The history of monarchy in Britain can be traced back to the 9th century. There are kings and queens from different dynasties, the most famous among which are **the House of Plantagenet**, **the House of Tudor and the**

House of Stuart. The present royal family is **the House of Windsor** since the time of King George V.

2 In 1953, after George VI died, his daughter Elizabeth was crowned as a young queen when she was 27 years old. From then on, she ruled Britain for nearly 70 years. As a monarch with the longest reign in history, Elizabeth II witnessed the change of government of 15 prime ministers, from **Winston Churchill** to Liz Truss. But Queen Elizabeth II was not the first queen in Britain's history. Throughout history, there have been several women who have challenged male power. Among these queens of England, two have exerted far-reaching influence on the growth and expansion of Britain. One is **Queen Elizabeth I** and the other is Queen Victoria.

3 Queen Elizabeth I ruled England from 1558 to 1603. She was called virgin queen because she remained unmarried and childless all her lifetime. But she has created an **unprecedented** Elizabethan Era[1], which is famous for the flourishing of the English Renaissance[2], led by William Shakespeare and **Christopher Marlowe**. Under her reign, England expanded its trading and colonies, making it a confident new power in the world.

unprecedented
adj. 前所未有的

4 Queen Victoria was **commemorated** by an enormous marble statue of her, which is seated at the front of Buckingham Palace. She ruled Britain from 1837 to 1901. Her reign of 64 years was longer than any other British monarch before her and her time was called Victoria Era. It was a period of industrial, cultural, political, scientific, and military development within the UK, and was marked by a great expansion of the British Empire. Her marriage to her cousin Prince Albert is a famous romantic court love. Their nine children married into royal and noble families across Europe, earning her the nickname "the grandmother of Europe".

commemorate
v. 纪念

5 The **throne** of the monarchy in Britain, which has been passed in **succession** in the past 1,000 years, has been broken only once, when between 1649 and 1660, King Charles I was beheaded and a republic was

throne
n. 王位
succession
n. 继任

established. Even though there was a **restoration** in 1660, people were not as enthusiastic about the monarch as before. The new monarch after the Glorious Revolution accepted the Bill of Rights, which limited the power of the king and confirmed the **supremacy** of the government.

restoration *n.* 复辟

supremacy *n.* 至高无上

6 Today, King Charles III is both the head of Britain and Commonwealth states, such as Australia, Canada and New Zealand. But the king has no real power and most of his powers are symbolic. Every law in the country is made in his name and all ministers are appointed by him. The most important job for the monarch is to represent the UK both at home and abroad and to set an example for other people.

7 Who are the members of the British royal family? Elizabeth II and her husband Prince Philip have four children—Prince Charles, Prince Andrew, Prince Edward and Princess Anne. Succession of the crown is founded on the hereditary principle. Queen's eldest son Prince Charles, also known as Prince Wales, has succeeded her throne in 2022. His ex-wife was Princess Diana, the Princess of Wales and her current wife is Queen Consort Camilla, the Duchess of Cornwall. Charles and Diana have two sons—William and Harry. Their elder son William, the Prince of Cambridge, is the first heir to the throne. Prince William got married to Catherine Middleton in 2011. Now the couple have three children, among whom Prince George is the second heir to the throne. The marriage of Prince Harry to American actress Meghan Markle has been attracting people's attention. In 2020, they decided to step back as senior members of British royal family, which was dubbed "Megxit[3]" by the public.

8 Members of British royal family have many public duties and responsibilities to fulfill. They should participate in all kinds of public activities and historical events to represent the royal family. But you may wonder: Where does the royal family get their money to support themselves? The British government supports the monarch and the royal family financially by means of **the Sovereign Grant**, which is intended

to meet the costs of the sovereign's official expenditures. Members of the royal family also receive an annual payment from the government to cover office costs. This is known as **Parliamentary Annuity**.

Cultural Terms

1. the House of Plantagenet 金雀花王朝（源于法国贵族，12 世纪起统治英国）
2. the House of Tudor 都铎王朝（15 世纪末及 16 世纪统治英国的王朝，被认为是英国历史上的黄金王朝，代表君主有亨利八世和伊丽莎白一世）
3. the House of Stuart 斯图亚特王朝（来自苏格兰，自 1603 年起统治整个不列颠岛）
4. the House of Windsor 温莎王朝（1917 年，面对“一战”中英国百姓的反德情绪，英王乔治五世将爱德华七世开创的萨克森—科堡—哥达王朝改名为温莎王朝）
5. Winston Churchill 温斯顿·丘吉尔（20 世纪初期到中期的英国政治家、外交家、军事家，“二战”时期的英国首相，领导英国取得了对抗德国的胜利）
6. Queen Elizabeth I 英国女王伊丽莎白一世（1558—1603 年任英格兰和爱尔兰女王，是都铎王朝的第五位也是最后一位君主，她终生未婚，带领英国打败西班牙成为海上强国，创造了一个繁荣强盛的伊丽莎白时代）
7. Christopher Marlowe 克里斯多弗·马娄（莎士比亚同期英国著名的剧作家、诗人、翻译家）
8. the Sovereign Grant 君主准许金（英国政府官方拨付皇室的经费，用于支付皇家的公务开支）
9. Parliamentary Annuity 议会年金（英国议会定期为皇室成员存入的账户经费，用于支付皇家成员的开支）

Cultural Notes

1. Elizabethan Era

伊丽莎白时代，指的是英格兰历史上由伊丽莎白一世女王统治的时期。历史学家经常将其描述为英格兰历史上的黄金时代。这一时期同样是英国文艺复兴的鼎峰，见证了诗歌、音乐和文学的蓬勃发展，威廉·莎士比亚和许多其他人创作的戏剧打破了传统的戏剧风格。伊丽莎白时代也是英格兰对外探索和扩张的时代，开启了英国成为欧洲强国的序幕。

2. the English Renaissance

英国文艺复兴。相对于欧洲其他国家来说，英国的文艺复兴起始较晚，通常指 15-16 世纪这个时期。英国文艺复兴受到欧洲文艺复兴的影响，主张“以人为本”，反对中世纪“以神为中心”的世界观，提倡积极进取、享受现世欢乐的生活理想。代表人物有托马斯·莫尔、威廉·莎士比亚、本·琼森等人。

3. Megxit

梅根退出，这是基于 “Brexit” 一词的词汇创新，指的是英国哈利王子的妻子梅根脱离英国皇室这一事件，曾一度令公众哗然。

Exercises

I. Matching

Directions: *Match the descriptions on the left side with the people on the right side.*

1. The nickname of ________ is “the grandmother of Europe”.	**A.** George V
2. The House of Windsor starts from ________.	**B.** King Charles III
3. ________ ruled Britain in Shakespeare’s time.	**C.** Queen Elizabeth I
4. Now, ________ is the first heir to the throne of Britain.	**D.** Queen Victoria
5. ________ is the present monarch of the UK.	**E.** Prince William

II. Writing

Directions: *Write a self-introduction about one of the following three queens in the tone of the first person. The introduction should include a life experience description, major achievements in ruling the countries and some personal stories (200–300 words).*

Queen Elizabeth I

Queen Victoria

Queen Elizabeth II

Group Game

Mini-drama: An Act of the Movie *The Queen*

The Queen is a biographical drama film which tells the life of Queen Elizabeth II and her royal family in 1997. There is a scene in the movie depicting Tony Blair's first visit to the Queen in Buckingham Palace and Queen's official appointment of the new prime minister. Watch the scene and act it out in the class. There can be four roles in your play—the queen, Tony Blair, Mrs. Blair and the housekeeper in Buckingham Palace. Scan the QR code to watch the film episode and download the actors' lines.

Episode in the movie *The Queen*

Post-class Thinking

Comparison and Analysis

Directions: *Five hundred years ago, Queen Elizabeth I helped England to become a European power. In the history of China, there emerged quite a number of outstanding emperors who had established China's leading position in Asia and even the world. Can you introduce one or two of them and talk about their accomplishments when ruling the country?*

Text C The Political System in the US

Pre-class Preparation

MOOC Watching

Watch the MOOC video "The Political System in the United States" to prepare for Text C.

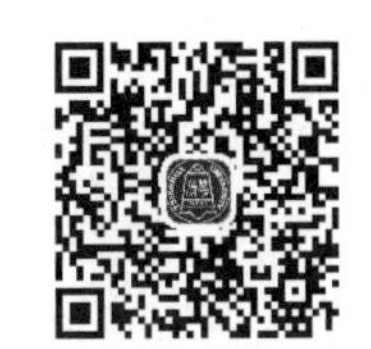

Pre-reading Questions

1. What are the three branches of the American federal government?
2. What are the differences between the political system in the US and that of other capitalist countries?

In-class Reading

The Political System in the US

1 After the United States declared its independence from Britain, the country set out to organize its own political system. Inspired by the French philosopher, **Montesquieu**, the power of the US federal government[1] is divided into three branches—legislative branch, executive branch, and judicial branch. The powers of the three branches are vested by the US Constitution in **the Congress**, the president, and **the federal courts**, including **the Supreme Court**, respectively.

★ **Three branches of the federal government**

2 In the US, the Congress functions as the legislative branch of the

US government. Legislative power of the Congress is vested in the two chambers of Congress: **the Senate** and **the House of Representatives**. The executive branch is headed by the president and is independent of the legislature. The judicial branch is composed of the Supreme Court and lower federal courts. The president's role is to **implement** laws after they have been passed. The role of the courts is to interpret the US Constitution[2] and federal laws and regulations. This includes resolving disputes between the executive and legislative branches.

implement
v. 贯彻，执行

★ Checks and balances

3 Checks and balances[3] is a principle of government to share power between separate political branches. The principle is applied primarily in constitutional governments. The system of checks and balances in government was developed to ensure that no branch of government would become too powerful. The US political system follows a principle of "checks and balances", which enables all three branches to mutually control each other.

4 In order to control the legislative power of the Congress, the president, who represents the executive power, is able to **veto** legislation passed in the Congress. The courts are also able to restrict the power of the Congress, and can declare the laws passed by the Congress unconstitutional. In addition to this, the president's power is restricted because the Congress has the power to **trump** a veto cast by the president regarding the passing of a law. The Congress can do this by passing such a law with a two-thirds majority. Further, the courts are able to declare the president's actions unconstitutional if the president acts beyond the scope of his authority.

veto
v. 否决

trump
v. 胜过，赢过

★ State governments and local governments

5 The US is a federal democratic republic[4]. The federal government created by the US Constitution is the typical feature of the American governmental system. However, most residents are also subject to a **state government** and various units of **local governments**. The latter includes

counties, municipalities, and special districts. State governments have the power to make laws on all subjects that are not granted to the federal government. These include education, family law, contract law, and most crimes. Unlike the federal government, which only has those powers granted to it in the Constitution, a state government has inherent powers to act unless limited by a **provision** of the state or national constitution.

provision
n. 条款

6 The laws in states vary from each other. For example, the legal age for drinking in some states is 21 and 18 in other states. Like the federal government, state governments have three branches: legislative branch, executive branch, and judicial branch. The chief executive of a state is its popularly elected governor, who typically holds office for a four-year term (in some states the term is two years). Except Nebraska, which has **unicameral** legislature, all states have a **bicameral** legislature, with the Upper House usually called the Senate and the Lower House called the House of Representatives, the Assembly or something similar. In most states, senators serve four-year terms, and members of the Lower House serve two-year terms. There are 89,500 local governments in the United States. The local governments directly serve the needs of the people, providing everything from police, health regulations, education, housing to public transportation.

unicameral
adj. 单院制的
bicameral
adj. 双院制的

★ **Political representation in the US and its problems**

7 Political representation[5] is an essential part of making sure that political institutions and democracy have taken their citizens' interests into account. However, concerns have been raised over the level of political influence held by different **demographic** groups in the US.

demographic
adj. 人口统计的

8 Women lack **proportional** representation in the US, bringing into question the extent to which women's issues are adequately addressed. **Racial and ethnic minorities** have also been disadvantaged by an absence of **equitable** representation, as white representatives feel difficult to

proportional
adj. 有比例的

equitable
adj. 公正的

fully understand the problems and situations faced by ethnic minorities. Although African Americans have won more elected positions and increased their overall political representation, they still lack proportional representation across a variety of different levels of government. Despite comprising 15% of the population in at least a quarter of House districts, **Latino** representation in the Congress has not correspondingly increased. Compared with the former two groups, Native and Asian Americans have different challenges and there are only a limited number of districts that are comprised of their small population. Therefore, their voices can hardly be heard and their political rights are often neglected due to a lack of political representation. The problems in American political representation lead to many noticeable social problems, such as sexism, social inequality and racial discrimination.

★ **American political parties**

9 The modern political party system in the US is a two-party system dominated by **the Democratic Party** and **the Republican Party**. These two parties have won every US presidential election since 1852 and have controlled the US Congress since at least 1856. From time to time, several other third parties have achieved relatively minor representation at the national and state levels.

10 The animal symbols of donkey and elephant have been used to represent the Democratic Party and the Republican Party respectively since the 19th century. The origins of the Democratic donkey can be traced to the 1828 presidential campaign. During that election campaign, opponents of Andrew Jackson called him **jackass**. Instead of feeling offended, Jackson was amused by it and included the image of donkey in his campaign posters. Later, Jackson defeated **incumbent** John Quincy Adams and became America's first Democratic president. In the 1870s, influential political cartoonist Thomas Nast helped **popularize** the donkey as a symbol for the entire Democratic Party.

jackass
n. 愚蠢的人

incumbent
adj. 现任的

popularize
v. 使通俗化

11 The Republican Party was formed in 1854 and six years later Abraham Lincoln became its first leader elected to the White House. An image of an elephant was featured as a Republican symbol in at least one political cartoon and a newspaper **illustration** during the Civil War (when "seeing the elephant" was an expression used by soldiers to mean experiencing combat). But it was not taken as a symbol of the whole party until Thomas Nast, the father of the modern political cartoon, used it in an 1874 *Harper's Weekly* cartoon.

illustration
n. 插图

Cultural Terms

1. Montesquieu 孟德斯鸠（法国启蒙运动思想家，也是西方国家学说奠基人）
2. the Congress 美国国会（美国的立法机构）
3. the federal courts 联邦法院（美国联邦政府的一部分，包括普通法院和专门法院）
4. the Supreme Court 最高法院（美国司法体系中最高级别的联邦法院）
5. the Senate 参议院（美国国会的两院之一，每州有两位议员代表）
6. the House of Representatives 众议院（美国国会两院之一，每州议员人数由州人口数决定）
7. state government 州政府（美国宪法规定 50 个州都具有一定的独立性，都有自己的宪法和法律）
8. local government 地方政府（美国州政府之下的县级等其他地方政府）
9. racial and ethnic minority 少数族裔群体
10. Latino 拉丁美洲人
11. the Democratic Party 民主党 （美国两大政党之一，俗称“驴党”）
12. the Republican Party 共和党 （美国两大政党之一，俗称“象党”）

Cultural Notes

1. the US federal government

美国联邦政府，美国的中央政府，由三部分组成：立法分支、行政分支、司法分支，其权力分别由国会、总统和联邦法院掌握，由《美国宪法》赋予。这些部门的权力和职责由美国国会法进一步定义，包括设立行政部门和次于最高法院的法院。联邦政府部门皆位于华盛顿特区。

2. US Constitution

《美国宪法》，世界上首部成文宪法，也是美国的根本大法。《美国宪法》于1787年在费城召开的制宪会议上获得代表批准，1788年正式生效并奠定了美国政治制度的法律基础。根据宪法，美国成为一个由多个具有一定独立性的州组成的联邦国家，同时也有一个联邦政府来为联邦的运作而服务。《美国宪法》为日后许多国家宪法的制定提供了成功的典范。

3. checks and balances

制约与均衡是美国联邦政府三权分立制度的内在核心和工作原理。立法、行政、司法三权彼此相互制约，防止某一分支的权力过于集中而形成专权。三大分支相互制约从而形成一种较为稳定的政治局面。

4. federal democratic republic

联邦民主共和国是指实施联邦制的共和制国家。共和制国家与君主制国家不同，是指拥有民选国家领导人，而非君主。在联邦共和国，联邦政府和各个地方政府之间有权力分工。虽然不同国家的具体权力分配不同，但通常联邦政府处理国防、货币政策等事项，而地方政府则处理基础设施维护、教育等政策。联邦政府与其他政体中央政府在政治生活上各方面均与有绝对主导权的单一制有所差异。

5. political representation

政治代表权，指当政治行为者考虑公民的最大利益时，使公民“出席”公共决策过程的活动。代表可以按照符合自己判断且维护公民最大利益的行为行事。在西方国家，许多弱势群体，如外来民族、有色人种、女性的政治代表等，会受到轻视，也带来一定的社会问题。

Exercise

Discussion

Directions: *Discuss the following topics with your partners. Then one or two members will give a speech representing the whole group.*

1. Consider and compare the power of the British monarch and the American president. What similarities do they have in their public duties and how do they differ in other aspects?
2. Have you heard of Black Lives Matter (BLM) Movement? It refers to a famous political and social movement against police brutality and racial violence against black people

in the US. Why do the black people still suffer from a lack of social equality with the Emancipation Proclamation released more than 150 years ago? What might be the deep social and political causes behind this phenomenon?

Post-class Thinking

Role-play

Directions: *Form a group of three. Three members in each group represent the three branches of the US federal government, i.e., the US Congress, the American President, the Supreme Court and other federal courts respectively. Introduce to each other your separate duties and rights and how you check and balance your powers. The group which presents the most systematic introduction and most detailed description wins.*

Supplementary Resources

1. Extensive Reading

Scan the QR codes to read Text D "Political Parties and Presidential Election in the US" and watch the MOOC video "Presidential Election in the US". Discuss the following questions with your partners: What is US presidential election? Who won the 2020 US presidential election?

Text D "Political Parties and Presidential Election in the US"

MOOC video "Presidential Election in the US"

2. Documentaries and TV Series

1) Documentary: *A History of Britain* （《英国史》）

A History of Britain is a BBC documentary series written and presented by Simon Schama, first transmitted in the UK from September 30, 2000. Schama believed that it was necessary to produce a historical documentary on Great Britain at that time. He argued that Britain was entering a new phase of its relationship with Europe and the rest of the world, and where it would end up depending a great deal on where it comes from.

2) Documentary: *Monarchy* （《君主制》）

Monarchy is a Channel 4 British TV series (2004–2007) by British academic David Starkey, charting the political and ideological history of the English monarchy from the Saxon period to modern times.

3) TV series: *The Crown* （《王冠》）

The Crown is a historical drama streaming television series about the reign of Queen Elizabeth II, created and principally written by Peter Morgan and produced by Left Bank Pictures and Sony Pictures Television for Netflix. *The Crown* has been praised by critics for its acting, directing, writing, cinematography, and production values, though its historical inaccuracies have received some criticism.

4) Documentary: *America's Great Divide: From Obama to Trump* （《美国大分裂：从奥巴马到特朗普》）

America's Great Divide: From Obama to Trump is a 2020 two-part television documentary film about the political divide between the US Democratic Party and Republican Party in the early 21st century.

5) TV series: *The House of Cards* （《纸牌屋》）

The House of Cards is an American political thriller streaming television series created by Beau Willimon. *The House of Cards* is set in Washington, DC, and is the story of Congressman Frank Underwood, a Democrat from South Carolina's 5th congressional district and House Majority Whip, and his equally ambitious wife Claire Underwood.

3. Books

狄更斯 . 2018. 英国简史 . 渊博译 . 杭州：浙江人民出版社 .

房龙 . 2017. 美国的故事 . 端木杉译 . 北京：北京时代华文书局 .

韩炯，姜静 . 2012. 白金帝国：英国皇室 . 北京：中国青年出版社 .

苏菲 . 2011. 英伦玫瑰：戴安娜 . 长沙：湖南师范大学出版社 .

文玉 . 2012. 女王伊丽莎白二世家族传 . 武汉：华中科技大学出版社 .

Chapter 6
An Overview of Education in the UK and the US

The UK and the US are both reputed for their education, especially higher education. It is commonly assumed that both countries have top-ranking higher institutions and world-renowned academic influence. This chapter will introduce the education systems of the UK and the US and their prestigious higher institutions first, and then introduce how to apply to the overseas colleges and universities and how to prepare for those important international tests.

Text A An Introduction to the Education Systems in the UK and the US

Pre-class Preparation

MOOC Watching

Watch the MOOC video "Education Systems in the UK and the US" to prepare for Text A.

Pre-reading Questions

1. What impresses you when mentioning British and American education?
2. What are the similarities and differences between the education system in China and that in Western countries?

In-class Reading

An Introduction to the Education Systems in the UK and the US

unexceptionally *adv.* 无一例外地

1 Today, nearly every nation **unexceptionally** attaches great importance to the development of education, for education plays a fundamentally decisive role in creation of better human beings and essentially a better society. Though sharing much in common, the education system differs somewhat from nation to nation, which is also true between the UK and the US.

★ The education system in the UK

2 The education system in the UK is divided into five Key Stages[1], Key Stage 1 (ages 5–7), Key Stage 2 (ages 7–11), Key Stage 3 (ages 11–14),

Key Stage 4 (ages 14–16) and Key Stage 5 (ages 16–18). The first two key stages belong to the primary education (ages 5–11), while Key Stage 3 and Key Stage 4 belong to the secondary education (ages 11–16), the legally compulsory education length for all children from about 5 to 16 years old previously. But today, students in England must remain in some form of education or training until the age of 18. That is to say, those aged between 16 and 18 may opt to study A-Levels[2] at Key Stage 5 or gain some form of training for **vocational** qualifications, such as AS-Levels[3] and NVQs[4].

vocational
adj. 职业的

3 At Key Stage 1, especially during the first year of the stage, schools pay attention to kids' **phonic** teaching and learning with an aim to improve their ability to read. At Key Stage 2, **the National Curriculum** centers around a more knowledge-oriented instruction on three core subjects, i.e., English, mathematics and science. Key Stage 3 is rather important since it's a period of education leading to the GCSE[5] national qualification. At the end of this stage, some students may choose to take the GCSE or other qualifications in advance. Key Stage 4 is the final stage of the previous compulsory education, and also the most common period for students to sit for the national assessment tests.

phonic
adj. 语音的

4 During the primary education, about 93% of children in England and Wales choose to go to **state schools**, while the rest 7% go to **private schools**. As for the secondary education, nearly 88% of pupils in England go to comprehensive schools[6], as do all pupils in Wales. Besides studying all the subjects taught in primary education, secondary school students are also required to learn at least one foreign language, take **citizenship** classes, and attend personal, social and health education as well.

citizenship
n. 公民权

5 Many students remain at school after the **minimum** leaving age of 16 for further education, extending into the sixth form[7] for another two-year post-GCSE academic education. They choose to study several subjects during the two years for the A-Level examinations. In the UK, students are commonly required to pass A-Levels for an **undergraduate** degree

minimum
adj. 最小的；最低的

undergraduate
n. 本科生

at universities, which generally admit those applicants who have at least three A-Levels with top grades. Chances will increase if the subjects they choose are highly related to their aimed university courses.

6 Higher education in Britain begins with a three-year bachelor's degree, followed by a one-year master's degree and the doctorate, a research degree that usually takes at least three years.

★ The education system in the US

federalism
n. 联邦制

7 The US follows **federalism** that has valued local governments a lot so that no country-level education system or curriculum applies to the entire country. In other words, education remains a local matter, guided by the Department of Education of the state. Nearly all students in Grades 1 to 12 can enjoy free education if they go to a **public school**. Compulsory education in the US generally covers children ranging from 6 to 16 or 18 years old, divided into 3 stages: elementary schools (ages 6–11), middle schools (ages 11–14), and high schools (ages 14–18).

arithmetic
n. 算数

algebra
n. 几何
geometry
n. 代数
pre-calculus
n. 初级微积分

8 Elementary schools begin with kindergarten and extend through Grades 1 to 5. Most children start their kindergarten life at the age of 5 and move on to Grade 1 at 6 years old. Each local school district determines the curriculum for their kids but with common emphasis on reading, writing, and **arithmetic** during primary education. Middle schools include Grades 6 to 8 and high schools grades 9 to 12. The duration at each stage may vary from state to state. Although the curricula also vary among different states, the same core subjects remain academically focused, like English language, sciences (biology, chemistry and physics), and mathematics (**algebra**, **geometry**, **pre-calculus** and statistics). Besides core subjects, high school students may choose to take some elective courses as well, such as music, art, or theater classes.

9 A student can only get his or her **high school diploma** (**HSD**) after he or she has successfully passed all of the required courses. Grades are given

to students for each course at the end of each semester. Schools in the US mostly use the letter grades "A" through "F", derived from a scale of 0–100. Generally speaking, "A" stands for excellence in academic performance, "B" means doing better than the average peers, "C" represents average, "D" means below the average and "F" means failure. A student who fails a required course must retake that course in the coming academic year. However, the passing grade differs from state to state, for instance, the "D" grade (60–70) is considered a failing grade in Texas or Virginia, while in Hawaii the "D" grade may be considered passing in certain classes, but failing in others.

10 After graduating from high school, students have the option of attending a two-year community college[8] if they don't want to go to a four-year university immediately. **Admission** to a community college is easy and the tuition is relatively cheap. Students there can earn an associate degree before they decide whether they want to transfer to a four-year university. In an American four-year college or university, the students who pursue a bachelor's degree are called "undergraduates", and those who pursue a master's or doctoral degree are "graduate students."

admission
n. 录取

Cultural Terms

1. the National Curriculum 全国统一必修课程
2. state school 公立学校（学生在校接受免费教育）
3. private school 私立学校（英国的伊顿公学、哈罗公学是著名的私立学校）
4. public school （美）公立学校（在英国指公学，属于私立学校）
5. high school diploma (HSD) 美国高中毕业证书

Cultural Notes

1. Key Stages

根据英国统一的国家课程大纲，整个中小学教育划分为 5 个关键阶段，每一阶段对应一个年龄段。课程大纲明确规定每一阶段的学生学习哪些内容，要求掌握哪些知识。世人所了解的英国教育通常指英格兰教育体系，威尔士教育遵循英格兰教育体系，而苏格兰体系相对独立。在学制结构方面，苏格兰体系采取的是“小学 7 年、中学 4 年、预科 1 年”的学制，而英格兰体系采取的是“小学 6 年、中学 5 年、预科 2 年”的学制。

2. A-Levels

General Certificate of Education Advanced Level 的缩写，即英国大学入学考试，相当于中国的高考。A-Levels 为 16–18 岁的学生开设，学制为 2 年，评估的等级是 A*–E，学生的成绩基本上是由第二年（13 年级）的期末考试来决定。在英国，学生凭 A-Levels 的成绩可以直接申报大学。

3. AS-Levels

完整的 A-Levels 学制为 2 年，包括 AS（12 年级）学年和 A2（13 年级）学年。AS-Levels 是指学生在 AS 学年结束的时候参加科目考试获得的分数。

4. NVQ

National Vocational Qualifications 的缩写，即国家职业资格证书。在英国，学生学习与某职业技能相关的课程并通过职业资格认证考试后获得证书，等同于我们国内的专科毕业证书。证书共分为 5 个级别，学生结合自身的实际工作和职业培训，从低级向高级考取证书。四级国家职业资格证书相当于学士学位，五级国家职业资格证书相当于硕士学位。

5. GCSE

General Certificate of Secondary Education 的缩写，即普通中等教育证书，英国学生从 16 岁左右开始参加普通中等教育证书考试。学生 16 岁以后面临分流：一部分选择几门课程继续学习 2 年，然后通过 A-Levels 考试，从而获得去大学深造的资格；另一部分通常以某种方式进入职业技术学院接受职业培训或教育。

6. comprehensive school

英国普通中学，20 世纪 60 年代在英国得到广泛推行。普通中学是公立中学，属于免费教育。此类学校不设入学考试，不论学生的能力水平如何均可入学。

7. the sixth form

中学六年级（16—18 岁的英国学生），这里指通过 GCSE 考试后的大学预科班。通常是经过 2 年的学习，通过 A-Levels 高水平考试的学生才有资格申请大学就读。

8. community college

美国社区大学，学制为 2 年，学生毕业后可获副学士学位（associate degree），随后转入四年制大学继续攻读 2 年，毕业后可获学士学位（bachelor's degree）。相较于四年制大学，社区大学具备入学灵活、学费较低、班级规模小、更注重个性化发展和实践经验等优势，受欢迎度较高。

Exercises

I. Diagram Sketching

Directions: *Based on Text A, sketch a brief diagram of the educational structure of the UK and the US respectively, mainly including the information about the educational stages and the age groups. In addition, draw a third diagram of the educational structure of China.*

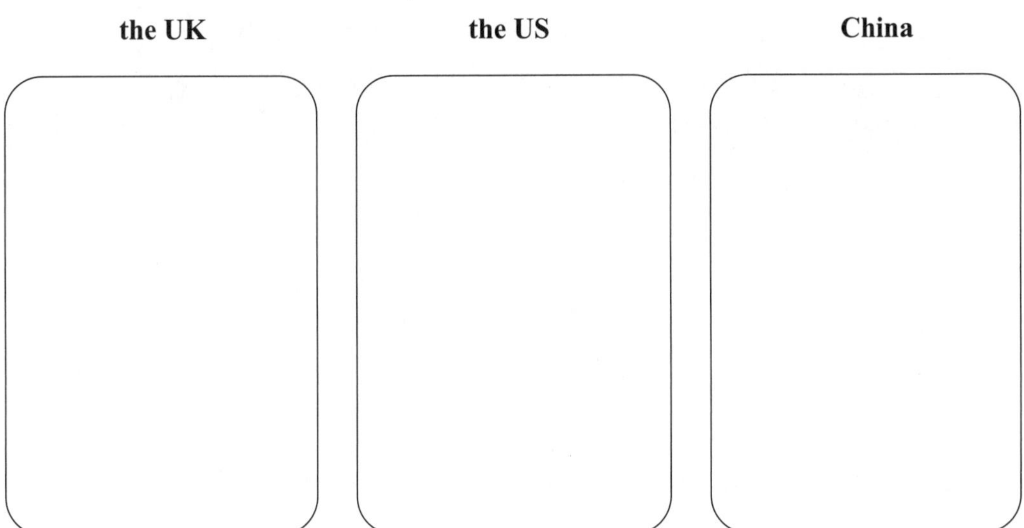

II. Findings Sharing

Directions: *Based on the three diagrams you've sketched above, try to compare them and share your findings with your classmates.*

____

____

____

In-class Game

Subject Hunting

Directions: *Circle a cluster of letters in the following table horizontally, or vertically, or diagonally to form a subject name, with example ① already offered. Write down the subject names you've hunted in the blanks below, marked with the same number as that used in the table for better indication. It's viewed as PASS if you figure out more than 12 subjects.*

a	b	l	e	g	p	h	i	l	o	s	o	p	h	y	h	p	p	t
n	e	c	k	i	t	r	e	e	n	g	i	n	e	e	r	i	n	g
h	i	s	t	o	r	y	g	g	e	d	r	a	m	a	h	u	m	n
i	b	o	o	s	t	e	r	a	m	e	e	c	e	s	①a	f	e	d
e	a	p	h	y	s	i	c	s	t	a	d	h	n	a	r	i	v	p
m	o	o	n	i	g	h	t	u	i	d	i	e	c	b	t	v	e	s
a	u	t	a	s	t	o	p	a	t	o	z	m	e	g	e	e	n	y
t	i	s	s	h	a	m	p	o	l	i	t	i	c	s	r	t	i	c
h	e	r	i	g	o	l	s	i	t	l	o	s	e	t	e	e	n	h
s	a	t	i	c	k	i	s	i	a	i	p	t	e	d	s	d	g	o
e	r	b	o	o	k	t	c	a	p	t	a	r	c	g	c	u	e	l
s	t	a	t	i	s	t	i	c	s	e	t	y	o	i	e	c	o	o
t	y	t	e	n	a	l	e	a	o	r	y	t	n	d	b	a	g	g
r	i	s	e	c	l	a	n	g	u	a	g	e	o	m	e	t	r	y
b	i	o	l	o	g	y	c	u	t	t	u	n	m	o	i	i	a	e
g	o	f	a	r	e	r	e	f	i	u	i	o	i	o	i	o	p	s
k	h	u	w	m	b	a	t	e	a	r	l	i	c	n	r	n	h	u
l	o	r	y	b	r	o	o	s	t	e	r	o	s	e	h	g	y	i
r	e	g	x	a	a	c	c	o	u	n	t	i	n	g	o	a	i	t

① art ② ________ ③ ________ ④ ________ ⑤ ________

⑥ ________ ⑦ ________ ⑧ ________ ⑨ ________ ⑩ ________

⑪ ________ ⑫ ________ ⑬ PASS

⑭ ________ ⑮ ________ ⑯ ________ ⑰ ________ ⑱ ________

⑲ ________ ⑳ ________ ㉑ ________ ㉒ ________ ㉓ ________

Post-class Thinking

Discussion

Directions: *To ensure education equality and narrow the gap between urban and rural schools, China put forward a number of educational policies or programs, such as Project Hope, and Spring Bud Project. What do you know about the two projects or beyond? Suppose you're invited to propose for the compulsory education of China, which aspects do you think need to be improved and why?*

Text B A Glimpse of Famous Universities in the UK and the US

Pre-class Preparation

MOOC Watching

Watch the MOOC video "Prestigious Higher Institutions in Britain and America" to prepare for Text B.

Pre-reading Questions

1. What higher institutions do you know about in Britain and America?
2. What majors or programs are representative of the college or university that you have mentioned?

In-class Reading

A Glimpse of Famous Universities in the UK and the US

1 Based on the Times Higher Education World Reputation Rankings[1] 2022, the US dominates the ranking table, with an absolutely high percentage in the overall top 200, 57 in total. The UK comes in second, with 28 universities in the top 200, headed by the Oxford University in the first place. In all, 10 universities from China rank in the top 200, Tsinghua University and Peking University, for the first time, entering the top 20.

2 Among the top universities around the world, most attention is generally drawn to the UK higher education led by the G5 Super Elite[2] and the US higher education led by the Ivy League[3]. The following will mainly introduce prestigious universities in the two countries.

★ **Prestigious universities in the UK**

3 The G5 Super Elite is made up of five best universities in the UK, Oxford University, Cambridge University, Imperial College London, UCL, and London School of Economics and Political Science. The **foremost** two are jointly named "Oxbridge", combined with Durham University to be named "Doxbridge". Oxford (1096), Cambridge (1209) and Durham (1832) are the three oldest schools in England, and also the main representative schools adopting the collegiate system[4].

foremost
adj. 最前的

4 Oxford University is composed of 39 colleges and **collegial** institutions. Based on the 2020 Norrington Table[5] ranking, *College Gazette*[6] ranked New College, St. Catherine's College, Queen's College, St. Peter's College and Merton College as the top five at Oxford. As for top-ranking majors, Oxford's classics, theology, and political science have traditionally

collegial
adj. 大学的

held the highest reputation in terms of scholarship and instruction since the Renaissance. Over the centuries, many prominent elites, including scientists, philosophers, politicians, explorers, and writers, have graduated from the university, like **Oscar Wilde**, **Adam Smith**, **John Locke**, **William Penn**, Albert Einstein and **Tony Blair**.

5 Cambridge, the second-oldest university in Britain, is known to be a prestigious university all around the world. Cambridge University consists of 31 autonomous colleges and over 100 academic departments. Currently, subjects like English language and literature, **archaeology** and **pharmacy** are classified into the top 10 in the world. In total, 121 **affiliates** of Cambridge University have been awarded Nobel Prizes since 1904. The latest winner is Professor Sir Roger Penrose[7], who won the Nobel Prize for Physics in 2020. Besides, many famous **alumni** help make Cambridge more reputed, just to name a few, Isaac Newton, Stephen Hawking, Charles Darwin, **Lord Byron** and **John Maynard Keynes**. Through such a long course of establishment and development, both Oxford and Cambridge have been grown up into prestigious lighthouses in higher education globally. In addition, both possess renowned scholarly institutions, libraries, museums, and publishing houses as well.

archaeology *n.* 考古学
pharmacy *n.* 药剂学；制药学
affiliate *n.* 附属机构
alumni *n.* （统称）校友(alumnus 的复数)

6 Ranked No.82 in the QS World University Rankings[8] (2022), Durham University is consistently ranked among the top universities in the UK. It shows great diversity and flexibility in social and academic community, with the staff and student bodies coming from more than 120 countries. Over 90% of subjects are ranked in the UK top 10, which confirms their outstanding teaching and learning standard. Durham University has a global reputation for excellence and **collaboration** to make an impact on the world, from improving people's health to supporting business.

collaboration *n.* 协作；合作

7 Scotland is also known for its rich cultural history. Around the 15th to 16th centuries, there were four **distinguished** schools in Scotland,

distinguished *adj.* 著名的；卓越的

University of St. Andrews (1410), University of Glasgow (1451), University of Aberdeen (1495) and University of Edinburgh (1583). The University of Edinburgh is ranked the first in Scotland and the fourth in the UK based on its reputation, research performance, and alumni impact. It's an internationally-focused university and welcomes students from all corners of the globe, the majority of whom come from China and the US. Its College of Medicine and **Veterinary** Medicine is reputed to be a world-leader in its field. A total of 21 Nobel **laureates** are affiliated with the university, and famous alumni include Charles Darwin, **David Hume** and **Gordon Brown**. The rest of the top Scottish universities are the University of Stirling, University of Dundee, Heriot-Watt University and University of Strathclyde, based on the 2021 edition of the QS World University Rankings.

veterinary *adj.* 兽医的
laureate *n.* 获奖者

8 British universities founded in the early 20th century are grouped into Red Brick Universities[9], mainly referring to six civic universities built in the major industrial cities of Great Britain. They are: University of Birmingham (1900), University of Liverpool (1903), University of Manchester (1903), University of Leeds (1904), University of Sheffield (1905) and University of Bristol (1909). Previously viewed as non-collegiate institutions, the six universities admitted applicants regardless of religion or background, but with the sole aim of teaching their students "real-world" skills, especially civic science and engineering. In other words, the six red bricks focused on practical knowledge over the academic research, which also distinguished them from the ancient English universities of Oxford and Cambridge and from the newer University of Durham as well. The term "red brick" originated from the distinctive red-bricked Victoria Building at the University of Liverpool, but now it is sometimes used more widely to mean any of the non-ancient universities.

9 In 1960s, another term "plateglass[10]" was coined, referring to 20 new universities established around the mid-20th century, such as Aston

University, University of Kent, Lancaster University and University of Warwick. The term is associated with the modern architectural style of the universities, often with wide expanses of plateglass in steel or concrete frames. This distinguished them from the (largely Victorian) Red Brick Universities and the older ancient universities.

10 Top universities in the UK jointly set up the Russell Group[11] in 1994, combining 17 world-class and research-intensive universities, including the G5 Super Elite, six Red Brick Universities, two from Scotland, and four other universities from England. Now with 24 members in total, the Russell Group is inserting huge social, economic and cultural impacts locally, across the UK and around the globe. For instance, 91% of research at the Russell Group is world-leading or internationally excellent, its research covering a large expanse, from medicine, health and life sciences to physical sciences, engineering and mathematics, from social sciences to arts and humanities.

★ Prestigious universities in the US

11 Across the Atlantic Ocean, the US is reputed to have the first-class higher institutions in the world, including universities and colleges. Universities in the US commonly fall into three types: public universities, private universities and research universities.

12 Universities are higher education institutions, usually lasting up to four years. The main difference between public universities and private universities lies in whether they are state-funded or not. Public universities are often bigger in size than private ones and lower in tuition costs. More part-time and **commuter** students tend to be enrolled by public universities, and international students will have to pay higher fees than domestic students at such universities. University of California, Los Angeles (UCLA) is a good example of public universities, No.1 in the Top Public Schools and No.20 in National Universities based on the 2022 edition of Best

commuter
n. 通勤者

selective
adj. 严格筛选的

Colleges[12]. It's most **selective** with an acceptance rate of 14%, and half the admitted applicants have an **SAT** score between 1,290 and 1,520 or an **ACT** score between 29 and 34. The tuition fee is $13,268 for in-state applicants and $43,022 for out-of-state ones. To name a few most popular majors at UCLA: Social Sciences; English Language and Literature/Letters; and History. University of California, Berkeley, University of Michigan, University of Virginia and University of California, Santa Barbara are the rest of the top public universities.

13 Not funded by the state government, private universities tend to have higher tuition fees than public ones. Private universities, either for-profit or non-profit, generally pay most attention to producing high-quality curriculums and education. However, those non-profit private universities commonly have a better reputation than for-profit ones. Bay Atlantic University (BAU) is one of the non-profit private universities, awarding many scholarships to both domestic and international students. For instance, it offers tuition price scholarship to any international student enrolled in a master's degree program at BAU with a GMAT score between 550 and 750.

14 Research universities can be either public or non-profit private universities. They are doctorate degree-granting institutions, focusing on academic research and high research activities. All the eight Ivy League universities belong to this type. The Ivy League, generally viewed as the counterpart of the G5 Super Elite in the UK, is actually an athletic union of sports teams from eight private institutions of higher education in the northeastern US: Brown University, Columbia University, Cornell University, Dartmouth College, Harvard University, Princeton University, the University of Pennsylvania, and Yale University.

bond
n. 纽带；联系

15 Since its establishment in the year of 1954, the **bond** between these universities has gone beyond sports, and has long been associated with academic excellence, selectivity in admissions, and social elitism. Ivy

League universities are ranked among the top universities worldwide and they enjoy a prestigious academic reputation. The students who have enrolled in the Ivy League universities are regarded as the most intellectual and promising young men and women in the world. Many prominent political leaders, Nobel Prize winners and social elites have received their higher education from the Ivy League universities. In addition to the generous **donation** from their successful alumni, Ivy League universities are also favored by the US government so that they receive the largest university financial **endowments** in the world.

donation
n. 捐赠

endowment
n. 资助

16 Harvard University, founded in 1636, is a private, non-profit institution at the top of the Ivy League. It's world-famous for the excellence of higher education, including the top-ranked schools, such as Business School, Medical School, Graduate Education School, School of Engineering and Applied Sciences, Law School and John F. Kennedy School of Government. Harvard University is ranked the second based on the Times Higher Education World Reputation Rankings 2022, only after Oxford. Harvard has ever cultivated eight US presidents and many Nobel Prize winners in all fields. Famous alumni include John F. Kennedy, Bill Gates, Barack Obama, **Noam Chomsky** and Mark Zuckerberg.

17 Besides the eight universities in the northeastern US, there are also many outstanding universities scattered around the rest of the country. The University of Chicago and Northwestern University are the leading higher institutions in the midwest. The University of Chicago was founded in 1890 by **the American Baptist Education Society** with the generous donation from John Rockefeller, an American business **magnate** and **philanthropist**. Only within a decade, it turned into one of the world's leading universities.

magnate
n. (尤指)产业大亨

philanthropist
n. 慈善家

18 In the west, Stanford University and the University of California in Los Angeles and Berkeley are also the top academic and professional institutions both nationwide and worldwide. Stanford University, one of the

world's top universities, is a private research institution in northern Silicon Valley[13], California. It offers the most popular majors as follows: Computer and Information Sciences and Support Services; **Interdisciplinary** Studies; and Engineering. Stanford's faculty and alumni have founded many famous companies including Google and Yahoo, which have exerted **tremendous** influence on the development of modern technology.

interdisciplinary *adj.* 跨学科的
tremendous *adj.* 巨大的

19 Apart from universities, colleges also play an important role in the US higher education, including liberal arts colleges and community colleges. Liberal arts colleges are mostly non-profit private colleges, putting more emphasis on an undergraduate and well-rounded education rather than research. Community colleges are primarily two-year higher education institutions, providing students with lower-level **tertiary** education, and eventually with associate degrees, diplomas, and certificates if they graduate as requested. Two-year community colleges become increasingly popular for lower tuition fees, immediate employment after graduation, and great availability of transferring to four-year schools.

tertiary *adj.* 第三级的

20 Nearly eight million students enrolled in at least one course at a two-year college during the 2018–2019 school year. Walla Walla Community College (WWCC) in Washington, Santa Barbara City College in California, and Lake Area Technique Institute in South Dakota are ranked as the top 3 community colleges in the US. Take Walla Walla Community College as an example: academic courses (100 level or higher) at WWCC are **transferable** to most four-year universities. In addition, it offers e-learning programs, so that students can get an associate degree entirely online or through a combination of online and on-campus courses.

transferable *adj.* 可转移的；可转录的

Cultural Terms

1. Oscar Wilde 奥斯卡·王尔德（1854—1900, 英国最伟大的作家与艺术家之一）
2. Adam Smith 亚当·斯密（1723—1790，英国经济学家、哲学家、作家）
3. John Locke 约翰·洛克（1632—1704，英国哲学家和医生，俗称“自由主义之父”）

4. William Penn 威廉·佩恩（1644—1718，北美殖民地时期宾夕法尼亚殖民地的开拓者，同时也是贵格会的主要支持者和宗教改革家）
5. Tony Blair 托尼·布莱尔（1953— ，英国政治家，1997—2007 年任英国首相）
6. Lord Byron 拜伦（1788—1824，英国 19 世纪初期伟大的浪漫主义诗人）
7. John Maynard Keynes 约翰·梅纳德·凯恩斯（1883—1946，英国经济学家，宏观经济学创立人，被称为“宏观经济学之父”）
8. David Hume 大卫·休谟（1711—1776，苏格兰不可知论哲学家、经济学家、历史学家）
9. Gordon Brown 戈登·布朗（1951— ，英国政治家，2007—2010 年任英国首相）
10. SAT 美国高中毕业生学术能力水平考试（或称美国高考，总分 1600 分）
11. ACT 美国大学入学考试（学科考试，总分 36 分）
12. Noam Chomsky 诺姆·乔姆斯基（1928— ，美国语言学家、哲学家、政治评论家）
13. the American Baptist Education Society 美国浸礼会教育协会

Cultural Notes

1. the Times Higher Education World Reputation Rankings

泰晤士高等教育世界大学声誉排名（简称 THE 世界大学声誉排名），由《泰晤士高等教育专刊》从 2011 年开始发布。该排行榜突出体现各高校在吸引人才、商业投资、科研团队等方面的竞争力。

2. the G5 Super Elite

G5 超级精英大学，又称 G5，是英国剑桥大学、牛津大学、帝国理工学院、伦敦大学学院和伦敦政治经济学院五所精英学校的并称。G5 是英国顶尖研究型大学的代名词，代表了英国最高水平的科研实力和经济实力。其中，剑桥大学、牛津大学、伦敦大学学院和帝国理工学院常年占据世界大学排行榜前十名。

3. the Ivy League

常春藤联盟，最初指的是美国东北部地区八所高校（七所大学和一所学院）组成的体育赛事联盟。后沿用“常春藤”这一名称，指由这八校组成的高校联盟，所有成员都是美国一流名校。

4. the collegiate system

学院制，指的是英国中世纪大学的一个传统运作模式。学院不是单纯的教育实体，也不是单纯提供住宿的场所，而是为学生提供一个运动、交际和适合居住的活动中心。学院的学生可以学习不同的学科，就读于不同的年级。英国目前现存三所学院制大学，分别是牛津大学、剑桥大学和杜伦大学，这也是英格兰最古老的三所大学，并称作“Doxbridge”。

5. Norrington Table

诺林顿排行榜，20 世纪 60 年代由牛津大学三一学院前院长诺林顿爵士设立。诺林顿评分基于本科学位等级，以百分比表示，用以衡量各学院学生的最终成绩表现。本排名主要为申请本科课程的学生提供相对性参考。

6. *College Gazette*

《大学公报》，是美国高等教育信息的可靠来源。每周都会发布关于顶尖学院和大学的新内容及招生建议和策略。《大学公报》发表的文章和排名已经被公认的出版物甚至学校自己认可和引用。

7. Sir Roger Penrose

罗杰·潘罗斯爵士（1931—），英国数学物理学家，牛津大学数学系名誉教授。他对广义相对论与宇宙学的贡献显著，因发现黑洞形成是广义相对论的可靠预测而获得 2020 年诺贝尔物理学奖。

8. the QS World University Rankings

QS 世界大学排名，由英国高等教育资讯和分析数据提供商 QS（Quacquarelli Symonds）发布，一般每年夏季更新排名。QS 世界大学排名是参与机构最多、世界影响范围最广的排名之一，与泰晤士高等教育世界大学排名、US News 世界大学排名和软科世界大学学术排名被公认为四大权威的世界大学排名。

9. Red Brick Universities

红砖大学，是指在大英帝国维多利亚时代于英格兰六大重要工业中心城市创立的、第一次世界大战前得到英国皇家许可的六所高校：伯明翰大学、利物浦大学、曼彻斯特大学、利兹大学、谢菲尔德大学和布里斯托大学。这六所大学均与英国工业革命有着极其密切的关系，在创立之初均为科学或工程技术类学院，为英国的工业化奠定了重要基础，同时也都是英国顶尖大学联盟——罗素大学集团的成员。

10. plateglass

平板玻璃大学，是 20 世纪 60 年代英国大学扩张浪潮的产物，包括《罗宾斯报告》发表前后成立的 20 所大学。该报告提出让更多的平民大众上大学，随之建立起一批新的高校，此外还有一些专科学院升级为大学，英国高等教育由此完全进入大众化时代。平板玻璃大学的名字主要源于新建大学广用平板玻璃的建筑特色。

11. the Russell Group

罗素大学集团，成立于 1994 年，是由英国 24 所研究型大学组成的高校联盟，因各位校长每年春季固定在英国伦敦罗素饭店举行研究经费会议而得名。罗素集团盟校包括六所金三角名校（G5、伦敦国王学院）、六所红砖大学、两所苏格兰大学（爱丁堡大学 、格拉斯哥大学）、卡迪夫大学（威尔士）和贝尔法斯特女王大学（北爱尔兰）以及其他八所英格兰大学（伦敦玛丽女王大学、诺丁汉大学、南安普顿大学、纽卡斯尔大学、华威大学、杜伦大学、埃克塞特大学、约克大学）。该集团与世界各国的高校联盟，如中国九校联盟、国际科技大学联盟、澳大利亚八校集团、环太平洋大学联盟、德国 U15 大学联盟等均保持合作关系。

12. Best Colleges

美国最佳大学排名，由《美国新闻和世界报道》发布，即每年 US News 推出的美国大学排名榜。该排名基于学生毕业率和师资资源等核心因素，分别提供四个总体排名：国立大学、文科学院、地方大学和地方学院。该排名旨在结合专家建议、排名和数据，为学生在择校时提供参考和支持。

13. Silicon Valley

硅谷，位于美国加利福尼亚北部，是当今电子工业和计算机业的王国。硅谷最早是研究和生产以硅为基础的半导体芯片的地方，因而得名。

Exercise

True or False

Directions: *Determine whether the following statements are true (T) or false (F).*

1. Oxford, Cambridge and UCL are the three oldest schools in England adopting the collegiate system.
2. College of Medicine and Veterinary Medicine of the University of Edinburgh is a world-leader in the medical field.
3. In terms of social prestige and academic achievement as well, the Ivy League in the US is somewhat equal to the G5 Super Elite in the UK.
4. The University of California in the midwest enjoys the top nationwide and worldwide fame.

5. The foundation of Google and Yahoo owes much to Stanford faculty and alumni.

In-class Game

Matching

Directions: *Different universities have different histories or traditions, which may also be read from their different logos. Do you recognize any logos of the ten universities shown in the following table? Match the universities (marked with letters A–J) with their logos (marked with numbers 1–10). You may write down the letters on the blanks corresponding to the numbers.*

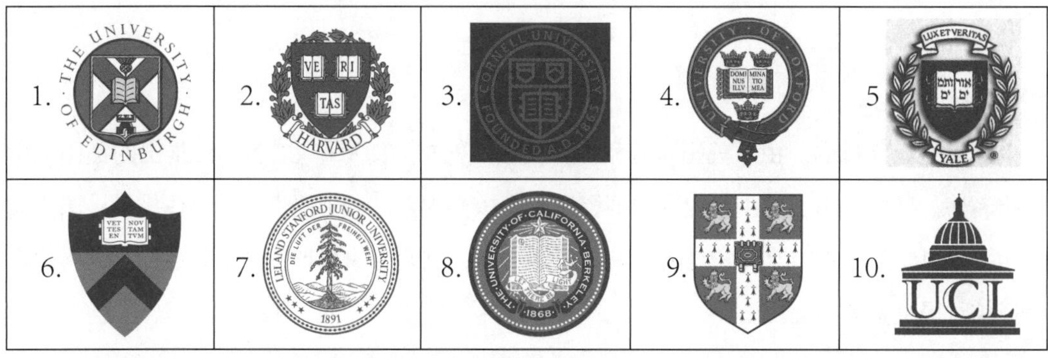

1. ________	**A.** Oxford University
2. ________	**B.** Stanford University
3. ________	**C.** Princeton University
4. ________	**D.** Cambridge University
5. ________	**E.** University of California, Berkeley
6. ________	**F.** Harvard University
7. ________	**G.** University College London
8. ________	**H.** Yale University
9. ________	**I.** University of Edinburgh
10. ________	**J.** Cornell University

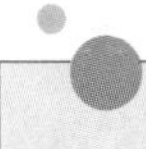

Post-class Thinking

Discussion

Directions: *What is the motto of your university or college? Pick three universities from the following pictures and search for their mottos respectively. Discuss with your partners both similarities and dissimilarities between the four mottos.*

1. Princeton University	2. Harvard University	3. Oxford University
4. Columbia University	5. Cambridge University	6. Yale University

The motto of my university /college:

____

The mottos of the universities displayed in the picture:

1. ______________________________

2. ______________________________

3. ______________________________

Text C How to Apply to Universities Overseas

Pre-class Preparation

MOOC Watching

Watch the MOOC video "How to Apply to Universities Overseas?" to prepare for Text C.

Pre-reading Questions

1. If you have a chance to study abroad, which university will you choose and why?
2. It's important for applicants to get themselves well prepared for a study abroad program. What do you have to take into consideration during the application procedure and why?

In-class Reading

How to Apply to Universities Overseas

1 The application process to universities overseas is complicated, **demanding**, and even **overwhelming** sometimes. As an applicant, you have to be mentally prepared for the challenge you're going to meet with. Once you have completed the application process, you are getting one big step closer to your dream school. It will be a great help if you stay organized throughout the application process, which will keep you less stressed on the one hand, and ensure that all of the procedures get fulfilled and all the required materials get prepared well and essentially sent to the target school on the other hand.

demanding *adj.* 要求高的
overwhelming *adj.* 压倒性的

★ **Making a plan**

2 The first thing you have to do before starting your application is to make a careful plan about how to find the schools that suit your needs best. In other words, you have to conduct a research, take careful notes of useful information, and **preferably** check with an experienced counselor from a registered studying abroad agency to see how your plan can be improved.

preferably
adv. 更合意地；最好是

3 Maybe you're supposed to be clear about all the following questions: Do I intend to pursue an undergraduate degree or a graduate one? What do I want to study for? Where can I find a strong academic program that best suits my needs? How much is my budget? What other factors do I have to consider that might affect my academic and social life while I study abroad, such as weather, food, and local customs?

★ **Searching information online**

4 Once you have **crystallized** your thought on the questions above, you can start searching online for the schools that currently offer the academic program you want to enroll in. Maybe the most effective way to start your online research on US schools is to view the website of US News. You may get information about the updated US colleges and graduate schools rankings, as well as the latest rankings of specific academic programs.

crystallize
v. 使明确

5 If you want to find the counterpart information about the schools in the UK, you can view the website of The Complete University Guide. Based on your research, make a list of the schools or programs you want to apply to. Thereafter you may start searching for the admissions requirements for international applicants on each school's official website.

★ **Application steps**

6 Now, the factual application may get started, generally following the steps below:

7 First, to submit an application for admission. The application form can

be submitted online, and usually the international applicants are asked to provide their personal and educational background in the application form.

8 Second, to submit two letters of recommendation from teachers, counselors, or advisers. As part of the application process, recommendation letters can help admissions officers get a better understanding of the applicants, so as to add extra merit to a college application.

transcript
n. 成绩报告单

9 Third, the original or certified copies of his or her secondary school **transcripts** or mark sheets are required for an applicant applying to an undergraduate degree. All the copies should be signed by the proper authorities. To get a graduate degree, the applicant should submit certified copies of his or her college transcripts or mark sheets. The documents need to be translated into English clearly and accurately if the original language is not English.

10 Fourth, international applicants are required to demonstrate their English language proficiency. It's highly advisable for the applicant to be first aware of what proficiency tests his or her target institutions require and recognize. Scores from the Test of English as a Foreign Language (TOEFL)[1] or the International English Language Testing System (IELTS)[2] exam are the recommended forms of proof. Most colleges in the US or the UK require minimum scores of 550 on the paper-based test or 80 on the Internet-based test in TOEFL. Band 6 or higher is required in IELTS. Most graduate programs generally demand higher scores.

11 Fifth, for an international applicant seeking an undergraduate degree in the US, SAT or ACT test scores are recommended to submit. These scores sometimes are not required for admission, but may help enhance the level of the applicant's academic scholarship. In recent years, some American schools have started to accept China's *gaokao* scores as entrance criteria. For those who wish to seek a graduate degree in the US, they need to submit GRE[3] test scores, or GMAT[4] scores for some graduate business and

management programs. However, GRE or GMAT tests are not required by most graduate programs in the UK.

12 Last but not least, both a curriculum vitae (CV[5]) and a personal statement or statement of purpose are required to submit in many schools. A CV is used mainly in academic circles, for an applicant may **elaborate** on the education, publications and some other academic achievements that he or she has received so far, often including his or her current academic focus. A personal statement or statement of purpose is an essay of prospective applicants' achievements, talents, interests and goals, typically in three or four paragraphs. In the essay, they need to clarify their purposes of study, and how they can connect their academic interests, future developments with the schools or programs they are applying to. For the applicants who pursue a graduate academic program, writing samples or publications in their academic fields of study are usually asked to submit, which may help improve their admissions odds.

elaborate
v. 详细描述

Cultural Notes

1. the Test of English as a Foreign Language (TOEFL)

   托福考试，面向非英语国家留学生，是由美国教育考试服务中心（Educational Testing Service，简称 ETS）研发的一个学术英语语言测试。托福考试通过检测参试者在英语听、说、读、写四个技能方面的表现，衡量参试者的真实学术语言能力。考试结果可用于本科及研究生阶段的院校申请。

2. the International English Language Testing System (IELTS)

   国际英语测试系统，简称雅思考试，是著名的国际性英语标准化水平测试之一。雅思考试有两种考试类型：学术类和培训类。学术类适用于出国留学申请本科、硕士及以上学位或获得专业资质。培训类适用于英语国家移民申请（如澳大利亚、加拿大、新西兰及英国），或申请培训及非文凭类课程的学习。

3. GRE

   GRE（Graduate Record Examination）即美国研究生入学考试，由美国教育考试服务中心主办。GRE 是美国各大学研究生院决定是否向申请人提供奖学金资助的重要参考条件之一，也是教授对申请者是否授予奖学金所依据的最重要标准 。

4. GMAT

GMAT（Graduate Management Admission Test）即研究生管理科学入学考试。美国、英国、澳大利亚等国家的高校都采用 GMAT 考试成绩来评估申请入学者是否适合在商业、经济和管理等专业的研究生阶段学习，从而决定是否录取。

5. CV

curriculum vitae 的缩写，原意指生活道路，现引申为简历，多指学术履历。CV 和 resume 相比较而言，CV 通常更为详细，一般两页纸或以上，内容更加全面；而 resume 通常不超过一页纸。在美国，CV 主要用于申请学术、教育、科研职位，或者申请奖学金等；而在欧洲、中东、非洲和亚洲等地，CV 则更常用于应聘工作。

Exercises

I. Summary

Directions: *Complete the following tasks as required.*

Based on Text C, an international applicant for higher education is suggested to consider and follow ________ steps:

Step 1 ____

Step 2 ____

Step 3 ____

…

II. Application Simulation

Directions: *Suppose that you have an opportunity to study overseas, and you may apply to any prestigious university in the world. What's your dream school? What's your dream major? Try to make a simulated application plan with the reference of what we have learned from Text C.*

Post-class Thinking

I. Comparison and Analysis

Directions: *Talk about the differences between college entrance exams/systems in China, the UK and the US. In addition, what do you think about* gaokao*? Do you think that China's* gaokao *provides a fair and transparent chance for test takers?*

II. Translation and Discussion

Directions: *"Life Education" was at the core of Tao Xingzhi's educational ideas, including three basic beliefs—"Life is education" "Society is school" "Teaching, learning and practice come together as one". Here are more famous quotes put forward by Mr. Tao as follows. Translate them into English and share with your partners your favorite quote based on your own understanding and experiences.*

Tao Xingzhi (1891–1946)

1. 发明千千万，起点是一问。

____

____

2. 好的先生不是教书，不是教学生，乃是教学生学。

____

3. 因为道德是做人的根本。根本一坏，纵然使你有一些学问和本领，也无甚用处。

4. 活的人才教育不是灌输知识，而是将开发文化宝库的钥匙，尽我们知道的交给学生。

5. 人像树木一样，要使他们尽量长上去，不能勉强都长得一样高，应当是：立脚点上求平等，于出头处谋自由。

Supplementary Resources

1. Extensive Reading

Scan the QR codes to read Text D "Making Yourself Aware of Some International Tests" and watch the MOOC video "An Introduction to Important International Tests". Then discuss the following questions with your partner:

1) What international tests are candidates required to pass if they plan to apply to a university overseas?

2) What do you know about the tests?

Text D "Making Yourself Aware of Some International Tests"

MOOC video "An Introduction to Important International Tests"

2. Documentaries

1) Documentary: *Childhood Elsewhere* (《他乡的童年》)

This documentary was made around the theme of childhood and growth, with a total of six episodes. Director Zhou Yijun is a well-known reporter in China. With the question of what is the "correct" way of education, she visited five countries—Finland, Japan, India, Israel and the UK. Finally, she returned to China to explore the Chinese people's own cognition and pursuit of growth. The film experiences the classroom from the perspective of children, feels the educational methods of different countries from the perspective of parents, and launches an exploration and reflection on education and growth from the history and culture of different societies.

2) Documentary: *Homo Academics* （《学习的人》）

The Korean documentary was filmed by four Harvard students with different cultural backgrounds. Focusing on the learning styles of people from different cultures, the documentary aims to answer the main question: What is the essence of learning? There exit both similarities and differences between foreign education and Chinese education, which are rooted in similar or very different traditions and cultures. Different cultures produce different education, which closely affects people's way of thinking and living.

3) Documentary: *Chinese School* （《中式学校》）

Made by the BBC, the documentary has three episodes in total. In the film, five Chinese teachers were invited to a middle school in Hampshire to conduct a one-month educational experiment of "Chinese teaching" for the students of the middle school. The cultural and educational differences between China and the West were also fully reflected in the experiment. At the same time, an upsurge of learning Chinese education was set off in the UK, because Chinese and Western education both have their own advantages and are worth learning from each other.

4) Documentary: *Do Schools Kill Creativity?* （《学校扼杀创造力吗？》）

In this TED education video, Ken Robinson, one of the most influential educators in the world, gives a humorous and vivid speech on establishing an educational system to cultivate creativity rather than stifle creativity. He tells the story of a child with ADHD who finally found herself in dance and realized her life value. It is worth pondering by all parents and teachers.

3. Books

Davidson, C. N. 2017. *The New Education: How to Revolutionize the University to Prepare Students for a World in Flux*. New York: Basic Books.

Deresiewicz, W. 2014. *Excellent Sheep: The Miseducation of the American Elite and the Way to a Meaningful Life*. New York: Free Press.

Kohn, A. 2004. *What Does It Mean to Be Well Educated?* Boston: Beacon Press.

Watanabe-Crockett, L. 2018. *Future-focused Learning: 10 Essential Shifts of Everyday Practice*. Bloomington: Solution Tree.

帕尔菲曼 . 2011. 高等教育何以为“高”：牛津导师制教学反思 . 冯青来译 . 北京：北京大学出版社 .

Chapter 7
Public Media in the UK and the US

The most common forms of public media are newspapers, magazines, radio, television, and the Internet. The UK and the US both have huge mass media systems. The UK has a diverse range of media providers, the most prominent being the publicly owned broadcaster, the British Broadcasting Corporation (BBC). The US has an advanced mass media industry, in which the biggest corporations include Warner Media, the Walt Disney Company, News Corp., Viacom, CBS and Comcast.

Text A Print Media: Newspapers and Magazines in the UK and the US

Pre-class Preparation

MOOC Watching

Watch the MOOC video "Print Media: Newspapers and Magazines in the UK and the US" to prepare for Text A.

Pre-reading Questions

1. Do you know any quality and popular newspapers in the UK?
2. What are the most influential newspapers and magazines in the US?

In-class Reading

Print Media: Newspapers and Magazines in the UK and the US

★ Newspapers and magazines in the UK

1 In general, all newspapers in Britain can be divided into two groups: quality papers[1] and popular papers[2]. Quality papers are normally **broadsheets** in format, whereas popular papers are largely **tabloids**, half size of broadsheets. The quality newspapers are also known as "heavies" because they carry more serious and in-depth articles of particularly political and social importance. Besides, they also carry financial reports, travel news and book and film reviews. Britain's "Big Three"—***The Times, The Guardian*** and ***The Daily Telegraph*** all belong to quality papers.

broadsheet *n.* 大幅报纸
tabloid *n.* 小报

The Times, in particular, is one of Britain's oldest and most influential national newspapers, but not the most popular. That **accolade** falls to *The Daily Telegraph*, which has a circulation twice as great as that of *The Times* and *The Guardian* together. Another two famous newspapers—***The Independent*** and ***The Financial Times*** are also quality papers.

accolade *n.* 荣誉

2 But if you are looking for more entertaining and less serious reports, popular papers will be a better choice. They are usually characterized by large headlines, a lot of big photographs, and personal aspects of news. The tabloids can also be divided into the **mass-market** titles, or "red tops", such as ***The Sun*** and ***The Daily Mirror***, and the middle-market papers, such as ***The Daily Express*** and ***The Daily Mail***. By the way, *The Sun* has the largest circulation among daily newspapers in the UK.

mass-market *adj.* 大众市场的

3 However, these differences are not absolute. To cater to the public's tastes and expand the circulation, some broadsheets like *The Independent* and *The Times*, have both changed to a **compact** format, not much bigger than that used by the tabloids, as they realize tabloids are easier to read and hold. Meanwhile, many of the broadsheets also provide stories about famous people.

compact *adj.* 紧凑的

Newspapers in the UK

4 Another thing you should know about British newspapers is that many daily papers now have Sunday editions, which are called Sunday newspapers[3]. Actually all newspapers in Britain, both the quality and popular ones, have their sister Sunday issues, for instance, *The Times* and

The Sunday Times, *The Guardian* and ***The Observer***, *The Daily Telegraph* and ***The Sunday Telegraph***. Reading Sunday papers is a popular **pastime** for Britons on weekends.

pastime
n. 消遣

5 Talking about British newspapers, have you ever heard of **Fleet Street** in London? Well, this place used to be home of the British press, although the national papers have now moved out because of the revolution in work practices. Even so, the term Fleet Street continues to be used as a **metonym** for the British national press.

metonym
n. 转喻

6 In addition to newspapers, magazines, periodicals and journals are also widely available in the UK. They cover a variety of interesting topics such as art, food, travel, lifestyles and sports, to target different groups of readers. The most famous British magazines include ***The Economist***, ***Nature***, ***New Scientist***, ***The Spectator***, ***The Radio Times*** and ***NME***, and they have achieved circulation worldwide. Among them, *The Economist* is the most influential and substantial periodical in the UK. Its primary focus is world news, politics and business, but it also runs regular sections on science and technology as well as books and the arts.

★ Newspapers and magazines in the US

7 Similarly, the publishing industry in the US is also well-developed. There are over 1,600 daily newspapers in the US and several thousand additional local weekly papers. ***The Wall Street Journal***, ***USA Today***, ***The New York Times***, ***The Los Angeles Times***, and ***Washington Post*** are the top-five best-selling newspapers.

8 By circulation, *The Wall Street Journal* is the largest newspaper in the US. Its main **rival**, in the business sector, is the London-based *Financial Times*, which also publishes several international editions. In its history, *The Wall Street Journal* has won more than 30 Pulitzer Prizes[4]. Pulitzer Prize is an American award for achievements in newspaper and online journalism, literature, and musical composition. But *The Wall Street Journal* is not the

rival
n. 竞争对手

only newspaper to have received the great honor. In fact, *The New York Times* has won the most Pulitzer Prizes by far. Meanwhile, its website is also the most popular American online newspaper website. Nicknamed as "the Old Gray Lady" due to its serious style, *The New York Times* is long regarded as a national "newspaper of record". Its motto is "All the News That's Fit to Print", highlighting the importance of honest **journalism**. Accordingly, its website has adapted it to "All the News That's Fit to Click".

journalism
n. 新闻业

Popular newspapers in the US

9 Apart from newspapers, the US also has a large magazine industry with hundreds of magazines serving almost every interest. The three leading weekly newsmagazines are ***Time***, ***Newsweek***, and ***US News and World Report***. *Time* is well known for naming a "Person of the Year", while *US News* publishes annual ratings of American colleges and universities. Other world famous magazines include ***National Geographic***, ***Science*** and ***Reader's Digest***. *National Geographic* is the official magazine of the National Geographic Society, which primarily contains articles about geography, history, and world culture. The proceeds from the magazine are used by the National Geographic Society to pursue cultural and wildlife research, and to produce their famous **documentary films**. *Reader's Digest* is an American general interest family magazine, which offers **condensed** articles from a wide variety of publications. It is published in seven foreign languages and reaches readers in many other countries.

condensed
adj. 缩编的；浓缩的

10 The US also has over a dozen major political magazines, including *The Atlantic* and *The New Yorker* among others. In entertainment, the magazines *Variety, The Hollywood Reporter, America Pioneer* and *LA Record* are very popular.

11 Finally, besides the hundreds of specialized magazines that serve the diverse interests and hobbies of the American people, like *Vanity Fair*, *Glamour*, *Vogue*, *Automobile* and *The Rolling Stone,* there are also dozens of magazines published by professional organizations for their members, such as *Communications of the ACM* (for computer science specialists) and *The ABA Journal* (for lawyers).

T Cultural Terms

1. *The Times*《泰晤士报》（英国第一主流日报，综合型日报）
2. *The Guardian*《卫报》（中产阶级和年轻人青睐的报纸，政治观点激进，偏左翼）
3. *The Daily Telegraph*《每日电讯报》（老牌英国报纸，一度是销量最高的报纸）
4. *The Independent*《独立报》（政治立场较为中立的英国报纸）
5. *The Financial Times*《金融时报》（主要报道财经类信息的英国高端报纸，售价昂贵）
6. *The Sun*《太阳报》（英国最著名的流行小报）
7. *The Daily Mirror*《每日镜报》（英国流行小报）
8. *The Daily Express*《每日快报》（英国快报系的旗舰报纸）
9. *The Daily Mail*《每日邮报》（英国发行的老牌报刊）
10. *The Sunday Times*《星期日泰晤士报》（《泰晤士报》的周日版）
11. *The Observer*《观察家报》（《卫报》的周日版）
12. *The Sunday Telegraph*《星期日电讯报》（《每日电讯报》的周日版）
13. Fleet Street 弗利特街（传统意义上英国媒体的总部）
14. *The Economist*《经济学人》（著名英国期刊，包含政治、经济、新闻的深度分析）
15. *Nature*《自然》（世界领先的综合性科学期刊，引用率最高的原创性科学杂志之一）
16. *New Scientist*《新科学家》（英国较新的国际性科学杂志）
17. *The Spectator*《旁观者》（英国历史最悠久的杂志，以政治评论为主）
18. *The Radio Times*《广播时报》（英国杂志，刊载电视与广播节目）

19. *NME (New Music Express)* 《新音乐快递》（英国著名的网络音乐杂志）
20. *The Wall Street Journal* 《华尔街日报》（美国发行量最大的报纸之一，侧重金融商业领域报道）
21. *USA Today* 《今日美国》（美国唯一的彩色版全国性报纸）
22. *The New York Times* 《纽约时报》（多次荣获普利策奖且具有全球影响力的美国报纸）
23. *The Los Angeles Times* 《洛杉矶时报》（美国发行量最大的报纸之一，在洛杉矶地区很有影响力）
24. *Washington Post* 《华盛顿邮报》（在华盛顿特区最具影响力的报纸）
25. *Time* 《时代周刊》（又名《时代》，美国最重要的杂志之一，已有几十位中国名人登上杂志封面）
26. *Newsweek* 《新闻周刊》（在美国仅次于《时代周刊》的新闻类杂志）
27. *US News and World Report* 《美国新闻与世界报道》（与《时代周刊》与《新闻周刊》齐名的新闻杂志）
28. *National Geographic* 《国家地理》（原名《国家地理杂志》，是美国国家地理学会的官方杂志，有多个语言版本）
29. *Science* 《科学》（美国科学促进会出版的英文学术期刊，全球顶级的科学类刊物之一）
30. *Reader's Digest* 《读者文摘》（美国知名月刊，全球最畅销的杂志之一）
31. documentary film 纪录片

Cultural Notes

1. quality papers

质量报纸，指具有严肃主题和内容的报纸，这类报纸过去常常采用大开本印刷，近来不少质量报纸也采用了小报体印刷。如英国的《泰晤士报》和《独立报》于 2004 年起采用小报形式印刷。质量报纸曾经是英国报纸的主流，近年来发行量一度处于下降趋势。

2. popular papers

通俗报纸，指内容大众化和通俗化的报纸，这类报纸通常采用小报体裁，较受普通大众的欢迎，销量也较高，代表性的英国通俗报纸包括《太阳报》和《每日镜报》等。

3. Sunday papers

周报是单独在周日发行的报纸，通常到了周日，平时发行的报纸会改为周报发行，如《泰晤士报》改为《星期日泰晤士报》,《卫报》改为《观察家报》,《每日邮报》改为《星期日邮报》。

4. Pulitzer Prizes

普利策奖，是美国奖励报纸、杂志、新闻报道和文学、音乐创作有杰出表现所设的奖项，被誉为新闻界的“奥斯卡金像奖”。1917 年，根据报业巨头、匈牙利裔美国人约瑟夫·普利策的遗愿设立普利策奖。

Exercises

I. Multiple Choice

Directions: *Below each statement there are four choices. Decide which of the following choices is the most appropriate answer.*

1. Which of the following is **NOT** one of the top three newspapers in the UK?

A. *The Times.* B. *The Guardian.*
C. *The Daily Express.* D. *The Daily Telegraph.*

2. Which of the following is a daily newspaper?

A. *The Observer.* B. *The Spectator.* C. *The Guardian.* D. *The Economist.*

3. Which of the following journals is from the US?

A. *Science.* B. *New Scientist.* C. *Nature.* D. *The Lancet.*

4. Which newspaper has won the most Pulitzer Prizes in the US?

A. *The Wall Street Journal.* B. *New York Times.*
C. *The Los Angeles Times.* D. *Washington Post.*

5. To know what will be broadcast on TV channels next week in the UK, one can read ________.

A. *New Musical Express* B. *The Radio Times*
C. *Newsweek* D. *The Hollywood Reporter*

II. True or False

Directions: *Decide if the following statements are true (T) or false (F).*

1. *The Sun* has the second largest circulation among British daily newspapers only after *The Times*.
2. *The Observer* is the Sunday edition of *The Guardian*.
3. *The Wall Street Journal* is nicknamed “the Old Gray Lady”.
4. *Time* is a popular American newspaper as popular as *The Times* in the UK.

5. If you like geography, you can read the Chinese edition of *National Geographic*.

Extended Discussion

Directions: *Discuss the following topics with your partners.*

What newspapers or magazines do you like to read in China? Introduce one or two of your favorite Chinese newspapers or magazines and talk about their themes, content, layout and circulation.

____

____

____

Post-class Thinking

Blank Filling

Directions: *Scan the QR code to fill in the blanks in the mind map of Text A and you will have a better understanding of the structure of the text.*

Text B Broadcast Media: Radio and TV in the UK and the US

Pre-class Preparation

MOOC Watching

Watch the MOOC video "Broadcast Media" to prepare for Text B.

Pre-reading Questions

1. Why is BBC acknowledged as No.1 broadcasting corporation in the UK?
2. Can you introduce some representative broadcasters in the US?

Broadcast Media: Radio and TV in the UK and the US

★ Radio and TV stations in the UK

1 There are around 600 licensed radio stations in the UK. The most prominent stations are the national networks operated by BBC. The British Broadcasting Corporation (BBC)[1] is a public service broadcaster, headquartered in Westminster, London, and it is the world's oldest national broadcaster and the largest broadcaster in the world by number of employees.

2 The BBC has ten national radio services, six stations in the "national regions", and 40 other local stations. Of the ten national radio services, five are most famous. They are BBC Radio 1, offering new music and popular styles and being notable for its **chart** show; BBC Radio 2, playing adult contemporary, country and soul music amongst many other genres; BBC Radio 3, presenting classical and jazz music together with some **spoken-word programming** of a cultural nature in the evenings; BBC Radio 4, focusing on current affairs, factual and other speech-based programming, including drama and comedy; and BBC Radio 5 Live, broadcasting 24-hour news, sport and talk programs. Financed almost wholly by viewers' license fees, the BBC runs no **commercials**, either sound or television. The BBC World Service radio network is broadcast in more than thirty languages globally.

chart
n. 排行榜

commercial
n. 商业广告

3 As for television services, the BBC operates several television channels in the UK. BBC One[2] and BBC Two are the **flagship** channels. Besides offering up-to-date coverage of national and international affairs, BBC also broadcasts a mixture of drama, light entertainment, films, sport and documentaries. Up to now, a great number of high-quality insightful documentaries have been produced to open the public's eyes. The BBC World Service is one of the world's largest international broadcasters, broadcasting news, speech and discussions in 28 languages. In addition, the BBC World Service also presents BBC Learning English program to help people learn British English, which provides very good learning resources for second language learners.

flagship
n. 旗舰；王牌

4 The BBC is good at **adapting** literary works to TV series. *Pride and Prejudice*, *Emma*, *Cranford*, *Sense and Sensibility*, *North and South* and *Sherlock Holmes* are all classic TV series that have won great reviews worldwide. BBC documentaries have won the favor of audience all around the world. Most of these documentaries are featured by authentic context and advanced filming techniques. Some of the best BBC documentaries include *Wild China*, *The Blue Planet*, *Planet Earth Season*, *Life*, *Africa* and *Seven Worlds One Planet*.

adapt
v. 改编

The photo of *Pride and Prejudice*

5 Different from BBC One and BBC Two, another three main channels in Britain—**Independent Television (ITV)**, **Channel 4** and **Channel 5**—are run by private commercial operators. They rely on advertising for their

revenue *n.* 收入

revenue. ITV is the major commercial public service TV network in the UK. As a strong competitor to the BBC, it has produced many hit dramas. One good example is *Downton Abbey*. Even the former first lady of the US Michelle Obama is a huge fan of this TV show.

Radio and TV stations in the US

syndicated *adj.* 多家销售的

6 As a whole, the American broadcast networks are the largest and most **syndicated** in the world. People can enjoy all sorts of game shows, soap operas, situation comedies (sitcom), dramas, reality shows, talk shows and miniseries on TV at any time. No doubt many Americans are addicted to TV and they are called "Couch Potatoes[3]".

stylized *adj.* 有艺术风格的

7 Of all the radio and television networks in the United States, **the National Broadcasting Company (NBC)**, **the Columbia Broadcasting System (CBS)** and **the American Broadcasting Company (ABC)** are called the "Big Three". Formed in 1926, NBC is the oldest major broadcast network in the US, which is also called "Peacock Network", due to its **stylized** peacock logo, created originally for color broadcasts. NBC has produced many TV plays that have contributed to American popular culture. *ER*, *Friends*, *Law and Order*, *The White House Situation*, *Apprentices*, *Las Vegas Situation* and *The West Wing* are loved by American and even global viewers.

8 The second broadcaster CBS, is sometimes referred to as "Eye Network" in reference to the shape of the company's logo. CBS has also presented many excellent programs like *How I Met Your Mother*, *Broke Girls*, *Criminal Minds*, *CSI*, *The Big Bang Theory*, *Survivor* and *The Amazing Race*.

9 The last broadcaster, ABC, or the "Alphabet Network", is owned by the Walt Disney Company and is part of Disney-ABC Television Group. Its flagship program is the daily evening newscast and its morning news talk show is also very popular. ABC has got hot programs including *Castle*, *Lost*,

Revenge, *Desperate Housewives*, *Grey's Anatomy* and *Modern Family*.

10 As a competitor to the "Big Three" television networks, **FOX News** became a fourth television network in the US since the 1990s. In the 2000s, it emerged as the most-watched American broadcast network largely boosted by its famous reality singing competition **American Idol**. By the onset of COVID-19 pandemic, boosted by a series of new TV shows and especially **the Super Bowl**, FOX has overtaken NBC to become the most-watched television in the 18-40 **demographic**.

demographic
n. 特定年龄段人口

11 Apart from the three large broadcasters, CW, VOA, CNN, HBO, and ESPN are also very popular. **The CW Television Network (CW)** is an American broadcast television network that is operated by The CW Network, LLC, a limited liability joint **venture** between ViacomCBS and WarnerMedia. That is how the CW network got its name. The following are the logos of current five major broadcast networks in the US.

venture
n. 企业

12 **Voice of America (VOA)** is the official external broadcast institution of the US federal government. Its program "VOA Learning English" aims to help global learners with their American English. **The Cable News Network (CNN)** is another world-famous broadcaster. It was the first channel to provide 24-hour television news coverage, and the first all-news television channel in the US. **Home Box Office (HBO)** is an American pay television network and the oldest **subscription** television service. It became the first television channel in the world to begin transmitting via satellite, providing entertainment programs which do not accept advertisements and editing to maintain their objectivity. **Entertainment Sports Programming Network (ESPN)** is an American multinational basic cable sports channel jointly by ESPN Inc. and The Walt Disney Company. In 2018, ESPN was available to approximately 86 million television households in the US and now ESPN broadcasts are in more than 200 countries.

subscription
n. 订阅

T Cultural Terms

1. spoken-word programming 口头节目（如脱口秀、采访名人的对话类节目）
2. Independent Television (ITV) 英国独立电视台（英国第二大无线电视提供商）
3. Channel 4 英国电视四台 （英国新兴独立品牌电视台）
4. Channel 5 英国电视五台 （英国独立电视频道）
5. The National Broadcasting Company (NBC) 美国全国广播公司
6. The Columbia Broadcasting System (CBS) 哥伦比亚广播公司
7. The American Broadcasting Company (ABC) 美国广播公司
8. FOX News 福克斯新闻 (面向中青年的收视率排名全国第一的电视频道)
9. American Idol 美国偶像（福克斯公司自 2002 年举办的美国大众歌手选秀赛）
10. The Super Bowl 超级碗（美国职业橄榄球大赛年度冠军赛）
11. The CW Television Network (CW) 电视联播网（美国排名前五的免费电视网）
12. Voice of America (VOA) 美国之音（美国最知名的国际广播）
13. The Cable News Network (CNN) 美国有线电视新闻网（专门播放新闻的电视新闻频道）
14. Home Box Office (HBO) HBO 联播网（美国一家付费有线和卫星联播网）
15. Entertainment Sports Programming Network (ESPN) 娱乐与体育节目电视网（播放体育节目的美国电视新闻网）

* Cultural Notes

1. The British Broadcasting Corporation (BBC)

英国广播公司，缩写及通称为 BBC，是英国主要的公共媒体机构，世界第一家由国家成立的广播机构，也是全球最大的新闻媒体。其前身为 1922 年成立的英国广播有限公司，于 1927 年获取皇家特许状而改组成立；身为英国的法定法人机构之一，现今受数字化、文化、媒体和体育部的监管。英国广播公司不营销广告，营运资金主要来自于英国国民所缴纳的电视牌照费。

2. BBC One

英国广播公司 1 台，是 BBC 的电视旗舰频道，该频道下属的 BBC 新闻频道在报道时将疫情与政治挂钩，在涉疆报道和疫情报道方面极力抹黑中国。2021 年，中国国家广播电视总局不允许 BBC 世界新闻台继续在中国境内落地，对其新一年度落地申请不予受理。

3. Couch Potatoes

"沙发土豆"是 20 世纪 70 年代创造出来的表达。"土豆"一词有双重含义：一是指终日在沙发上看电视的人就像"种在沙发的土豆"一样纹丝不动；二是指这类人一般总是在看电视的同时不停地吃炸土豆片。说某人是"沙发土豆"，通常是批评这种不健康的方式。"沙发土豆"的生活方式早在 20 世纪 60 年代开始在美国流行，后又传到西方各国，成为极其重要的"致胖因素"，对人们的形象和健康带来严重的不利影响。"couch potato"这个表达简洁形象，广为传播。1993 年，"couch potato"被收入《牛津英语词典》。如今，"沙发土豆"不仅是美国人的词汇，也逐渐被全世界读者接纳。

Exercises

I. Blank Filling

Directions: *After reading Text B and watching the MOOC video, fill in the following blanks.*

1. The two flagship channels of the British Broadcasting Corporation are BBC One and ________.
2. The BBC World Service presents BBC Learning English program to help people learn ________.
3. ________ is also called "Peacock Network" due to its stylized peacock logo.
4. VOA is the official ________ broadcast institution of the US federal government.
5. Those people who are addicted to TV and eat a lot of junk food are described by Americans as "________".

II. Matching

Directions: *Match the names of radio and TV stations in the left column with the features they have in the right column.*

1. BBC ________	**A.** It is the oldest major broadcast network in the US, which is also called "Peacock Network".
2. NBC ________	**B.** It is a major commercial public service TV network in the UK besides BBC.
3. VOA ________	**C.** It is the first channel to provide 24-hour television news coverage, and the first all-news television channel in the US.
4. ITV ________	**D.** It is the world's oldest national broadcaster and the largest broadcaster in the world by number of employees.
5. CBS ________	**E.** It is separated from NBC and now is part of Disney-ABC Television Group.
6. ABC ________	**F.** It is the official external broadcast institution of the US federal government.
7. CNN ________	**G.** It is sometimes referred to as "Eye Network" in reference to the shape of the company's logo.

Post-class Thinking

Comparison and Analysis

Directions: *Public media is a mirror of society. It provides information about what is going on around the world and also conveys the sound of the nation and the people. Do you know any famous public media in China and how do they play their role in expressing Chinese people's attitude in the international arena? What are the differences between Chinese and Western public media in the collection, production and spread of news?*

____

____

____

____

Text C Digital Media in the UK and the US

Pre-class Preparation

MOOC Watching

Watch the MOOC video "Digital Media" to prepare for Text C.

Pre-reading Questions

1. What forms of media are called digital media and what are your most familiar digital media forms in China?
2. What are the most influential digital media providers in the UK and the US?

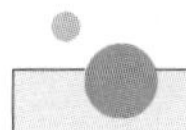

In-class Reading

Digital Media in the UK and the US

1 Digital media[1] refers to any communication media in which data can be created, viewed, distributed, modified, and preserved on a digital electronics device. This includes text, audio, video, and graphics that are transmitted over the Internet, for viewing on the Internet. With the Internet connecting the whole world, digital media has **permeated** almost every aspect of our lives. Digital media has had a significantly broad and complex impact on society and culture.

permeate *v.* 渗透

2 According to a new survey in 2021, American people spend more than 13 hours per day with digital media, including digital video, smartphones,

CTV, **subscription OTT** (over-the-top media service), and digital audio. In this sense, digital media has posed great challenges to print and broadcasting industries, which forces people to transform these traditional media industries as a result.

3 Digital media, especially social media[2], has already become an integral part of people's life. Digital media makes use of interactive technologies and allows the creation or exchange of information, via virtual communities[3] and networks. Thanks to social networking services, it is now possible to share interests and activities across geographic borders. Among numerous social networking services, the most famous in Britain and America include **Facebook**, **Twitter**, **Google**, **LinkedIn**, **Instagram**, **Pinterest**, **Vine**, and **Tumblr**. They play an essential role in the daily lives of the British and American people. Other popular platforms are sometimes referred to as social media services, such as YouTube, WhatsApp, LINE, Snapchat, and Viber. Wikis are examples of **collaborative** content creation.

collaborative *adj.* 合作的

★ Meta

4 Meta[4] Platforms, also known as Meta for short, is formerly known as Facebook, Inc. In October 2021, the co-founder and CEO of Facebook announced that the parent company of Facebook would change its name to "Meta". The name change reflects that the company has shifted its long-term focus to the metaverse, a digital extension of the physical world featured by social media, virtual reality and **augmented reality**. Now Meta is an American multinational technology **conglomerate** based in California of the US. The company is the parent organization of Facebook, Instagram, and WhatsApp, among other **subsidiaries**. Meta is one of the world's most valuable companies and is considered one of the five biggest technology companies in the US , alongside Amazon, Google, Apple, and Microsoft.

conglomerate *n.* 大型企业集团

subsidiary *n.* 附属公司

5 The **predecessor** of Meta is Facebook, which is a social networking website intended to connect friends, family and business associates.

predecessor *n.* 前身

Facebook was founded on February 4, 2004, by a Harvard University student named Mark Zuckerberg and his fellow students. Originally as a college networking website, Facebook later grew into one of the largest networking sites. Facebook can be accessed from devices with Internet connectivity and users can post text, photos and multimedia which is shared with any other users. Facebook has been among the most downloaded mobile apps in and out of the US. In 2021, **Alexa Internet** ranked Facebook seventh in global Internet usage.

★ **Twitter**

6 Twitter is another popular online social networking service. It enables users to send and read short messages called "**tweets**". Twitter was created in March 2006 by Jack Dorsey, Evan Williams, Biz Stone and Noah Glass. It rapidly gained worldwide popularity after its launch. Tweets were originally restricted to 140 characters, but was doubled to 280 for non-CJK languages[5] in November 2017. Audio and video tweets remain limited to 140 seconds for most accounts. In 2013, it was one of the ten most-visited websites and has been described as "**the SMS of the Internet**". As of 2019, Twitter had more than 330 million monthly active users. Twitter is a some-to-many microblogging service, given that the vast majority of tweets are written by a small minority of users.

★ **YouTube**

7 YouTube is an online video platform owned by Google. In total, users watch more than one billion hours of YouTube videos each day, and hundreds of hours of video content is uploaded to YouTube servers every minute. YouTube provides several ways to watch videos, including the website, the mobile apps, and permits other websites to **embed** them. Available content includes music videos, video clips, short and documentary films, audio recordings, **movie trailers**, **live streams**, and video blogs. Most content is generated by individuals, but media corporations also

embed
v. 使嵌入

publish videos. Besides watching and uploading, registered users can comment on videos, rate them, create playlists, and subscribe to other users.

★ LinkedIn

8 LinkedIn is an American business and employment-oriented online service that operates via websites and mobile apps. Launched on May 5, 2003, the platform is mainly used for professional networking, and allows job seekers to post their CVs and employers to post jobs. Since 2016, it has been a wholly owned subsidiary of Microsoft. As of February 2021, LinkedIn had 740 million registered members from 150 countries. LinkedIn allows members (both workers and employers) to create profiles and "connect" to each other in an online social network which may represent real-world professional relationships. Through LinkedIn, people can stay in touch with business contacts and search for potential employers. Therefore, many American students now use LinkedIn to hunt for jobs.

★ TikTok

9 TikTok is a short-form video hosting service owned by ByteDance. As the founder of Douyin, the most popular short video platform in China, ByteDance planned on Douyin expanding overseas.

10 They developed the application called TikTok in the international market in September 2017. TikTok has gained global popularity since its launch and hosts user-submitted videos ranging in duration from 3 seconds to 10 minutes. In October 2020, TikTok's mobile downloads worldwide surpassed 2 billion. Morning Consult, the famous global decision intelligence company, named TikTok the third-fastest growing brand of 2020, after Zoom and Peacock. Cloudflare, the web performance and security company, ranked TikTok the most popular website of 2021, surpassing Google. TikTok and Douyin have almost the same user interface but no access to each other's content. The two products are similar, but their features are not identical. Douyin has multiple functions such as buying, booking hotels, and making geo-tagged reviews. Despite

attempts to ban TikTok in the United States, this application is developing fast and will launch more features to protect the privacy and safety of users, support mobile and PC streaming, as well as create more connections between video creators and followers.

11 Compared with print media, the mass media, and other **analog** technologies, digital media is easy to copy, store, share and modify. This quality of digital media has caused disruptive innovation in many industries, especially journalism, publishing, education, entertainment, and the music business. Digital media has also allowed individuals to become content creators. Anyone with access to computers and the Internet can participate in social media and contribute their own writing, art, videos, photography and commentary to the Internet. User-generated content raises issues of privacy, **credibility**, **civility** and compensation for cultural, intellectual and artistic contributions. The **ubiquity** of digital media and its effects on society suggest that we are at the start of a new era in industrial history, called the Information Age, perhaps leading to a paperless society in which all media are produced and consumed on computers.

analog
adj. 模拟的

credibility
n. 可靠度

civility
n. 礼貌，礼仪

ubiquity
n. 普遍存在

T Cultural Terms

1. CTV 电视网
2. subscription OTT 订阅过顶内容服务（通过互联网向观众提供的流媒体服务）
3. Facebook 脸书（美国一家社交媒体传播公司，由扎克伯格创建）
4. Twitter 推特（美国一个微博客和社交网络服务平台）
5. Google 谷歌（美国的一家互联网搜索、云计算、广告公司）
6. LinkedIn 领英（美国一家社交网络服务网站，可发布求职信息，专为商业人士创建）
7. Instagram 彩色相机（Facebook 公司一款免费提供在线图片及视频分享的社群应用软件）
8. Pinterest 缤趣（美国的手机和网络应用程序，服务图片分享类的社交网站）
9. Vine（Twitter 旗下发布短视频的社交网络平台，已被关闭）
10. Tumblr 汤博乐（美国一家轻博客社交网络平台）
11. virtual reality 虚拟现实（用电脑模拟产生三维空间的虚拟世界，让用户感觉身临其境）

12. augmented reality 增强现实（将计算机生成的文字、图像、三维模型、音乐、视频等虚拟信息模拟仿真后，应用到真实世界中，实现对真实世界的“增强”）
13. Alexa Internet 亚马逊一家子公司（主要从事网络流量分析并提供网站排名，已于 2021 年 12 月停止服务）
14. tweet 推文（指推特上发布的文章）
15. the SMS of the Internet 互联网短信服务
16. movie trailer 电影预告片
17. live stream 直播流

Cultural Notes

1. digital media

数字媒体，是指可对信息和数据进行数字化编码的媒体形式，包括计算机程序和软件、数字影像、数字视频、互联网网页、数据和数据库、数字音频、电子书等。与数字媒体相对的是实体书、报纸、杂志等平面媒体，以及图片、录音带等模拟介质。

2. social media

社交媒体，是指人们进行创作、分享、交流互动的虚拟社区和网络平台。社交媒体与一般的社会大众媒体最显著的不同，是可以让用户享有更多的自主选择权利。社交媒体能够以多种不同的形式来呈现，包括文本、图片、音乐和视频。

3. virtual community

虚拟社区，是模仿真实人类社区构建的虚拟网络社群。用户在虚拟社区也可以跨越地理的限制发布信息、分享资讯、建立友谊、相互支持。Howard Rheingold 于 1993 年出版的 *The Virtual Community* 一书中提出“虚拟社区”一词。

4. Meta

元宇宙，希腊语中的表达是“beyond”，表达未来主义的动机。Meta 的前身是美国知名社交网站 Facebook，2021 年 10 月 28 日创立者扎克伯格宣布 Facebook 改名为 Meta。如今的 Meta 是美国一家经营社交网络服务、虚拟现实、元宇宙等产品的互联网科技公司，总部位于美国加州门洛帕克，旗下拥有 Facebook、Instagram、WhatsApp 等社交软件。

5. CJK languages

汉语、日本语、朝鲜语非兼容表意音文字，是对中文、日文、韩文曾经或现今所使用过的汉字统称。有时也将越南文字包括进来，统称为“CJKV（Chinese-Japanese-Korean-

Vietnamese）。由于 CJK 文字与字母文字编码方式不同，国际社会有时会采取不同的处理方式，如 Twitter 于 2017 年开始放宽了推文的字数限制，增加至 280 个字符，但 CJK 文字仍为 140 个字符。

Exercises

I. Multiple Choice

Directions: *Below each statement there are four choices. Decide which of the following choices is the most appropriate answer.*

1. Which of the following is **NOT** one of the five biggest technology companies in the US?

   A. Meta. B. Twitter. C. Google. D. Microsoft.

2. In 2017, tweets were originally restricted to 140 characters, but were doubled to ________ for non-CJK languages.

   A.160 B. 180 C. 240 D. 280

3. With the help of ________, people can stay in touch with business contacts and search for potential employer.

   A. Facebook B. Twitter C. LinkedIn D. WhatsApp

4. Which of the following is one of the ten most-visited websites and has been described as "the SMS of the Internet" ?

   A. Facebook. B. Instagram. C. Twitter. D. YouTube.

5. Which of the following digital media platforms is owned by Google?

   A. Twitter. B. YouTube. C. LinkedIn. D. Instagram.

II. True or False

Directions: *Determine the following statements are true or false.*

1. Digital media includes text, audio, video, and graphics that are transmitted over the Internet.
2. The website of *New York Times* is a form of print media.
3. Facebook was founded on February 4, 2004, by a Yale University student named Mark Zuckerberg and his fellow students.
4. Wikis are examples of collaborative content creation.
5. Since 2016, YouTube has been a wholly owned subsidiary of Microsoft.

Critical Thinking

Directions: *Digital media in China has developed rapidly in recent years and many new platforms have emerged such as WeChat, Microblog, Tiktok, QQ, Bilibili, etc. Compare the following Chinese and American digital media platforms and find out their similarities and differences.*

1. WeChat v.s. Facebook

___

2. Microblog v.s. Twitter

___

3. Bilibili v.s. YouTube

___

Post-class Thinking

Discussion

Directions: *Discuss the following topic with your partners.*

Amusing Ourselves to Death, written by Neil Postman, was published in 1985. Neil Postman alerts us that the real and present dangers of entertainment, such as the media of television, shape our lives and ways we live and prevent us from realizing our real goals. In the age of digitalization, we are surrounded by information from all kinds of social media, which provide us convenience but also deprive us of a sense of self. What should be correct attitude towards social media in the 21st century?

Supplementary Resources

1. Extensive Reading

Scan the QR codes to read Text D "TV Series and Movies in the UK and the US" and watch the MOOC video "Films in the UK and the US". Think of the following question: Do you like watching British or American movies and TV series? Introduce your favorite ones to your partners.

Text D "TV Series and Movies in the UK and the US"

MOOC video "Films in the UK and the US"

2. Documentaries, TV Series and Film

1) Documentary: *The Rise of the Murdoch Dynasty* （《默多克王朝的崛起》）

The Rise of the Murdoch Dynasty is a BBC documentary series broadcast in 2020. It is about the business empire Rupert Murdoch built and his political influence, the News International phone hacking scandal and his children's battles to succeed him.

2) TV series: *The Morning Show* （《早间新闻》）

The Morning Show is an American drama streaming television series in which Jennifer Aniston and Reese Witherspoon play the roles of hard-working and ambitious anchors of a famous American morning TV show. It provides an inside look at the lives of the people who help America wake up in the morning, exploring the unique challenges faced by the men and women who carry out this daily televised ritual.

3) Film: *The Social Network* （《社交网络》）

The Social Network is a 2010 American biographical drama film adapted from Ben Mezrich's 2009 book *The Accidental Billionaires*. The film portrays the founding of social networking website Facebook and the resulting lawsuits.

3. Books

Cullen, J. 2013. *A Short History of the Modern Media*. Hoboken: Wiley-Blackwell Publishing.

Sklar, R. 2002. *A World History of Film*. New York: Harry N. Abrams.

陈旭光，苏涛 . 2014. 美国电影经典 . 北京：对外经贸大学出版社 .

端木义万 . 2011. 美国传媒文化 . 北京：北京大学出版社 .

顾悦 . 2011. 美国电影概览 . 南京：东南大学出版社 .

Chapter 8
A Culinary Adventure of the UK and the US

The history of British and American cuisine is not so profound as that of Chinese cuisine. With immigrants coming from all corners of the world and the improvement of cooking techniques, a big variety of foods are now available in the UK and the US, including Chinese, Indian, Italian, French and Spanish dishes. The variety of foods reflects the population diversity of the UK and the US today. This chapter will introduce traditional food and national drink in the UK, as well as fast food culture and cuisine of mixed flavors in the US.

Text A Traditional Food in the UK

Pre-class Preparation

MOOC Watching

Watch the MOOC video "Traditional Food: Most Delectable Cultural Heritage" to prepare for Text A.

Pre-reading Questions

1. What's your favorite food or dish and why?
2. Is it true that people cook different food for different seasons or climates? Illustrate your point of view based on your life experience.

In-class Reading

Traditional Food in the UK

1 Surrounded by the ocean water, the UK enjoys mild climate and rich rainfall, creating **lush** grasslands and agricultural land. Quality meat and vegetables are the main ingredients for the British people. Besides meat and vegetables, fish and chips is best known as the iconic English dish. The fish is commonly deep fried in flour **batter** and is eaten with golden chips. Traditionally, the fish and chips is covered with salt and malt **vinegar** and wrapped in newspapers. However, wrapping food in newspapers is now banned under EU **hygiene** regulations.

lush
adj. 草木繁茂的

batter
n. 面糊（煎料）

vinegar
n. 醋

hygiene
n. 卫生

2 Under the cultural influence of foreign settlers, trading countries and

colonies, the British food and style of cooking were constantly changing and evolving. If it wasn't for the two World Wars, British cuisine could have gone much further. However, wars broke out and supplies of many goods became short. Food **rationing** policies were then put in place to deal with the tough situation, which eventually led to the poor reputation of British food until the 1970s.

rationing
n. 配给制

3 After being overlooked by other countries for years, the increase in wealth and foreign travel from the 1980s onwards witnessed a corresponding improvement in food in the UK. The 1990s saw the rise of the celebrity chef and emphasis on organic **produce**. Now the British do have a wide and varied cuisine. It is funny that curry from India has become one of the Britain's favorite foods. Some traditional dishes such as roast beef and Yorkshire pudding[1], **Cornish pasties**, steak and kidney pie[2], **bread and butter pudding**, **treacle tart** remain popular to this day. Although these dishes are traditionally British, they are constantly being changed and evolved by using different ingredients. Besides, some other dishes have interesting names, like **Toad-in-the-Hole**, **Spotted-Dick**, **bubble and squeak**, **bangers**[3] **and mash**.

produce
n. 产品；（尤指）农产品

4 Although British cuisine is often mocked by other nationalities as boring, simple and unhealthy, the **full English breakfast** is renowned all over the world. It is a centuries-old British breakfast tradition, an icon of British **culinary** culture. In the UK, there is an old saying, "To eat well in England you should have breakfast three times a day." However, little information is available for its origin, but most people believe that it's originated in the rural England. A full breakfast in the morning can provide the working class with enough energy for a whole day.

culinary
adj. 烹饪的

5 A traditional English breakfast is quite varied in food, usually composed of eggs, bacon, sausages, fried bread, baked beans, black pudding, tomatoes and mushrooms. Without doubt, different flavors can be found throughout the country depending on the regions and the preferences of the local

people. Despite its enormous reputation, nowadays, a typical English breakfast is more likely to be a bowl of cereals, a slice of toast, orange juice or a cup of coffee. Another interesting thing about the full English breakfast is that although it is traditionally served at breakfast time, it is also popular at other time, usually replacing lunch. Many British and Irish cafes and pubs serve the meal at any time as an "all-day breakfast".

veritable *adj.* 十足的

stuffing *n.* 填料

gravy *n.* 肉汁

patriotic *adj.* 爱国的

ballad *n.* 民谣

6 Sunday Roast[4], also called Sunday dinner or Sunday lunch, is another national culinary pride in Britain. It's traditionally served on Sundays when people get a break from a week's hard work, so families or friends have time to gather together to enjoy the **veritable** feast. Believe it or not, Sunday Roast is even often compared to a less grand version of the Christmas dinner. A typical Sunday Roast usually consists of roasted meat, roast potato or mashed potato, accompanied with some other foods like Yorkshire pudding, **stuffing**, vegetables and **gravy**. The most common joints are beef, lamb or pork, and chicken is popular as well. The English **patriotic ballad** called *The Roast Beef of Old England*[5] substantially impresses us that British people like roast beef a great deal.

7 A classic British Christmas dinner draws people to the peak of Christmas day, as well as the highlight of the year. The dinner usually features a roast turkey with vegetables, followed by Christmas pudding, and then Christmas cake, perfect with a cup of tea or a glass of wine! Most importantly, the roast turkey is viewed as the king of the table on Christmas day because to prepare such a special dish needs lots of patience and love.

British Christmas dinner

Cultural Terms

1. Cornish pasties 康沃尔馅饼
2. bread and butter pudding 面包牛油布丁
3. treacle tart 蜜糖果馅饼
4. Toad-in-the-Hole < 英 > 面拖烤香肠（也叫 Sausage Toad）
5. Spotted-Dick 葡萄干布丁
6. bubble and squeak 卷心菜煎土豆
7. bangers and mash 香肠土豆泥
8. full English breakfast 豪华英式早餐

Cultural Notes

1. roast beef and Yorkshire pudding

烤牛肉加约克郡布丁，被称为“英国的国菜”。布丁通常作为餐后甜点，但约克郡布丁却是主菜中的开端；烤牛肉是鸡蛋加牛奶和面，与牛肉、土豆一起烤制的菜肴。

2. steak and kidney pie

牛排腰子饼，是一种以英国传统方式烹制的肉馅饼，内夹炒过的腰子和酒煮洋葱，风味极佳。

3. bangers

bangers，是一个口语词，在英国可指任何形状或口味的香肠。两次世界大战期间，因为可供食用的肉类都比较少，英国人在香肠中加入了更多肥肉和廉价的填料，加热时这些肥肉和填料迅速膨胀，导致香肠在锅中剧烈爆裂。这就是为什么人们叫它们 bangers 即“砰砰”的原因，也就是说，当人们烹饪香肠时，它们会发出砰砰的声音。

4. Sunday Roast

英国星期日烤肉，据说起源于工业革命时代的约克。礼拜天去教堂之前，约克人把肉放入烤箱慢烤，等从教堂回来就能食用。通常烤的就是猪肉、牛肉或羊肉，食用时配上约克布丁和几种煮好的蔬菜，并浇上勾了芡的肉汁。

5. *The Roast Beef of Old England*

《啊！昔日英格兰的烤牛肉》，是 18 世纪英国小说家、戏剧家亨利·菲尔丁（Henry Fielding）写的叙事诗。诗中慨叹，英国人吃烤牛肉的那些日子，“境界更高尚、鲜血更浓郁”，且“士兵更勇敢、朝臣更英明”。后来由作曲家理查德·莱弗里奇（Richard Leveridge）

修订，成为英国广为传唱的爱国民谣，英国皇家海军和美国海军陆战队在用餐时，都会演奏这首曲子。

Exercise

Matching

Directions: *Match the names and the foods.*

1. Spotted-Dick ________
2. steak and kidney pie ________
3. Cornish pasties ________
4. banger and mash ________
5. roast beef and Yorkshire pudding ________
6. Toad-in-the-Hole ________
7. treacle tart ________
8. bubble and squeak ________

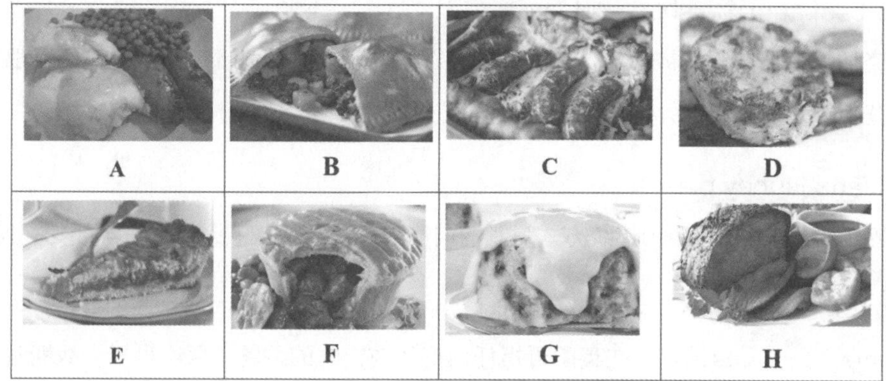

Post-class Thinking

Discussion

Directions: *What cooking ways or styles are used in Western and Chinese food preparation? You're suggested to compare the verbs used in describing food preparation processes and discuss their differences between Chinese and Western culture. And then introduce a traditional food of your hometown, with a focus on both ingredients and procedures in food making.*

Text B An Introduction to the Tea Culture in the UK

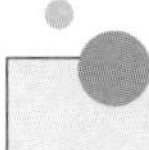

Pre-class Preparation

MOOC Watching

Watch the MOOC video "Tea: A National Drink in Britain" to prepare for Text B.

Pre-reading Questions

1. What do British people like to drink in their daily life besides water? What about you?
2. Why is beer called "liquid bread"?

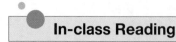

In-class Reading

An Introduction to the Tea Culture in the UK

1 The right pairing of food and drink can create wonderful taste experiences. Drinks can not only get rid of the thirst, but also bring many amazing effects. For example, some drinks like coffee can make people more excited and productive, while tea does good to human health. Similar to food, drinks also convey a lot of messages about culture.

2 Every nation in creation has its respective favorite drink. France is famous for its wine, and beer in Germany. Turkey has its coffee and they serve it blacker than ink. Russia goes for **vodka** and England loves its tea. Believe it or not, tea is the national drink in the UK. It is said that in every single day, the British drink about one hundred and sixty-five million cups of tea, almost three cups per person.

vodka
n. 伏特加（烈性酒）

3 How much British people love tea can also find the answer from **Samuel Johnson** (1709–1784), a famous English writer. During the 18th century, tea was still a relatively novel drink in England. Johnson was both a great lover of tea and a cheerleader for tea. He even described himself as "a hardened and shameless tea-drinker, who has, for twenty years, diluted his meals with only the **infusion** of this fascinating plant; whose kettle has scarcely time to cool; who with tea amuses the evening, with tea **solaces** the midnight, and, with tea, welcomes the morning".

infusion
n. 沏成的饮料
solace
v. 慰藉；使快乐

4 Tea didn't arrive in Britain until the early 17th century, when King Charles II married the Portuguese princess, Catherine of Braganza, who was the great tea lover. Under the influence of the new queen, tea drinking soon became quite a trend among the **aristocracy** of England. It was not until 1717 that the first tea shop for ladies was opened by **Thomas Twining**

aristocracy
n. 贵族

(1675–1741). However, tea was then a **luxury** product, for only the upper class could afford it. Tea, therefore, became something to show off. In case of theft, teas were usually locked in tea containers and only prepared by the host or hostess. When a tea party was served, it became quite a fashion for the host and hostess to display their delicate china pots and cups, silver teakettles and elegantly carved tea jars and tea tables. Soon, the upper class's **enthusiasm** for tea spread to the middle class.

luxury *n.* 奢侈品

enthusiasm *n.* 热情

5 To avoid taxation and cater for the increasing need, **smuggling** and **adulteration** appeared. By the late 18th century, it was estimated that more tea was smuggled into Britain than was brought in legally. Finally in 1784, the Prime Minister, **William Pitt**, cut down the **duty** on tea. In this way, legal tea became much more affordable but not cheap enough, so adulteration continued for many years. Because of that, black tea gained more popularity than green tea for fear that poisonous chemicals would be added to make green tea the right color.

smuggling *n.* 走私（罪）

adulteration *n.* 掺杂；掺假

duty *n.* 税

6 More and more tea shops began to open throughout England, making it available for everyone to drink tea. Along with their increasing love of teas, the British gradually developed their tradition of afternoon tea. Henry James once wrote in *The Portrait of a Lady*[1], "There are few hours in life more agreeable than the hour dedicated to the ceremony known as afternoon tea." What's interesting is that the famous ceremony was originally an idea of Anna Maria Russell[2], the seventh Duchess of Bedford. She intended merely to drive off the hunger first because at that time dinner was often served late after 8 o'clock in the evening. Later Anna invited her friends to join her and the whole upper class slowly followed suit.

7 A traditional afternoon tea ceremony usually prepares a selection of **dainty** sandwiches, freshly baked **scones** served with cream and fruit jam, cakes and **pastries**. Besides, tea or coffee is also provided, served with milk and sugar. Obviously, afternoon tea is a mini meal to fill in the long gap between lunch and dinner, not just a drink. Afternoon tea is customarily

dainty *adj.* 精致的

scone *n.* 烤饼，司康饼

pastry *n.* 油酥糕点

served on low and comfortable chairs, hence the name "low tea". However, high tea[3], as a matter of fact, is a substantial evening meal originally for the working class. At that time, people usually sat on the high back dining chairs while served at the table.

8 In turn, British people's great welcome of drinking tea gives birth to the booming British market offering large varieties of teas. Currently, there are almost 1,500 teas in Britain, all varying in style, taste, and color. However, their teas are imported, mainly from China and India. **Darjeeling**, **Ceylon Tea** and **Assam** from India are viewed as the three most important types popular in the UK, while **Lapsang Souchong** and **Yunnan Tea** are the two favorite China teas. Lapsang Souchong growing on the hills in north Fujian wins the favor of British people due to its smoky **aroma** and flavor. Yunnan Tea is a black tea from Yunnan Province, which the British think is similar to Assam in taste and makes an excellent breakfast tea.

aroma
n. 芳香

Cultural Terms

1. Samuel Johnson 塞缪尔·约翰逊（1709—1784，英国作家、文学评论家和诗人）
2. Thomas Twining 托马斯·川宁（1675—1741，英国商人，也是英国茶商的创始人）
3. William Pitt 小威廉·皮特（1759—1806，英国政治家，英国历史上最年轻的首相）
4. Darjeeling 大吉岭红茶（产自印度，被誉为“红茶中的香槟”）
5. Ceylon Tea 锡兰红茶（产自斯里兰卡，又称“西冷红茶”“惜兰红茶”）
6. Assam 阿萨姆红茶（产自印度，口味浓郁，含有麦芽甚至坚果香气）
7. Lapsang Souchong 武夷山正山小种（世界红茶的鼻祖，以独特的松烟香和桂圆汤味而著称）
8. Yunnan Tea 云南红茶（简称滇红，以茶味浓、强、鲜为特色）

Cultural Notes

1. *The Portrait of a Lady*

《一位贵妇的画像》，是亨利·詹姆斯的早期代表作，发表于1881年，被西方批评家视为美国现代小说的一个开端。

2. Anna Maria Russell

安娜·玛丽亚·罗素，贝德福德公爵夫人（1783—1857），英国女贵族。她于 1837—1841 年间担任维多利亚女王的寝室女官（Lady of the Bedchamber），首创英国“下午茶”这种餐饮文化。19 世纪，晚餐通常在晚上 19:00—20:30 供应。安娜发现下午 16:00—17:00 喝喝茶、吃点零食不仅能提神，还能消除饥饿感，于是她开始邀请朋友和她一起喝茶和吃糕点。这一做法很快流行，后来又从上层社会广泛传播到普通大众的生活中。由此可见，下午茶从最初为满足“小需求”而提供的茶和小吃，转变为今天独特的饮食文化和社交礼仪。

3. high tea

原指工人们在下午 17:00—18:00 喝的下午茶，一般搭配容易果腹的食物，如土豆、肉类等。在英格兰北部、苏格兰和大部分威尔士那些传统的重工业、矿山、船厂以及农庄地区很流行，工人们吃饱后可以继续工作。区别于上流社会在下午 16:00 享用的下午茶（low tea），high tea 更像是正餐的茶点，因坐在较高的餐桌椅上食用而得名。

Exercises

I. True or False

Directions: *Determine whether the following statements are true (T) or false (F).*

1. The casual pairing of food and drink can create wonderful taste experiences.
2. Food conveys messages about culture of a certain region, so do drinks.
3. Samuel Johnson was an extreme tea lover and he lived merely on tea for twenty years.
4. Tea used to be enjoyed only among the upper class.
5. The tradition of afternoon tea was originated from Portugal.
6. A traditional afternoon tea is also nicknamed “high tea”.

II. Matching

Directions: *The tea market offers teas of a great variety, and here are listed some common teas in English. Which teas do they refer to in Chinese?*

III. Survey Report

Directions: *Select a certain tea and conduct a relevant survey, and then make a report on the tea, including its origin, history, ingredients, function, drinking traditions, merits and demerits, etc. In addition, make a comparison about tea drinking tradition between the UK and China.*

Post-class Thinking

Blank Filling

Directions: *Scan the QR code to fill in the blanks of the mind map of Text B and you will have a better understanding of the structure of the text.*

Text C Facts About Fast Food in the US

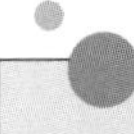

Pre-class Preparation

MOOC Watching

Watch the MOOC video "American Fast Food: A Blessing or a Curse" to prepare for Text C.

Pre-reading Questions

1. What shops or foods does fast food remind you of? What effects does fast food have on your health?
2. Why is the fast food industry growing steadily? List the most popular fast food chain stores in your city.

In-class Reading

Facts About Fast Food in the US

1 "The Melting Pot" used to be a term **metaphorically** generalizing the self-image of the American society. It traditionally referred to the newly-born country welcoming people from various races, countries, and religions to **assimilate** into America. When it comes to food, "the Melting Pot" is even much truer. On the table of American families, it's very common to find almost every kind of ethnic food, **interwoven** with the fact of the US being an immigration country. However, this also makes it difficult to find a typical American food.

metaphorically *adv.* 比喻地

assimilate *v.* (使)同化；吸收

interweave *v.* (过去分词为 interwoven) 交织

2 In spite of this, there is no denying that millions of Americans consume a large quantity of fast food every day, and what's more, they sell it all over the world. There are close to 50,000 fast food chains across the US, and American fast food restaurants are located in over 100 countries. It's easy and convenient for Americans to satisfy almost any appetite at a quick service restaurant, from burgers to **tacos**, from Vietnamese noodles to **kebabs**, from egg rolls to fried rice, from sushi to **pad Thai**.

taco
n. 墨西哥煎玉米粉卷（以肉、豆等作馅）

kebab
n. 烤肉串

3 McDonald's undoubtedly enjoys the most fame and prevalence, but it is not the first fast food restaurant set up in the US. White Castle is the first one, which is a hamburger joint opened in 1916. In the 1920s, the fast food service in the US began to grow parallel to the car industry, i.e., food being served out of a window and into an automobile. Americans became more and more fond of **curb service**, which soon gained popularity and spread nationwide to deliver food from the restaurant to waiting customers outside in their cars. By the 1940s, the waitresses had begun to wear **roller skates** to speed service. Drive-through windows also followed so that people could order and eat food right in their cars. By the 1950s, the fast food industry boomed, while fast food **franchises** also became quite popular thanks to the standardized menus, **signage**, and advertising.

roller skates
溜冰鞋

franchise
n. 特许经销权

signage
n.（统称）标志，标识

4 Americans truly love fast food. According to a research report from **the National Center for Health Statistics** in 2018, more than 1 in 3 US adults eat some type of fast food every day. McDonald's, the world's largest chain of hamburger, feeds more than 46 million American customers daily, which is more than the entire population of Spain. However, behind its popularity, fast food is also globally criticized for causing **obesity**. Released by the **CDC**, 36% American adults and 17% American youth under 19 are either overweight or obese. If left ignored, obesity will then surpass smoking as the leading cause of preventable death in the US.

obesity
n. 肥胖症

5 Despite people's increasing criticism of fast food and advancing awareness of health, fast food is still everywhere. Why are so many people still choosing

to eat fast food although knowing clearly how unhealthy fast food is? The answer lies in the fact that it is inexpensive, convenient, available and filling. McDonald's, Starbucks, Taco Bell, Burger King, Subway, Wendy's, Pizza Hut and KFC have already become household brands not only in the US, but also in many other countries. Not just in restaurants, fast food can also be found in street **vendors**, food trucks, delivery services, sports **arenas**, and even **convenience stores** and gas stations.

vendor
n. 小贩；摊贩
arena
n. 圆形运动场

6 Among all these brands, which fast food chains are the most popular among consumers? You may get the answer immediately at a glance of the rankings of the top 15 quick service giants in the US in 2019 (see Table 8-1). McDonald's ranked No. 1 with over $40 billion in sales, almost double that of the second-largest fast food chain, Starbucks. Studies show that parents and young children form the biggest customers of McDonald's, and more interestingly, a higher percentage of females enjoy eating at McDonald's in the US. By comparing burgers, pizza, chicken, and other food categories, burger joints remain the most popular fast food item, i.e., burgers are king.

Table 8-1 The 15 most popular fast food chains in the US in 2019

Ranking	Company	Category	US Sales
1	McDonald's	Burger	$40.41
2	Starbucks	Snack	$21.55
3	Chick-fil-A	Chicken	$11.00
4	Taco Bell	Global	$11.00
5	Burger King	Burger	$10.30
6	Subway	Sandwich	$10.00
7	Wendy's	Burger	$9.87
8	Dunkin'	Snack	$9.22
9	Domino's	Pizza	$7.10
10	Panera Bread	Sandwich	$5.93
11	Chipotle	Global	$5.52
12	Pizza Hut	Pizza	$5.38
13	KFC	Chicken	$4.82
14	Sonic Drive-In	Burger	$4.69
15	Arby's	Sandwich	$3.89

7 As long as the society is still on the go, the market will remain huge for fast food. But with increasing concern on the significance of both nutrition and health, consumers are now trying their best to eat healthy fast food. As a result, a new challenge has been posed in front of fast food industry, that is, a must to provide much healthier and more nutritious food to the people who are always in a hurry.

Cultural Terms

1. pad Thai 泰式炒河粉
2. curb service （美）路边餐饮服务
3. the National Center for Health Statistics 美国国家卫生统计中心
4. CDC 美国疾病控制中心（Centers for Disease Control）
5. convenience store 便利店（常为 24 小时营业）

Exercises

I. True or False

Directions: *Determine whether the following statements are true (T) or false (F).*

1. "The Melting Pot" is a typical American dish which mixes different foods.
2. McDonald's is the first fast food restaurant set up in the US.
3. The growth of fast food in the US is closely related to the car industry.
4. Being criticized as the leading cause of obesity, fast food becomes less and less popular in the US than before.
5. It's estimated that obesity will likely become the leading cause of preventable death in the US.
6. Fast food industry remains confident in producing better food for consumers.

II. Reordering

Directions: *The text mentions that Americans may satisfy almost any appetite at a fast food restaurant, from burgers to tacos, from Vietnamese noodles to kebabs, from egg rolls to fried rice, from sushi to pad Thai. Have a try to arrange the following foods in the same order as mentioned in the text.*

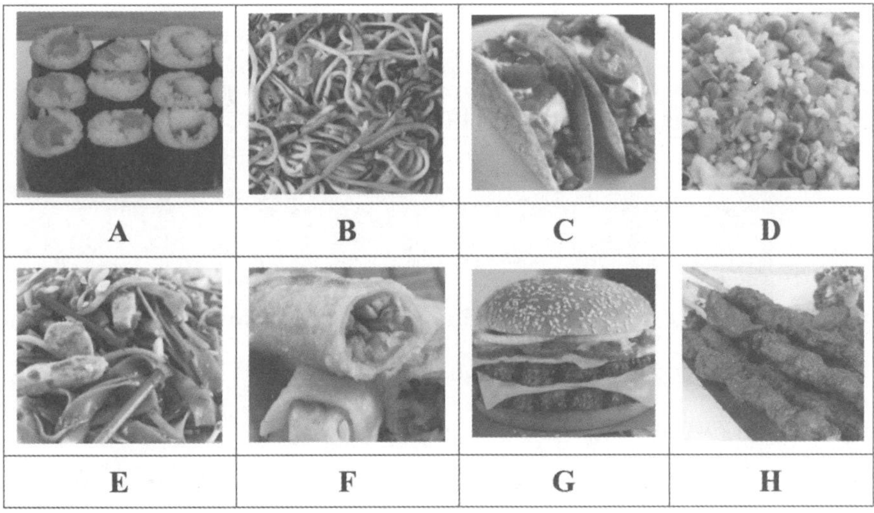

Reordering: ____→ ____→ ____→ ____→ ____→ ____→ ____→ ____

Post-class Thinking

Critical Thinking

Directions: *Choose one position and come up with views and evidence to support this position.*

How often do you eat fast food? Is it an essential part of your life? Form two groups within the class to debate whether people can get rid of fast food or not.

Position A: People can get rid of fast food.

Position B: People cannot get rid of fast food.

The debate process should go as follows:

- The two sides make opening statements;
- Side A presents its arguments;
- Side B rebuts Side A's arguments and presents its arguments;
- Side A rebuts Side B's arguments;
- The two sides make closing statements.

Hint: Focus on the cause and effect between fast food culture and fast rhythm of life.

Supplementary Resources

1. Extensive Reading

Scan the QR codes to read Text D "Various Facets of American Cuisine" and watch the MOOC video "American Cuisine: A Mixture of Flavors". Then discuss the following questions with your partner:

1) How many meals do you have every day? When do you eat and what do you eat most of the time?

2) Have you ever eaten any special food for a specific purpose?

Text D "Various Facets of American Cuisine"

MOOC video "American Cuisine: A Mixture of Flavors"

2. Documentaries

1) Documentary: *That Sugar Film* (2014) （《另类糖影》）

That Sugar Film is an Australian documentary starring and directed by Damon Gameau in 2014. It focuses on the hidden sugar in foods, and further discovers the bitter truth about sugar, i.e., the effects of a high sugar diet on a healthy body. *That Sugar Film* may change the way you think about "healthy" food.

2) Documentary: *Food Matters* (2008) （《健康饮食》）

Food Matters is a documentary directed by James Colquhoun and Carlo Ledesma, aiming to discover how the food we eat can help or hurt our health. Several leading experts in nutrition and natural healing have been interviewed and they point out two facts. One is that not every problem needs costly and major medical treatment. The other fact is that we have some alternative therapies that can be more effective, more economical, less harmful and less invasive. In other words, the film helps people rethink the belief systems given by modern medical and health care establishments.

3) Documentary: *Fed Up* (2014) （《甜蜜的负担》）

The 2014 film *Fed Up* is an advocacy documentary, directed by Stephanie Soechtig. The film aims to examine the obesity epidemic in America and the role that food industry plays in aggravating it. Obesity is endangering our children, largely resulted from increased sugar consumption. Soechtig enlists both emotional and visual techniques, as well as satirical humor, to attract our attention and wake us up to the central problems related to obesity.

3. Books

Freedman, P. 2019. *Food: The History of Taste*. New York: Thames & Hudson.

Mason, L. 2004. *Food Culture in Great Britain (Food Culture Around the World)*. Westpoint: Greenwood.

McDonald, M. R. 2009. *Food Culture in Central America (Food Culture Around the World)*. Westpoint: Greenwood.

Petrini, C. 2004. *Slow Food: The Case for Taste (Arts and Traditions of the Table: Perspectives on Culinary History)*. McCuaig, W. (trans.). Columbia: Columbia University Press.

梁实秋 . 2012. 雅舍谈吃 . 长沙：湖南文艺出版社 .

Chapter 9
Arts in the UK and the US

Art reflects reality and conveys emotion in a creative way. Various forms, including language, writing, painting, music and body, are used to express art. Visual art is one of the most common arts, such as sculpture, painting and photography. The UK has a long history of art development and has produced rich art forms, while the US has formed a unique artistic style in a relatively short historical development. This chapter will introduce architecture, painting, pop art and theater in the UK and the US.

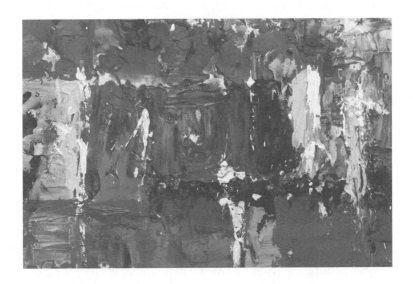

Text A Architectural Styles in the UK and the US

Pre-class Preparation

MOOC Watching

Watch the MOOC videos "Baroque and Gothic Architectures in Britain" and "American Modern Architecture" to prepare for Text A.

MOOC video "Baroque and Gothic Architectures in Britain"

MOOC video "American Modern Architecture"

Pre-reading Question

Do you know about any architectural styles? Name some buildings in correspondence to the styles you mention.

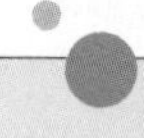

In-class Reading

Architectural Styles in the UK and the US

1 Architecture, an embodiment of art and technique, serves both **utilitarian** and **aesthetic** ends. Different historical periods naturally give birth to different types of architecture, which is closely related to its culture and society as well.

utilitarian *adj.* 实用的
aesthetic *adj.* 审美的

★ Gothic style

2 Gothic architecture, originated in France around the mid-12th century, is mainly characterized by rib **vault**, flying **buttress**, and pointed **arch**. The three features are advantageous to make buildings taller and more elaborate, such as Westminster Abbey in London, the site for royal coronation, burials and weddings.

vault
n. 拱顶；拱
buttress
n. 扶壁
arch
n. 拱门

3 **Lincoln Cathedral** (begun in 1192) is famous as the first mature example of the early English Gothic style, especially for its **nave** and **choir**. The Chapter House of **Wells Cathedral** (finished by 1306), the meeting place for cathedral affairs, is **octagonal** in shape and delicately decorated with sculpture. Along with the evolution of Gothic architecture, the size of the windows was progressively enlarged. Thus, more light would shed into the interiors, and meanwhile larger space was spared for the stained glass, typically in dark blue and bright **ruby** red.

nave
n. 教堂正厅
choir
n. （教堂）唱经楼；唱诗席
octagonal
adj. 八边形的
ruby
adj. 红宝石的

4 The **flamboyant** style is characteristic of the late Gothic architecture, while in England, the builders refused this style and used an upright rectangle for walls and windows. **King's College Chapel at Cambridge** presents the masterpiece of this style, in which the fan-shaped spreading panels are in amazingly beautiful accord with the rectangular panels of the walls and windows.

flamboyant
adj. 绚丽夺目的

King's College Chapel at Cambridge

★ Baroque style

5 Baroque style originated in Italy after Renaissance, which impressed people with abundant ornaments and various arts decoration. As it spread

throughout Europe, Baroque became a style demonstrating power and was adopted by rulers and the Catholic Church. English Baroque was a response to the European Baroque style and developed into a unique style to England after the Great Fire of London[1] in 1666.

6 Architect **Christopher Wren** took the lead and started to reconstruct churches using the Baroque style. St. Paul's Cathedral, completed at the end of the 17th century, was viewed as one of the best examples in this category, emphasizing bold spaces, domes, and large masses. The Baroque style was later termed Rococo[2], as a reaction against grandeur and symmetry in the 18th century. In comparison, one of the principal differences is that Baroque emphasizes symmetry while Rococo emphasizes **asymmetric** designs.

asymmetric
adj. 不对称的

The Dome of St. Paul's Cathedral

★ **Neoclassical style**

7 By the end of the 18th century, however, **Neoclassical** style had replaced Rococo to a large extent. A revival of classical architecture, Neoclassical architecture developed a new taste for antique simplicity, in contrast to the excesses of the Rococo style. It generally featured grand scale and simple **geometric** forms. Besides, it showed a preference for both columns and blank walls.

Neoclassical
adj. 新古典主义的

geometric
adj. 几何的

8 Neoclassicism thrived in Europe and the US, with examples appearing in almost every major city. Different from Rococo, Neoclassical architecture typically had a flat quality, both the White House in Washington and **the Bank of England** in London serving as notable examples of this style.

The White House in Washington

★ **Modernist architecture**

9 At the turn of the 20th century, modernist architecture appeared, emphasizing the principle of "Form follows function". Consequently skyscrapers emerged in the US, which oriented towards function to meet the ever-increasing demand for **accommodations** accompanied with high urbanization. **Louis Sullivan's Wainwright Building** in 1891 is an excellent early example, a ten-story U-shaped building with wide glass windows ensuring the light of inside offices. The skyscraper is regarded as America's unique contribution to the world history of architecture.

accommodations *n.* 住处

10 After 1900s, New York City assumed leadership in the development of skyscrapers. The adoption of steel framework made their **soaring** heights possible, along with other advances in engineering and technology. **Woolworth Building**, designed by **Cass Gilbert**, was the tallest building in the world when completed at 792 feet and 55 floors. Not only was the building remarkable in height, but also the external details in Gothic style embodied America's increasing power in business and economy. That's why some critics even called Woolworth Building "the Cathedral of Commerce".

soaring *adj.* 高耸的

★ **Art Deco**

11 Art Deco[3] is a term referring to a design movement, which influenced art, fashion, **homewares**, and building styles in both Europe and the US in the 1920s and 1930s. Architects were inventive in their design

homewares *n.* 家居用品

approach, seeking to create fresh and modern structures. They tended to use contrasting colors boldly and applied various geometric details, including V-shape, pyramids, **sunbursts** or **florals**. In addition, decorative geometric windows and doors, spires or tower-like structures were often used to make a simple square building seem more splendid.

sunburst
n. 旭日形设计
floral
n. 花卉

12 Hugely welcomed by American architects and engineers, the Art Deco style exerted a profound influence on the design of many architectural projects of the era, skyscrapers ranking the top of the list. Some of the most amazing Art Deco skyscrapers in the US include **the Empire State Building** (443 meters), **the Chrysler Building** (319 meters), **American International Building** (290 meters), **General Electric Building** (195 meters), **the Foshay Tower** (185 meters) and so on. The Chrysler Building is one of the finest examples of Art Deco skyscraper architecture, built in 1930 with the design of **William Van Alen** (1883–1954).

The Chrysler Building

★ American modernism

13 Besides the focus on commercial and economic development, American modern architecture also features the style and tendency of "organic" architecture, with an attempt to integrate a building with its

natural surroundings. For the purpose of integrating house and site, **Frank Lloyd Wright** turned away from the traditional boxlike design and built in **the Prairie States** with the horizontal character of the prairie itself. In order to achieve organic unity among all parts of the house, Wright integrated lighting and heating into the ceiling and floor, and designed built-in bookcases, shelves, and storage drawers.

14 Various architectural styles come into being in different historical periods to meet the change of the society, such as the up-to-date technology, people's aesthetic tastes and standards, attitudes toward the world, factual concerns of human life and their expectations of the nature. In addition to the six architectural styles mentioned above, brutalist architecture[4], postmodernism[5], neomodernism[6], high-tech architecture, green architecture[7] and smart buildings[8] emerge one after another across the globe as the times require.

T Cultural Terms

1. Lincoln Cathedral 林肯大教堂（建于 1072—1092 年，是英格兰最大的教堂之一）
2. Wells Cathedral 韦尔斯大教堂（建于 1175—1490 年，因其美丽的外观而被评为英格兰最美丽和最具诗意的教堂之一）
3. King's College Chapel at Cambridge 剑桥大学国王学院礼拜堂（中世纪晚期英国建筑，以其堂内的管风琴和扇形拱顶天花板而闻名）
4. Christopher Wren 克里斯多佛·雷恩（1632—1723，英国皇家学会会长，天文学家和著名建筑师）
5. the Bank of England 英格兰银行（英国的中央银行）
6. Louis Sullivan 路易斯·沙利文（1856—1924，第一批设计摩天大楼的美国建筑师之一）
7. Wainwright Building 温莱特大厦（现代摩天楼的设计原型，视为首座成功应用钢框架结构的大楼）
8. Woolworth Building 伍尔沃斯大楼（位于美国纽约，建于 1913 年）
9. Cass Gilbert 卡斯·吉尔伯特（伍尔沃斯大楼的建筑师）

10. the Empire State Building 帝国大厦（美国纽约的地标建筑物之一，是装饰艺术风格建筑）
11. the Chrysler Building 克莱斯勒大厦（受克莱斯勒汽车制造公司的委托而建造，美国纽约典型的装饰艺术建筑）
12. American International Building 美国国际大厦（位于美国纽约，建于 1930—1932 年）
13. General Electric Building 通用电气大楼（位于美国纽约曼哈顿，建于 1929—1931 年，属装饰艺术风格）
14. the Foshay Tower 佛谢大厦（以华盛顿纪念碑为原型，位于明尼苏达州明尼阿波利斯市，于 1929 年完工，是装饰艺术风格建筑的典范，现为酒店）
15. William Van Alen 威廉·凡艾伦（1883—1954，克莱斯勒大厦的设计者）
16. Frank Lloyd Wright 弗兰克·劳埃德·赖特（1867—1959，美国著名建筑师，提出“有机建筑论”）
17. the Prairie States 美国中西部大草原各州（如蒙大拿州、怀俄明州、达科他州、内布拉斯加州和堪萨斯州）

Cultural Notes

1. the Great Fire of London

伦敦大火，发生于 1666 年 9 月 2–5 日，是英国伦敦历史上最严重的一次火灾，烧掉了许多建筑物，包括圣保罗大教堂，但解决了伦敦自 1665 年以来的鼠疫问题。

2. Rococo

洛可可艺术，18 世纪产生于法国并遍及欧洲，该艺术形式具有轻快、精致、细腻、繁复等特点。洛可可在构图上有意强调不对称，其工艺、结构和线条具有婉转、柔和的特点，其装饰题材有自然主义的倾向，被广泛应用在建筑、装潢、绘画、文学、雕塑、音乐等艺术领域。

3. Art Deco

艺术装饰风格，演变自 19 世纪末的新艺术运动，是当时欧美（主要是欧洲）中产阶级追求的一种艺术风格，以线条优美、图案典型、色彩明亮等为主要特征。后期经考古发现，远东、中东、希腊、罗马、埃及与玛雅等古老文化的物品或图腾，也都成为 Art Deco 装饰的素材来源。

4. brutalist architecture

野兽派建筑，源自法语“béton-brut”（本意为“原始混凝土”）。流行于20世纪50年代中期至70年代中期，主要用于学校、公共住房、教堂和政府大楼等公共机构的建筑。所用原料往往是原始的、未完成的状态，而且通常是实心的块状结构。巴比肯中心和巴比肯屋村是英国野兽派建筑的典型案例。

5. postmodernism

后现代主义，在建筑方面是指20世纪中期现代主义以后各流派建筑的总称，包含了多种风格的建筑。美国建筑师斯特恩提出后现代主义建筑有三个特征：装饰的采用；具有象征性或隐喻性；尊重环境，与现有环境相融合。

6. neomodernism

新现代主义，兴起于20世纪80—90年代，既具有现代主义的功能和理性主义的特征，又具有其独特的个人表现和象征性风格。新现代主义被认为是在混乱的后现代风格之后的一个回归过程，重新恢复现代主义设计和国际主义设计的理性的、次序的、功能性特征。

7. green architecture

绿色建筑，遵循因地制宜的原则，结合建筑所在地域的气候、环境、资源、经济和文化等特点，重在关照建筑全寿命期内的安全耐久、健康舒适、生活便利、资源节约、环境宜居五类指标等性能。

8. smart buildings

智能建筑，主要具备三大基本功能：建筑设备自动化 (Building Automation，BA)、通信自动化 (Communication Automation，CA) 和办公自动化 (Office Automation，OA)，即“3A”智能建筑。

Exercise

Question Answering

Directions: *Answer the following questions in brief based on Text A.*

1. What are the three typical characteristics of Gothic architecture?

____

2. How can you differentiate Baroque and Rococo?

3. Why did skyscrapers appear in America?

4. What does Art Deco refer to?

5. What is the main feature of American modernism?

Critical Thinking

Directions: *Choose one position and come up with views and evidence to support this position.*

Between form and function, which goes first for architecture?

Position A: Form goes first.
Position B: Function goes first.

The debate process should go as follows:

- The two sides make opening statements;
- Side A presents its arguments;
- Side B rebuts Side A's arguments and presents its arguments;
- Side A rebuts Side B's arguments;
- The two sides make closing statements.

Post-class Thinking

Comparison and Analysis

Directions: *The Imperial Palace (the Forbidden City) in Beijing is the world's largest royal palace. Buckingham Palace is the official home of the British* *royal family in London and the White House is the official home of US president in Washington, DC. Make a comparison among the three buildings from the perspective of architectural style.*

The Imperial Palace

Buckingham Palace

The White House

Blank Filling

Directions: *Scan the QR code to fill in the blanks in the mind map of Text A and you will have a better understanding of the structure of the text.*

Text B Paintings in the UK and the US

Pre-class Preparation

MOOC Watching

Watch the MOOC video "English Visual Art During Tudor Monarchy and American Frontier Paintings" to prepare for Text B.

Pre-reading Questions

1. Do you agree that painting is a kind of language? If your answer is positive, what elements does painting have?
2. When talking about painting, whose artworks come to your mind? Introduce them in brief.

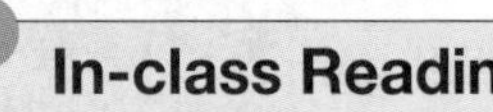

In-class Reading

Paintings in the UK and the US

1 Creating certain aesthetic patterns by combining relevant elements, painting helps the painter express ideas and emotions in a two-dimensional visual language. The elements of this language, including lines,

shapes, colours, tones and textures, are used in proper ways to produce corresponding works of art. They are presented in various volume, space, movement, and light on a flat surface to narrate a theme, to represent real or supernatural phenomena, or to create entirely abstract visual relationships.

★ **Paintings in the UK**

2 England's visual art has gone through different phases and trends over the centuries. Medieval English painting had a strong national tradition and it at times even influenced the rest of Europe. After England's break with the Roman Catholic Church, the Tudors[1] favored Netherlandish and German artists. Religious painting thus had no place in England and instead portrait **miniature** flourished. The artists of the Tudor court in the Renaissance and their **successors** before the Civil War were however imported talents, mostly portraitists, like **Rubens** and **Van Dyck**. **Sir Godfrey Kneller**, a German-born artist, continued to be a court portrait painter after the Restoration[2].

miniature
n. 小画像
successor
n. 继任者

3 Hans Holbein the Younger, an appointed court painter to Henry VIII in the year of 1532, shaped the taste of the English court and upper classes. By 1526, he had mastered the **unparalleled** skill to create the physical presence of a sitter. It's Holbein who helped maintain the images of Henry VIII and Elizabeth I alive until today. The two English Tudor monarchs held the "iconic status" for the great pains they took over their public images. Henry's confident pose and athletic **strut** conveyed that he's a man of great power. Elizabeth's carefully cultivated image left an impression of beauty of that era. Even in today's **image-soaked** consumer culture, the Tudor brand still enjoys widespread and lasting recognition in the market.

unparalleled
adj. 无比的
strut
n. 趾高气扬的步态
image-soaked
adj. 重视形象的
sobriety
n. 持重

4 **Samuel Cooper** and **Peter Lely** flourished not only under the Puritans, but also after the Restoration. Cooper's early works demonstrated the broader handling characteristic of the Stuart Dynasty[3] and the **sobriety** typical of the Commonwealth. Lely's paintings were notable for the deep

tone, rich color and sensual elegance.

5 The 18th century saw its art beginning to reflect middle-class living and attitudes. As the newly rich middle classes in the UK prospered, many of the paintings that emerged in the UK reflected Enlightenment[4] values, including an interest in social progress, and faith in reason and science. The English School[5], founded in c.1750, was the dominant school of painting in England to mark the rise of a national tradition but closed about 100 years later. **William Hogarth**, an early representative of the English school, believed that art should contribute to the improvement of society. His painting *Marriage Contract*, via showing an arranged marriage between the son of a lord and the daughter of a wealthy merchant, criticized and mocked the concept of marriage based on **aristocratic intrigue** rather than love.

aristocratic
adj. 贵族的
intrigue
n. 密谋策划

6 **Richard Wilson**, another early representative of the English school, started to found the English landscape tradition. Widely known as "the father of English landscape", Wilson added a delicate sense of light and distance and a grand design to the English tradition. Besides, **Turner**, **Constable**, **Crome**, **Cotman**, **Muller**, and **De Wint** summed up the best of English landscape oil painting during the first half of the 19th century. Among those **foregoing** artists, Turner, Cotman, and De Wint worked equally beautifully in water-colour, and were all leaders of the English water-colour school. Comparatively speaking, water-colour painting of the early 19th century in England had been **exploited** the most extensively and successfully, constituting one of the chief glories of English art.

foregoing
adj. 前述的

exploit
v. 发挥

★ Paintings in the US

7 *The Declaration of Independence* issued in 1776 marked the official establishment of the American national identity. Part of the new nation's history and civilization had been written visually by American artists and painters.

8 America's first well-known school of painting—the Hudson River School[6] was born in 1820. Their directness and simplicity of vision

influenced and inspired many later artists. Furthermore, impressed by the westward expansion of land and the **transcendent** beauty of frontier landscapes, American artists chose to depict rural America, such as its sea, mountains and people.

transcendent *adj.* 超凡的；卓越的

9 **Thomas Cole**, one of the founders of the Hudson River School, had worked as an **itinerant** painter by 1820. On his trips around New York, Cole sketched and painted the landscape, with a belief that a too close focus on factual accuracy was not real art. His painting *The Oxbow* conveys to us a contrast between the wild and the civilized, and further expresses that the former would eventually give way to the latter.

itinerant *adj.* 巡回的

The Oxbow

10 Though controversy became a way of life to American artists for a period of time after World War I, many American artists rejected the modern trends imitating the European influences. Instead, they chose to adopt academic realism in depicting America's urban and rural scenes. As a matter of fact, before Europeans came, rich and complex art traditions had been thriving among many **indigenous** tribes. They used complex geometric forms and patterns to depict the natural world and narrate ancestral and mythological stories. Naturally, the strong sense of national identity had soon been inherited by the first native American art movement, over 25 **Iroquois** artists expressing their tribe's beliefs, history, fashion, and lifestyle via drawing, painting, and printmaking. This successfully exerted major influences on foreign artists.

indigenous *adj.* 本地的

Iroquois *n.* 易洛魁人；易洛魁族人

11 Abstract **impressionist** artists worked with mixed media. Beginning in the fall of 1946, **Jackson Pollock** worked in a barn, where he placed his

impressionist *adj.* 印象派的

canvases on the floor so that he could work on them from all four sides. He also began to use house paints along with conventional oils, dripping them onto his canvases with sticks and brushes through a variety of fluid arm and wrist movements. *Autumn Rhythm* was one of his best works. The work shows no trace of the **Cubist** influence, **Picasso**'s chief legacy to modern art. Pollock's creativity resonated with the very world in which exciting and **chaotic** elements began **oozing** out at that time.

Cubist
adj. 立体派的

chaotic
adj. 混乱的

ooze
v. 泄漏；渗出

Autumn Rhythm

12 Between the year of 1955 and 1965, Pop Art prevailed in America. Andy Warhol and Roy Lichtenstein are the **pivotal** figures of American Pop Art, reproducing with satiric care, everyday objects and images of American popular culture.

pivotal
adj. 关键性的；核心的

13 Either British painting or American painting has its own history and contribution to the world art. They were first influenced by European art but later developed their own school of painting, leaving a far-reaching impact on the foreign art to a large extent. Similarly, they both express concern over the national tradition or national identity, holding the firm belief that art serves the improvement of society.

T Cultural Terms

1. Rubens 鲁本斯（1577—1640，17 世纪佛兰德斯画家，巴洛克画派早期的代表人物）
2. Van Dyck 凡·戴克（1599—1641，比利时画家，英国宫廷首席画家）
3. Sir Godfrey Kneller 克内勒爵士（1646—1723，德国画家，英国宫廷画师）
4. Samuel Cooper 萨木尔·库珀（1609—1672, 英国巴洛克时期细密画画家）
5. Peter Lely 彼得·莱利爵士（1618—1680，荷兰肖像画家）

6. William Hogarth 威廉·荷加斯（1697—1764, 英国著名画家、版画家、讽刺画家和欧洲连环漫画的先驱）
7. Richard Wilson 理查德·威尔逊（1714—1782, 英国风景艺术的先驱）
8. Turner 特纳（1775—1851，英国画家及图形艺术家）
9. Constable 康斯特布尔（1776—1837，19 世纪英国风景画家）
10. Crome 克罗姆（1768—1821，浪漫主义时期的英国风景画家）
11. Cotman 科特曼（1850—1920，英国风景画、肖像画和室内装饰画家）
12. Muller 穆勒（1812—1845，英国油画家，以其风景画和人物画而闻名）
13. De Wint 德·温特（1784—1849，荷兰裔英国画家，19 世纪早期英国主要水彩画家之一）
14. Thomas Cole 托马斯·科尔（1801—1848，哈德逊河画派的创始人）
15. Jackson Pollock 杰克逊·波洛克（1912—1956, 美国抽象表现主义绘画大师）
16. Picasso 毕加索（1881—1973，西班牙画家、雕塑家，现代艺术的创始人）

Cultural Notes

1. the Tudors

都铎王朝 (1485—1603)，是在亨利七世 1485 年入主英格兰、威尔士和爱尔兰后所开创的一个王朝，统治英格兰王国及其属土周围地区。都铎王朝直到 1603 年伊丽莎白一世去世为止, 共经历了五代君主, 历经 118 年。都铎王朝处于英国从封建主义向资本主义过渡时期, 被认为是英国君主专制历史上的黄金时期。

2. the Restoration

王朝复辟。1649 年开启英国共和国时期，克伦威尔担任“护国公”，实行有利于人民与资产阶级的政策。但是，克伦威尔于 1658 年去世，两年后查理一世之子查理二世恢复王位，即 1660 年斯图亚特王朝复辟。

3. the Stuart Dynasty

斯图亚特王朝，该王朝于 1371—1714 年统治苏格兰，于 1603—1714 年统治英格兰和爱尔兰。该王朝共有六代君主，詹姆斯一世、查理一世、查理二世、詹姆斯二世、威廉三世和玛丽二世以及安妮女王。

4. Enlightenment

启蒙运动，指发生在 17—18 世纪的一场资产阶级和人民大众的反封建、反教会的思想文化运动。启蒙运动有力批判了封建专制主义、宗教愚昧及特权主义，宣传自由、民主和平等的思想。

5. the English School

英国学派，英国的主要绘画流派，贯穿 18 世纪下半叶和 19 世纪上半叶，它的建立标志着一种民族传统的兴起。

6. the Hudson River School

哈德逊河派，即哈得逊河画派、美国风景画派，活跃于 1820—1880 年。画家托马斯·科尔被认为是哈德逊河派的创始人。

Exercise

Blank Filling

Directions: *Complete the following blanks based on Text B.*

1. The Enlightenment values reflected in the 18th-century British paintings mainly include ________ and ________.
2. ________ is widely known as "the father of English landscape".
3. Turner, Cotman and De Wint worked successfully not only in ________ , but also in ________.
4. American artists chose to depict their rural landscape because they were impressed by the ________ and the transcendent beauty of ________ during the 19th century.
5. Abstract impressionist artist ________ made ________ in 1946, one of his best works.

In-class Game

Directions: *What do you see from the following six paintings? Share your understanding with your partners in brief. Can you tell the names of the following paintings and their painters?*

1 2 3 4

5

6

1. ______________________ painted by ______________________.
2. ______________________ painted by ______________________.
3. ______________________ painted by ______________________.
4. ______________________ painted by ______________________.
5. ______________________ painted by ______________________.
6. ______________________ painted by ______________________.

Post-class Thinking

Discussion

Directions: *Discuss with your partners what you think is the most important characteristic for an artwork to become accepted and famous and why. Support your point of view with examples.*

Blank Filling

Directions: *Scan the QR code to fill in the blanks in the mind map of Text B and you will have a better understanding of the structure of the text.*

Text C Getting to Know About Pop Art in the UK and the US

Pre-class Preparation

MOOC Watching

Watch the MOOC video "Pop Art in Britain and America" to prepare for Text C.

Pre-reading Questions

1. What does the word "pop" mean in your knowledge?
2. Have you ever heard about Pop Art? What do you know about it?

In-class Reading

Getting to Know About Pop Art in the UK and the US

1 Pop Art, the art of popular culture, coincided with the globalization of pop music and youth culture during the post-WWII consumer boom. Though different in styles, paintings and sculptures in the 1950s and the

1960s all showed a common interest in mass-media, mass-production and mass-culture. The **incorporation** of **commonplace** objects like comic strips, soup cans, road signs, and even hamburgers into the work of art as subject matter made the public hard to take it seriously at first, but it had become one of the most recognized art movements by the end of the 20th century.

incorporation *n.* 结合；并入
commonplace *adj.* 平凡的；普通的

★ British Pop Art

2 Pop Art started in the UK and the word "Pop" was first coined by the British art critic **Lawrence Alloway** in 1954, who used it to describe a new type of art inspired by the imagery of popular culture. Furthermore, he founded the Independent Group together with **Richard Hamilton** and **Eduardo Paolozzi**, aiming to explore radical approaches to **contemporary** visual culture between 1952 and 1955. Paolozzi created a series of **collages** from American magazines in the late 1940s, conveying an ironic and critical attitude towards the all-American lifestyle. One of his artworks, titled *I Was a Rich Man's Plaything*, was such a part of the collage series and also the first visual artwork to use the word "Pop" **explicitly**.

contemporary *adj.* 当代的
collage *n.* 拼贴画
explicitly *adv.* 明确地

3 Some young British artists in the 1950s satirized but also envied the more inclusive and youthful American culture which was greatly influenced by mass media and mass production, so they relied on Pop Art to express their search for change by using Dada[1] collages and **assemblages**. In other words, British Pop artists adopted a similar visual technique, creating seemingly **irrational** combinations of random images to stimulate an echo in their society.

assemblage *n.*（人或物的）组合
irrational *adj.* 不合理的

4 The Pop Art Movement aimed to blur the boundaries between "high" art and "low" culture via paintings or sculptures. The artists thought that art might borrow any object from any cultural source. Thus, with a belief that everything was inter-connected in mind, Pop artists sought to make those connections literal in their artwork.

5 Richard Hamilton's collage of 1956, *Just What Is It That Makes Today's*

Homes So Different, So Appealing?, is such a representative imagery. This collage presents a different modern home furnished with modern household appliances, such as vacuum cleaner and television, and decorated with **cutouts** from magazine advertisements. Besides, the home was constructed by a body-builder and a **burlesque** dancer. The imagery created by Hamilton appreciated the great convenience brought by modern technology on the one hand, but criticized the **decadence** caused by American post-war consumerism on the other.

cutout
n. 剪切图
burlesque
n. 滑稽娱乐
decadence
n. 贪图享乐

★ **American Pop Art**

6 Although Pop Art started in the UK, it is essentially an American movement, evolving in a slightly different way from its British counterpart. By the mid-1950s, many American artists felt Abstract Expressionism[2] had become too **introspective** and elitist. Thus, they reintroduced the images in the concrete world as elements in creation with an attempt to reverse this trend. That's to say, they tried to pull art back from the **obscurity** of abstraction into the real world again. Around 1955, two remarkable artists, **Jasper Johns** and **Robert Rauschenberg**, emerged, whose art is seen as a bridge between Abstract Expressionism and Pop Art.

introspective
adj. 内省的
obscurity
n. 费解；晦涩

7 In Jasper Johns' eyes, subject and object in his art are both the same thing, art and life equally the same thing, so we needn't distinguish them. He led people not to look upon a painting as a representation or illusion but as an object with its own reality. He used "found images" or **iconography** of familiar signs, including flags, targets, letters and numbers, to create art, viewing them as "pre-formed, conventional, **depersonalized**, factual, exterior elements". In addition, his subjects provided him with a structure upon which he could explore the visual and physical qualities of his medium, resulting into a careful balance between representation and abstraction.

iconography
n. 图示法
depersonalize
v. 使不掺杂个人感情

8 Similarly, Robert Rauschenberg also used "found images" in his art,

but sometimes he even used real objects. With an aim to mirror people's life and psychology which were profoundly influenced by mass-media, he experimented with contemporary images gathered from newspapers, magazines, television and film, which he could reproduce in any size and color on a canvas or print. His paintings, to a large extent, capture the hidden power inserted by mass-media via combining images to suggest some kind of ironic **allegory**.

allegory
n. 讽喻

9 The artist who personifies Pop Art more than any other is **Andy Warhol**, deriving his subject matter from the imagery of mass-culture. He took advantage of second-hand images of celebrities and consumer products in his creation, for he thought they had an internal **banality** that made them more interesting. Warhol saw this aesthetic of mass-production as a mirror of contemporary American culture: "What's great about this country is that America started the tradition where the richest consumers buy essentially the same things as the poorest." His paintings of Marilyn Monroe are the most famous icons of Pop Art, reflecting mass **inclination** to celebrities. *Marilyn Diptych* is one of the first art products transforming conventional painting into the silk-screening[3] photographic images onto canvas.

banality
n. 平庸；平淡乏味

inclination
n. 倾向；趋势

10 **Roy Lichtenstein** developed an instantly recognizable style of Pop Art—**comic strip**, which is a style in a fixed format, usually black outlines, bold colors and tones expressed by **benday dots**. His comic strip plays an elaborate game with illusion and reality. For instance, *Oh, Jeff... I Love You, too... But...* embodies the contrast between comic-book emotions and real-life vividness. The issue of what is real and unreal in our media-soaked culture was just coming to awareness in the early 1960s.

11 In sum, Pop Art selected commonplace objects and people of everyday life as its subject matter, far from such traditional "high art" themes as morality, mythology, and classic history. But it's the images drawn from mass media and popular culture that shifted the Abstract Expressionism in

the direction of modernism. The incorporation of common imagery from real life has pushed Pop Art to become one of the most identifiable styles of modern art.

Cultural Terms

1. Lawrence Alloway 劳伦斯·阿洛韦（1926—1990，英国艺术评论家，创名了“波普艺术”）
2. Richard Hamilton 理查德·汉密尔顿（1922—2011, 英国著名艺术家）
3. Eduardo Paolozzi 爱德华多·包洛奇（1924—2005, 意大利裔英国雕塑家）
4. Jasper Johns 贾思培·琼斯（1930— ，美国当代艺术家）
5. Robert Rauschenberg 罗伯特·劳森伯格（1925—2008，战后美国波普艺术的代表人物）
6. Andy Warhol 安迪·沃霍尔（1928—1987，波普艺术的倡导者和领袖，也是对波普艺术影响最大的艺术家之一）
7. Roy Lichtenstein 罗伊·利希滕斯坦（1923—1997，美国画家，波普艺术大师）
8. comic strip 连环漫画
9. benday dots 本戴点（20 世纪 50 — 60 年代连环画采用的印刷圆点）

Cultural Notes

1. Dada

达达主义艺术，源于法语 dada，表示婴儿牙牙学语期间对周围事物的纯生理反应。1916—1924 年在欧美许多城市兴起，其主要表现为否定理性和传统文化，崇拜虚无主义。一般通过照片剪接或与纸片、抹布拼贴，去追求艺术表现的偶然性。达达主义艺术对 20 世纪西方现代艺术的发展产生了重大影响。

2. Abstract Expressionism

抽象表现主义，是指一种结合抽象形式和表现主义画家情感价值取向的非写实性绘画风格。它发展于 20 世纪 40 年代中期的纽约，画风多半大胆粗犷、尖锐且尺幅巨大。画作色彩强烈，并经常出现偶然效果，例如让油彩自然流淌而不加限制来作画。

3. silk-screening

丝网版画，属于孔版印刷，用绷有丝网的框板进行印花。这种印刷技术起源于 2000 多年前的中国，将涂料在框板上进行刮压，进而从网孔漏至印刷物上而形成图案，在商业和艺术上均被广泛使用。在美国，以安迪·沃霍尔 (Andy Warhol) 为首的众多艺术家都赏识这种制作成品的优点，并擅用丝网版画进行创作。

Exercises

True or False

Directions: *Determine whether the following statements are true (T) or false (F).*

1. The word "Pop" was first coined by the British art critic Richard Hamilton in 1954.
2. Paolozzi's collages conveyed an appreciative and critical attitude towards the all-American lifestyle.
3. The Pop Art Movement aims to make art by borrowing any object from any cultural source believing that everything is inter-connected in mind.
4. Both Jasper Johns and Robert Rauschenberg used "found images" in their art to mirror people's life and psychology.
5. Both British and American Pop Art showed a common interest in mass-media, mass-production and mass-culture.
6. Roy Lichtenstein developed comic strip, which is a style in a flexible format.
7. The Pop Art Movement via paintings or sculptures derived from mass culture objects and media stars was to blur the boundaries between "high" art and "low" culture.
8. Since started in Britain, Pop Art was a typical British movement.

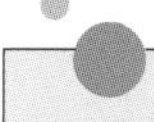

Post-class Thinking

Discussion

Directions: *After reading the text above, you may have known somewhat about the Pop Art. Why do you think Pop Art prevails in both the UK and the US? State your comment on one of the following three famous works of art and discuss whether you like such an art form in your own life.*

Eduardo Paolozzi (1924–2005), *I Was a Rich Man's Plaything*, 1947 (collage)	Robert Rauschenberg (1925–2008), *First Landing Jump*, 1961 (mixed media)	Roy Lichtenstein (1923–1997), *Oh, Jeff...I Love You , Too... But...*, 1964

Supplementary Resources

1. Extensive Reading

1) Scan the QR codes to read Text D "An Introduction to English Theatre and American Theater" and watch the MOOC video "English Theater and American Cinema". Then discuss the following questions with your partner: Which plays or playwrights do you know about? What's the relationship between theater and cinema?

Text D "An Introduction to English Theatre and American Theater"

MOOC video "English Theater and American Cinema"

2) Scan the QR codes to watch the following two video clips, one from Shakespeare's *Romeo and Juliet* and the other from Tang Xianzu's masterpiece *The Peony Pavilion*. After watching, compare the two dramas and discuss their differences, including scene setting, characterization, genre of lines and acting techniques, etc.

Romeo and Juliet

The Peony Pavilion

2. Documentaries

1) Documentary: *How Much Does Your Building Weigh, Mr. Foster?* (2010) （《您的建筑重几何，福斯特先生？》）

The documentary, directed by Carlos Carcas and Norberto Lopez Amado, attempts to trace the rise of Norman Foster, one of the world's top architects, and his pursuit of improving life through design. This film depicts his original ideas and how his dream inspired the design of iconic projects, including the world's largest buildings like Beijing Airport, German Parliament and Hearst Tower in New York.

2) Documentary: *Abstract: The Art of Design* （《抽象：设计的艺术》）

Abstract: The Art of Design is a Netflix original documentary series highlighting artists in the field of design. By visiting eight artists and designers from all over the world, such as Nike shoe designer Tinker Hatfield and *New Yorker* illustrator Christoph Niemann, the documentary helps people understand their attitudes towards design and creation, so as to explore the relationship between brand, design, creativity and the future.

3) Documentary: *Ways of Seeing* (《观看之道》)

The documentary is adapted from the works of film writer John Berger, with a total of four episodes. They critically review aesthetics under the Western culture by showing the changes of visual art and the hidden ideology behind it. John Berger believes that works of art, especially visual works of art, can truly reflect the current social consciousness and cultural form.

4) Documentary: *The Impressionists* (《印象派大师》)

This is a three-episode, three-hour mini documentary. Claude Monet, Edgar Degas, and Pierre Auguste Renoir are three representative impressionist artists. The documentary restores their creation scene at that time through the most influential works of the three and the close friendship among the three, combined with the form of film stories.

3. Books

Toman, R. 2013. 哥特艺术 : 1140—1500 年中世纪的视觉艺术 . 北京 : 北京美术摄影出版社 .

菲利帕 · 格里高利 . 2012. 都铎王朝 . 重庆 : 重庆出版社 .

马克 · 盖特雷恩 . 2014. 认识艺术 （全彩插图第 8 版）. 北京 : 世界图书出版公司 .

西蒙 · 沙马 . 2015. 艺术的力量 . 北京 : 北京美术摄影出版社 .

英国 DK 公司 . 2013. 伟大的旅程 : 一生必看的 103 个建筑 . 北京 : 北京美术摄影出版社 .

Chapter 10
Festivals and Holidays in the UK and the US

Festivals and holidays are an integral part of folk culture, which are of commemorative significance. They differ from each other in the origin, development and celebration. Some originate from traditional customs, some from religious rituals, and others from the purpose of commemorating an important figure or an influential event. Due to the historical ties, the UK and the US show both commonness and differences in their holidays and festivals. This chapter will introduce major festivals and holidays shared by both the UK and the US, as well as some specific days either in the UK or in the US.

Text A Three Common Public Holidays in the UK and the US

Pre-class Preparation

MOOC Watching

Watch the MOOC video "Holidays Shared by Britain and America" to prepare for Text A.

Pre-reading Questions

1. Which festivals or holidays are celebrated in both the UK and the US?
2. Christmas is viewed as the grandest holiday in the life of westerners. What traditions do you know about Christmas celebration?

In-class Reading

Three Common Public Holidays in the UK and the US

1 Festivals and holidays generally impress people with great joy and celebrations of all kinds. Entering the 21st century, **interaction** or even integration between different cultures is also becoming more and more frequent across the world. Various festivals and holidays in different places, a part of folk culture, tend to be introduced or transmitted from one location to another. Based on a long historical connection and communication, the UK and the US celebrate a number of common holidays, among which are three public holidays, i.e., Christmas Day, New Year's Day and Easter Day.

interaction *n.* 相互作用；相互影响

★ **Christmas Day**

2 Though it has **tremendous** religious importance of celebrating the birth of Jesus Christ on December 25, Christmas Day has been a popular holiday with non-Christians as well. The day involves various celebration activities.

tremendous *adj.* 巨大的

3 In the US, the arrival of Christmas features parades, gift giving, holiday displays, and lights galore. As it is the darkest time of year in the northern **hemisphere**, Christmas Day also turns into a celebration of light. Thus, decorating the house with colorful lights becomes very popular for every family. Besides, a Christmas tree is a must to decorate the living room. Whether it is artificial or natural, a **conifer** tree is commonly seen. On top of it are usually the heart-shaped leaves of ivy, which was said to represent Jesus coming to the Earth. The most noticeable one is a National Christmas Tree lit up by the president at the beginning of December.

hemisphere *n.* 半球

conifer *n.* 针叶树

4 In the UK, people spend the full afternoon with family watching the Christmas programs, especially the monarch's Christmas speech, broadcast **simultaneously** on the two biggest TV channels in the UK, BBC and ITV at 3:00 p.m. This tradition has been more than 60 years, ever since the first speech in 1957. The monarch reviews the year and gives a Christmas message usually speaking of tolerance and forgiveness. Towards evening, the whole family sit around and enjoy a heavy Christmas meal of turkey full of **trimmings**, followed by Christmas pudding for dessert. After dinner comes the most exciting tradition of exchanging presents. English families traditionally leave a glass of **sherry** and a slice of mince pie out there for **Father Christmas** to warm up on Christmas Eve. The next morning, children get thrilled to see what presents Father Christmas will leave for them under the Christmas tree.

simultaneously *adv.* 同时地

trimmings *n.* （菜肴的）配料

sherry *n.* 雪利酒（烈性葡萄酒，原产自西班牙南部）

The Queen's Christmas speech

★ **New Year's Day**

5 New Year's Day, marking the fresh start of a brand-new year, falls naturally on January 1 of the solar calendar, almost **unanimously** celebrated throughout the world.

unanimously
adv. 全体一致地

6 For American and British people, January 1, a week after Christmas, is universally a day for them to have fun and enjoy celebration. The holiday generally reaches the climax late on New Year's Eve with big fancy parties, plenty of parades and firework shows. Times Square[1] in New York is definitely a most popular place on New Year's Eve, since there is commonly a grand New Year party for the entire nation. People **plunge** into the square to **usher** in the coming year, giving each other best wishes. In the UK, the River Thames in London is an ideal place for people to gather along to watch the fireworks. Especially the moment when Big Ben chimes midnight, the crowds will join together holding hands and singing the traditional song *Auld Lang Syne*[2].

plunge
v. 猛冲向
usher
v. 引入

Rose parade on New Year's Day in the US

7 **Hogmanay**, in Scotland, just refers to New Year's Eve. There is also a prevalent **superstition** and custom that the first person to enter a house on the New Year's Day will bring them luck. What's more, if the First Footer has dark hair, like us Chinese, he or she will be most welcome and well-treated on that day as he or she is believed to bring them good luck for the whole year!

superstition
n. 迷信观念（或思想）

8 To welcome the year to come, it's a **prevailing** tradition for people to make New Year's **resolutions** carrying a good wish of moving forward with a better self. Due to the fact that health, safety and life quality become common concerns, people generally have quite similar New Year's resolutions, say, to conduct a healthy living style, to quit smoking, or to lose the extra pounds put on over Christmas. However, most often than not, people make the resolutions mostly in a tongue-in-cheek way, i.e., something not actually to be obeyed.

prevailing
adj. 流行的
resolution
n. 正式决定

★ **Easter Day**

9 Easter Sunday or Easter Day is among the most important religious holidays. For Christians, the holiday is centered on the **resurrection** of Jesus Christ with special events held in churches. For non-Christians, holding **secular** events also brings great fun!

resurrection
n. 复活

secular
adj. 现世的；世俗的

10 Apart from the midnight masses on Christmas, one of the most prevalent religious traditions is Easter services that take place at the break of a day. Some churches hold elaborate parades or at least social gatherings for the fellow churchgoers. In the meantime, the non-religious are inclined to have family gatherings or picnic, taking it as merely a celebration of the spring. Another secular event is giving each other eggs, regarded as a symbol of the resurrection and new life of Jesus Christ after his **crucifixion**. Eggs are often painted in bright colors like pink, blue, and yellow. And for children, chocolate eggs, or eggs with chocolate inside are especially preferable. A popular activity is Easter Egg Hunt[3], i.e., eggs are usually

hidden in public places, and then people, mostly children will start to look for them. The more eggs, the more fun.

Easter Egg Hunt

craze
n. 狂热

11 On Christmas children show **craze** for Santa Claus, for they hold the firm belief that it is Santa Claus who brings them the presents. Interestingly and similarly, the **Easter Bunny** is considered to bring the eggs at Easter. In addition, chocolate figures in the shape of bunnies are popular gifts at Easter, alongside the traditional eggs.

12 To sum up, the UK and the US celebrate three common public holidays, namely Christmas Day, New Year's Day and Easter Day. Among the three, Christmas aims to commemorate the birth of Jesus Christ while Easter the resurrection of Jesus Christ, though both have a religious origin, they're also popular among non-Christians.

T Cultural Terms

1. Father Christmas 圣诞老人（Santa Claus）
2. Hogmanay （苏格兰的）除夕及其欢庆活动
3. crucifixion 耶稣受难（指耶稣被钉死在十字架上）
4. Easter Bunny 复活节兔子（兔子多产，象征春天的复苏和新生命的诞生）

* Cultural Notes

1. Times Square

时代广场，美国纽约市曼哈顿的一块繁华街区，被称为“世界的十字路口”。原名为朗埃克广场，后因《纽约时报》早期在此设立的总部大楼而更名为时报广场。它附近聚集了近40家商场和剧院，是繁盛的娱乐及购物中心。

2. *Auld Lang Syne*

《友谊地久天长》，古苏格兰方言诗歌，大意为“逝去已久的日子”。这首诗歌后来被谱成了乐曲，并译成多国语言在全球各地传唱。

3. Easter Egg Hunt

复活节寻彩蛋活动，源于蛋孕育着新生命，象征着复活。最初是将蛋从山坡上滚下，最后一个捡到完整不破的蛋的人获胜。现在换成了五彩的塑料蛋，并在蛋里面装上糖果，把彩蛋藏放在草地上让小朋友去寻找。

In-class Game

Directions: *Traditional Christmas songs are largely associated with its religious origin and Christmas spirit. Do you know any Christmas songs and can you sing them? Christmas is to the Westerners what the Spring Festival is to the Chinese. What songs do the Chinese people like to sing to welcome Chinese Lunar New Year?*

Christmas songs:

____

____

Songs to welcome Chinese Lunar New Year:

____

____

Critical Thinking

Directions: *Choose one position and come up with views and evidence to support this position.*

Today, festivals and holidays often go side by side with big sales either offline or online, diluted by a commercial atmosphere to a large extent. Do you think that today's festivals and holidays have lost their truly original meaning and become commercialized?

Position A: Festivals and holidays nowadays have lost their true meaning.

Position B: Festivals and holidays nowadays have not lost their true meaning.

The debate process should go as follows:

- The two sides make opening statements;
- Side A presents its arguments;
- Side B rebuts Side A's arguments and presents its arguments;
- Side A rebuts Side B's arguments;
- The two sides make closing statements.

Post-class Thinking

Comparison and Analysis

Directions: *Every nation has its own festivals and holidays associated with its own origin and history. Christmas, Easter, Valentine's Day and Halloween are typical Western holidays while the Spring Festival, the Lantern Festival, the Qingming Festival and the Mid-Autumn Festival are all typical Chinese festivals. Make a comparison of festivals and holidays between China and the West in terms of origin and history, and then share your findings with your classmates.*

Text B Memorable Days in the US

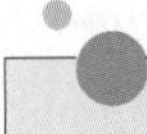

Pre-class Preparation

MOOC Watching

Watch the MOOC video "Uniquely Celebrated American Holidays" to prepare for Text B.

Pre-reading Questions

1. What typical holidays are celebrated in the US?
2. How do Americans celebrate their traditional holidays?

Memorable Days in the US

1 In the US, the federal law establishes 10 public holidays, eight of which are uniquely American holidays. Among the eight American holidays, six are commemorative of important historical figures, while the other two are related to national origins: Thanksgiving and the Fourth of July.

★ Martin Luther King Jr. Day[1]

2 Falling on the third Monday of January, Martin Luther King Jr. Day is a federal holiday set aside in honor of the civil rights leader—Martin Luther King Jr., who devoted himself to ending racial **segregation** and achieving racial equality instead in the US.

segregation
n. 隔离政策

3 Soon after Martin Luther King Jr. was assassinated in 1968, a bill to make his birthday a holiday to commemorate him was proposed, but was not passed until 1983. However, many states resisted the holiday or tried to term it otherwise, such as "Human Rights Day" in Utah. Though celebrated for the first time in 1986, it was not officially observed by all states until 2000. Americans usually join the marches and parades on this day, and some schools remain open and teach students the life and work of Martin Luther King Jr. In addition, Americans are now encouraged to donate some of their time as volunteers in citizen action groups.

★ Presidents' Day

4 The day was originally celebrated on February 22, George Washington's

birthday, to remember the most important American figure in the District of Columbia. It was signed into law in 1879 and expanded to the whole country in 1885. Later, a bill was proposed to produce more three-day weekends, Washington's birthday was shifted from February 22 to the third Monday of February, while the name of the holiday was changed into **Presidents' Day**. In effect, Washington and Lincoln are given equal recognition as two of America's most famous statesmen. The date shift enables itself to fall between their two birthdays, i.e., February 12 and February 22.

5 Now, Presidents' Day is popularly viewed as a day to honor all American presidents, past and present; however, this view encounters some lawmakers' objection, arguing that it'll **minimize** the legacies created by George Washington and Abraham Lincoln to group them together with any other president.

minimize
v. 减少

★ Memorial Day & Veterans Day[2]

6 **Memorial Day** & Veterans Day are two major US federal holidays closely tied to military **personnel**, commonly marked by parades, educational events and gathering. Both holidays evolve over the years. Memorial Day was first held on May 30, and the date was shifted to the last Monday of May in 1971. Furthermore, Memorial Day evolves from a day originally in honor of those lost in the Civil War, to a day in **remembrance** of those fallen from other wars in general.

personnel
n.（组织或军队中的）全体人员

remembrance
n. 回忆；纪念

7 Veterans Day was originally called Armistice Day, commemorating the end of World War I. Since an **armistice** was put into effect actually on November 11, 1918, the day of November 11 was set aside to honor veterans of the First World War (WWI). The word "armistice" was thereafter changed to "veterans" in 1954, while there are no more surviving combat veterans from WWI, the day has been expanded to pay **tribute** to American veterans of all wars as well as peacetime veterans.

armistice
n. 休战；停战协定

tribute
n. 悼念；致敬

★ Independence Day

8 The Declaration of Independence drafted by Thomas Jefferson was adopted on July 4, 1776, symbolizing the birth of American independence. **Independence Day** is celebrated with various festivities ranging from parades and concerts to more casual family gatherings and barbecues.

9 The American flags are flowing across the land, "The Star-Spangled Banner" is being sung and people are mostly dressed in red, white and blue. When the night falls, fireworks displays in New York City and Washington, DC will be staged and also televised nationally.

★ Labor Day

10 Dating back to 1894, Labor Day became a federal holiday dedicated to American workers on the first Monday in September. But it was first held in 1882 as a result of the Central Labor Union's desire to create a holiday for workers.

11 Besides celebrating laborers, it also means the last break before the fall session of school starts. Many teams start their first football game on or around the Labor Day weekend. Thus, to some extent, Labor Day symbolizes the unofficial ending of the summer vacation but the official beginning of the football season.

★ Columbus Day

12 **Columbus Day**, also called **Indigenous** Peoples' Day, has been celebrated on the second Monday in October since 1971. The day was observed to commemorate Christopher Columbus, who first arrived in Americas on October 12, 1492. In 1937 it became a national holiday by presidential **proclamation**. Though celebrated nationwide, it is especially popular among Italian Americans in honouring his achievement over the years, for Columbus was a native Italian although his explorations were sponsored by Spanish monarchs. During the latter half of the 19th

indigenous
adj. 本地的

proclamation
n. 宣言；公告

century, the day began to be observed in cities with large numbers of Italian Americans.

embellish
v. 修饰；美化

13 On this day, parades are **embellished** with cultural and religious images and symbols specific to Italian-Americans. In addition, floats depicting the ships of Columbus are often included in the public ceremonies and festivities.

Columbus Day parade

★ Thanksgiving Day

14 Along with Independence Day, Thanksgiving Day is also the first-celebrated and the most ancient holiday in the US. Falling on the fourth Thursday of November, Thanksgiving Day was originally celebrated for thanking God for blessings, dating back to 1620 when the **pilgrim** fathers arrived in America and made a good harvest the next year with the help of Indians. At first, Thanksgiving Day was not fixed, but decided upon by every state. It was not until 1863 during the Civil War did Abraham Lincoln establish Thanksgiving as a national holiday. Even though officially born during this war, it's more associated with the initially good relationship between the first European immigrants and the native Americans.

pilgrim
n. 清教徒前辈移民

15 Today, Thanksgiving is all about having a feast with family and giving thanks. Turkey is the traditional main course with yams, potatoes, **cranberries** and pumpkin pies. Since football is another tradition, people usually watch the football game while preparing the Thanksgiving meal.

cranberry
n. 蔓越莓

Thanksgiving meal

Cultural Terms

1. Presidents' Day 总统日 (美国法定假日，在二月份的第三个星期一，纪念华盛顿和林肯的生日)
2. Memorial Day 阵亡将士纪念日 (美国假日，通常为五月的最后一个星期一)
3. Independence Day 美国独立纪念日 (7 月 4 日，美国国庆日，纪念 1776 年美国宣布脱离英国)
4. Columbus Day 哥伦布日（纪念哥伦布于 1492 年首次登上美洲大陆，时间是 10 月 12 日或 10 月的第二个星期一）

Cultural Notes

1. Martin Luther King Jr. Day

马丁·路德·金纪念日，简称为 MLK 日，是唯一一个纪念美国黑人的联邦假日。马丁·路德·金，美国民权运动先驱，致力于为黑人争取平等权益。他是将“非暴力”和“直接行动”作为社会变革方法的最突出倡导者之一。1986 年 1 月 20 日，美国各地第一次庆祝这个假日, 不过大家对于纪念日定在他生日那天还是逝世那天, 一直争议不休。最后,里根总统于 1986 年宣布 1 月的第三个星期一为联邦法定假日。现在，时逢假日，美国学校通常组织学生参加志愿者公益活动，比如为穷人提供饭菜、去黑人小学做大扫除等。

2. Veterans Day

老兵节，美国法定假日之一，源于第一次世界大战。战争后期，交战双方商定从 1918 年 11 月 11 日 11 点开始休战，这一天被视为世界大战实际结束的日子。1919 年，美国总统威尔逊宣布 11 月 11 日为“休战日”。1938 年，美国通过法律将休战日设为法定假日，全国休假一天。1954 年，二战老兵艾森豪威尔总统签署命令，正式把该节日的名称从“休战日”改为“老兵节”，用以纪念美国历史上所有参战的军人。

Exercise

Question Answering

Directions: *Answer the following questions briefly based on Text B.*

1. Martin Luther King Jr. Day was not accepted by all fifty states right away. When did all fifty states adopt the day?

____

____

2. Why do some lawmakers object Presidents' Day being viewed as a day to honor all American presidents?

____

____

3. Veterans Day was originally called Armistice Day. Why did the name change?

____

____

4. Why is Columbus Day especially popular among Italian Americans?

____

____

5. July 4 is the Independence Day of the United States. Why are Americans mostly dressed in red, white and blue on that day?

____

____

Post-class Thinking

Discussion

Directions: *Generally speaking, festivals or holidays are associated with some significant moments, events, or occasions. Nowadays, some new holidays have been set up on our calendar. Can you name some special days that are now also observed in China? If you're invited to suggest a new holiday, which day will you choose and how will you name it?*

Text C Typical British Holidays: In Memory of the Saints

Pre-class Preparation

MOOC Watching

Watch the MOOC video "Uniquely Celebrated British Holidays" to prepare for Text C.

Pre-reading Questions

1. It's customary to set aside a specific day to commemorate the influential figures in history. What holidays in Britain are associated with important historical figures?
2. How do people in the UK celebrate the holidays? Are they also celebrated outside the UK?

In-class Reading

Typical British Holidays: In Memory of the Saints

1 Besides Christmas Day, New Year's Day and Easter Day, British people also celebrate many other special days, such as Epiphany[1], Burns Night[2], Valentine's Day, Pancake Day[3], Bonfire Night[4] and so on. Apart from all of these holidays, the four countries of the UK each has a specific day to commemorate their own patron saints, St. George's Day in England, St. Andrew's Day in Scotland, St. David's Day in Wales, and St. Patrick's Day in Northern Ireland.

★ St. George's Day (April 23)

2 St. George, born around 280 AD, is widely known for saving humans

from an evil dragon. According to the legend, there was once a dragon guarding the only well in Silene Town. People there had no choice but to offer a human sacrifice every day to the dragon in return for water. One day when St. George visited Silene, he struggled with the dragon bravely and finally succeeded in killing it. In order to show their gratitude to St. George, the inhabitants of the town all **converted** to Christianity. However, on April 23, 303, St. George was executed for his disagreement with the Roman Pope.

convert
v. (使) 皈依

3 Now people usually commemorate April 23 with parades, dancing and some other activities. St. George's cross, a red cross on the white background, regarded as the representation of the Day, forms the image of the flag of England, and furthermore part of the national flag of the UK. On St. George's Day, flags bearing St. George's cross are seen flowing on top of the buildings. Additionally, it is also used as a national symbol by sports fans, worn or painted on their faces at international matches.

★ St. Andrew's Day (November 30)

4 November 30 is celebrated in Scotland as its national day. The story of Saint Andrew varies, mainly known as a fisher first and then an **apostle** of Jesus Christ. St. Andrew's Day marked the victory and the new nationhood won by Scotland in fighting against the invading Germanic Angles. According to the legend of Scotland, St. Andrew exerted divine power and unexpectedly led Scotland to win the battle in spite of the other side's **overwhelming** odds. In consequence, the X-shaped cross where St. Andrew was **crucified** became the image of Scotland's flag, i.e., a white cross over a blue background, named St. Andrew's Cross.

apostle
n. 信徒，使徒（耶稣十二门徒之一）

overwhelming
adj. 势不可挡的；压倒性的

crucify
v. 把（某人）钉（或捆）在木十字架上处死

5 On St. Andrew's Day, the Scottish flag is flown across the country and special dances and festivals are held by the Scots, among which traditional Scottish culture is playing an increasing role, including food, music, **recitations**, and dancing specific of the local culture. Traditional food served on the occasion might include **cullen skink**, haggis[5], lamb, **neeps and tatties**. Ceilidh[6] (a Gaelic word, meaning "to party" "to visit") is a traditional Scottish country gathering involving Scottish folk music mixed with modern

recitation
n. 朗诵

pop music, dancing, and storytelling when and where people often wear the traditional iconic kilt. Not only in Scotland, variations of St. Andrew's Day are also celebrated in such other countries as Romania, Germany, Austria, Poland, and Russia due to the immigrants with their own Scottish roots. St. Andrew's Day falls on the last day of November, also marking the beginning of winter festivals such as Hogmanay and Burns Night.

★ St. David's Day (March 1)

6 St. David, the patron saint of Wales, died on March 1, 589. The day was later set aside for honoring St. David, who was said to spread Christianity throughout Wales. He built a good number of churches and finally became an **archbishop**. According to the legend, St. David led a simple life, living on only **leeks** and water as a strict **vegetarian**. This may well explain why the leek is viewed as a national symbol of Wales. His last words to his followers similarly have a great influence on the Welsh people: "Be joyful, keep the faith, and do the little things that you have heard and seen me do."

7 On St. David's Day, people will conduct various traditional activities such as parades, **choral** recitals, church services, or Welsh literature readings. The Welsh flag with a red dragon on a white and green background is flying around March 1 and people usually pin a **daffodil** or a leek to their clothes to pay tribute to St. David.

archbishop
n. 大主教
leek
n. 韭葱（威尔士民族的象征）
vegetarian
n. 素食主义者
choral
adj. 合唱的；唱诗班的
daffodil
n. 黄水仙（威尔士的民族象征）

St. David's Day parade in Colwyn Bay

★ St. Patrick's Day (March 17)

8 St. Patrick's Day is a cultural and religious celebration held on March

17, the traditional death date of Saint Patrick (c. 385–c. 461). He was worshipped as the foremost patron saint of Ireland. Now the Day is not only to commemorate Saint Patrick and the arrival of Christianity in Ireland, but also to celebrate the heritage and culture of the Irish in general.

attire *n.* 服装
shamrocks *n.* 三叶草
diaspora *n.*（任何民族的）大移居

9 Celebrations customarily involve public parades and festivals, Irish traditional music sessions, and the wearing of green **attire** or **shamrocks**. Saint Patrick's Day parades began in North America in the 18th century. Not until the 20th century did it spread to Ireland. Today, St. Patrick's Day is also widely celebrated in the UK, the US, Canada, Brazil, Argentina, Australia and New Zealand, especially amongst Irish **diaspora**.

pagan *adj.* 异教徒的；非基督教的

10 St. Patrick's Day is celebrated as a public bank holiday[7] in both Northern Ireland and the Republic of Ireland. The most representative color of the Day is green, the color of the shamrock, which is viewed as the most common symbol of the Day. Saint Patrick is said to have used the shamrock, a three-leaved plant, to explain the Holy Trinity to the **pagan** Irish. Many people dress themselves up in green to celebrate the holiday, green clothes, green hats and even green glasses. In addition, it's also a wonderful time to enjoy popular Irish food or drink, such as Irish brown bread, **corned beef** and cabbage, Irish coffee, Irish potato soup, Irish stew and Irish cream chocolate mousse cake.

T Cultural Terms

1. cullen skink 苏格兰鲜鱼浓汤
2. neeps and tatties 萝卜和土豆泥
3. corned beef 英式传统盐腌牛肉

Cultural Notes

1. Epiphany

主显节，1 月 6 日纪念贤士朝拜耶稣的日子，即 1 月 6 日。“主显”（Epiphaneia）一词的希腊文原意是：一位神出现，使人肉眼可以看见；或是一位被当作神崇拜的皇帝，到其王国的某一城市拜访，使当地的居民能看见他。按照传统习俗，东正教徒会跃入冰冷刺骨的水中“净化”灵魂。

2. Burns Night

彭斯之夜，纪念苏格兰诗人罗伯特·彭斯的诞辰日，即 1 月 25 日，是苏格兰最重要的节日之一。为了纪念彭斯，很多英国餐馆和酒吧都会在这天举办“彭斯之夜”主题的庆祝活动。传统的彭斯晚宴包括吟唱彭斯诗篇、发表演说、享用苏格兰美食。

3. Pancake Day

煎饼节，英国的一个传统节日，通常是 2 月或 3 月的一个周二。该节日源于 1445 年的英国白金汉郡的奥尔尼镇，一个主妇煎煎饼的时候，突然想起要去教堂做礼拜。于是她就端着煎锅冲出门，中途还给煎饼翻了几次面，生怕煎饼煎煳。所以，煎饼日这一天英国各地都会举行煎饼赛跑活动。

4. Bonfire Night

篝火之夜，也叫盖伊·福克斯之夜（Guy Fawkes Night），英国的一个传统节日。每年 11 月 5 日晚，英国人通常制作假人“盖伊”，把它放到篝火上焚烧，借以庆祝 1605 年天主教反叛分子炸毁议会大厦的阴谋失败。

5. haggis

肉馅羊肚，苏格兰的一种本地风味菜。在羊肚里填满切碎的羊肉、燕麦片、杂碎以及香料之后将羊肚封紧，然后煮成油光发亮的棕色。

6. Ceilidh

同乐会，一种传统的盖尔人的社交聚会。早期人们通常讲故事、吟诗、弹唱和诵对，近代跳舞也融入聚会活动中并流行起来。这种舞蹈被称作凯利舞，由来自加拿大、美国、新西兰的苏格兰和爱尔兰后裔广泛传播，并且当地都有传统的聚会和舞蹈比赛活动。

7. bank holiday

银行假日，即银行放假不营业的日子，英国的法定公众假日（自 1871 年被承认）。银行假日每一年的具体日期由政府公布。

Exercise

True or False

Directions: *Determine whether the following statements are true (T) or false (F).*

1. The flag of England is an X-shaped cross on the white ground.
2. St. David was said to live on only leeks and water as a strict vegetarian.
3. St. Andrew's Day is also celebrated in some other countries like Romania, Germany, Australia, Poland, and Russia.
4. St. Patrick's Day is celebrated as a public bank holiday in the whole UK.
5. The leek is viewed as the national symbol of Wales and the shamrock as the most common symbol of the St. Patrick's Day.

Post-class Thinking

Discussion

Directions: *Based on Text C, we know that some specific days are related to certain saints with their legendary stories. Are there any special days in China similarly related to certain people, authentic or legendary? If yes, please introduce some of the special days briefly.*

Supplementary Resources

1. Extensive Reading

Scan the QR codes to read Text D "An Introduction to Three Shared Non-public Holidays" and watch the MOOC video "Non-public Holidays Shared by Britain and America". Then discuss the following questions with your partner:

1) Holidays are generally grouped into two categories: public holidays and non-public holidays. What's the difference between the two types?

2) What non-public holidays are celebrated in both the UK and the US? How do people usually celebrate the days?

Text D "An Introduction to Three Shared Non-public Holidays"

MOOC video "Non-public Holidays Shared by Britain and America"

2. Documentaries

1) Documentary: *European Festivals* (《欧洲节日大观》)

The documentary is led by Rick Steves to visit France, Germany, Italy, Spain, Switzerland, Norway and other European countries to experience the local traditional culture. The top ten European festivals are introduced by the documentary, focusing on the happy and festive atmosphere of singing and dancing, traditional food, picturesque scenery and fireworks.

2) Documentary: *Cook, Eat, Repeat, Christmas Special* (《美食·品味·重复——圣诞特辑》)

The documentary, produced by BBC, records the inspiration of beautiful chef Nigella to share her favorite recipes and delicious food. *Christmas Special* shares the melody of Christmas cooking, rhythm of delicious food and repeated pleasure.

3) Documentary: *Chinese New Year—The Biggest Celebration on Earth* (《中国新年：全球最大庆典》)

The documentary, produced by the BBC, records the Chinese people returning home for the Spring Festival. It introduces the Chinese Spring Festival from the aspects of local customs and celebrations, and shares the lively and joyful atmosphere of the festival.

3. Books

Hatfield, S. 2017. *Chasing Christmas: Sweet Western Holiday Romance*. Fresno: CreateSpace Independent Publishing Platform.

耿卫忠 . 2006. 西方传统节日与文化 . 太原 : 书海出版社 .

胡晓红，徐少保，曹易娟 . 2020. 中国传统民俗节日文化之韵 : 汉英对照 . 长春 : 吉林大学出版社 .

王辉云 . 2013. 闲聊美国节日的历史和文化 . 北京 : 生活 · 读书 · 新知三联书店 .

朱子仪 . 2005. 西方的节日 . 上海 : 上海人民出版社 .